Illustrated Book of QUESTIONS & ANSWERS

PUBLICATIONS INTERNATIONAL, LTD.

Louis Weber, C.E.O.
Publications International, Ltd.
7373 North Cicero Avenue
Lincolnwood, Illinois 60646

Manufactured in USA.

ISBN: 0-7853-1683-3

Library of Congress Catalog Card Number: 95-72997

CONSULTANTS

Anna J. Austin, Ph.D., is an Associate Professor, Chairperson of Elementary Education Department, and Co-Chairperson of the division of Early Childhood and Elementary Education at the National-Louis University.

Michael Boersma holds a Master of Arts degree in the History of Science from the University of Wisconsin at Madison and is the Science Exhibit Developer at the Museum of Science and Industry in Chicago.

Martin F.J. Flower holds a Ph.D. in volcanology/geochemistry from the University of Manchester, UK. He is a former editorial board member of *Geology* magazine and was a research associate for the Smithsonian Institution, Museum of Natural History. He is managing editor of *Earth Science Reviews* and is a professor of geological sciences at the University of Illinois, Chicago.

David Hollander, Ph.D., is an Assistant Professor of Geological Sciences at Northwestern University and continues to do research and to guest lecture throughout the world.

David A.R. Kristovich, Ph.D., earned his Doctorate degree in Meteorology at the University of Chicago. He currently works as Assistant Professional Scientist, Office of Cloud and Precipitation at Illinois State Water Survey, Illinois State University.

Michael Lieber, Ph.D., is an Associate Professor of Anthropology at the University of Illinois at Chicago and has authored many publications in various fields of anthropology.

William Purcell, Ph.D., is an Assistant Research Professor at Northwestern University and has received many fellowships and grants to guest lecture and conduct research.

Rosalind B. Resnick is the author of *Exploring the World of Online Services,* a coauthor of *The Internet Business Guide,* and publisher of the monthly electronic newsletter *Interactive Publishing Alert.*

Mark Rosenthal holds a Master of Arts degree in Zoology from Northeastern University and is the Curator of Mammals at the Lincoln Park Zoo in Chicago.

Wayne Schmidt is the director of The National Museum of Transportation in St. Louis and is the former Executive Director of the Intrepid Sea-Air-Space Museum in New York.

Ronald Singer, D.Sc., is a Professor of Anatomy and Anthropology at the University of Chicago and has received numerous awards, research grants, and fellowships.

Janet R. Taylor, Ph.D., served as a Master Gardener at the Chicago Botanic Garden Plant Information Service and has written and edited several publications on botany.

Roy L. Taylor, Ph.D., is the Executive Director of Rancho Santa Ana Botanic Garden and Professor of Botany at Claremont Graduate School. He formerly served as Director of the Chicago Botanic Garden and President of the Chicago Horticultural Society.

Deborah S. Tynes is the Science Specialist for grades K-4 in the Shaker Heights City School District in Ohio.

Thomas Wisniewski holds a Master of Music Degree from Northern Illinois University and is a Professor of Music Education at the University of Illinois at Champaign-Urbana.

ILLUSTRATORS:

Keith Batcheller: How Do We Use Machines to Communicate?; **Amy Paluch Epton:** How Do We Use Machines to Communicate?, How Does the Earth Change?, Where Does Energy Come From?, What Are Plants?; **Leonard Freeman:** How Does the Earth Change?; **Brad Gaber:** How Do We Use Machines to Communicate?, How Does the Earth Change?, Where Does Energy Come From?; **Michael Gardner:** What Is Astronomy?, How Do We Use Machines to Communicate?, How Does the Earth Change?,Where Does Energy Come From?; **Margaret Gerrity:** How Does the Human Body Work?; **Dale Glasgow:** What Is Astronomy?; **Dale Gustafson:** How Do We Transport People and Products?; **Zbigniew Jastrzebski:** How Do We Use Machines to Communicate?, How Does the Earth Change?,Where Does Energy Come From?, What Are Plants?; **Bruce Long:** What Are Animals?, What Are Plants?; **Kay Salem:** How Do We Use Machines to Communicate?; **Richard Stergulz:** What Are Animals?, What Are Plants?; **Don Wieland:** What Are Animals?, How Do We Transport People and Products?; **Kurt Williams:** What Are Animals?

CONTENTS

What Is **ASTRONOMY**?

The Universe • Galaxies • Stars • The Solar System • Comets and Asteroids • The Moon • Eclipses • Telescopes • Spacecraft

→ PAGE 6

How Does the **EARTH CHANGE**?

Structure of the Earth • Crust and Plates • Earthquakes • Volcanoes • Underwater Formations • Rock Formation • Seasons • Atmosphere • Water Cycle • Clouds • Rain • Hail • Lightning • Snow • Hurricanes • Tornadoes • Climate and Ecosystems • Pollution

→ PAGE 34

What Are **PLANTS**?

Types of Plants • Deciduous Trees • Coniferous Trees • Flowering Plants and Pollination • Water Plants • Photosynthesis • Carnivorous and Parasitic Plants • Uses of Plants

PAGE 60

What Are **ANIMALS**?

Dinosaurs • Animal Groups • Protozoans • Simple Animals • Crabs and Lobsters • Mollusks • Sea Stars • Worms • Spiders • Insects • Fish • Amphibians • Reptiles • Birds • Mammals • Animals of Interest

→ PAGE 78

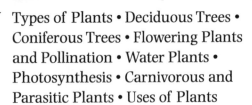

How Does the HUMAN BODY WORK?

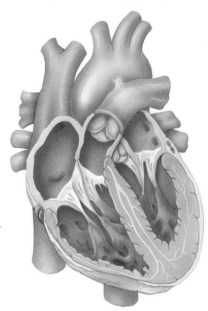

Cells • Skin • Muscular System • Skeletal System •
Nervous System • Circulatory System •
Respiratory System • Digestive System • Eye • Ear

PAGE 126

How Do We TRANSPORT PEOPLE & PRODUCTS?

Airplanes • Helicopters • Balloons and Blimps •
Boats • Trains • Trucks • Fire-Fighting
Equipment • City Services Equipment •
Construction Equipment • Farm Machinery

PAGE 144

Where Does ENERGY COME FROM?

Energy • Hydroelectric
Power • Nuclear Power •
Solar Power • Wind Power •
Oil and Natural Gas • Coal

PAGE 166

How Do We Use MACHINES TO COMMUNICATE?

Radio • TV/VCR • Satellites/Broadcasting •
Compact Disc • Internet • Telephone • Fax Machine

PAGE 180

What Is ASTRONOMY?

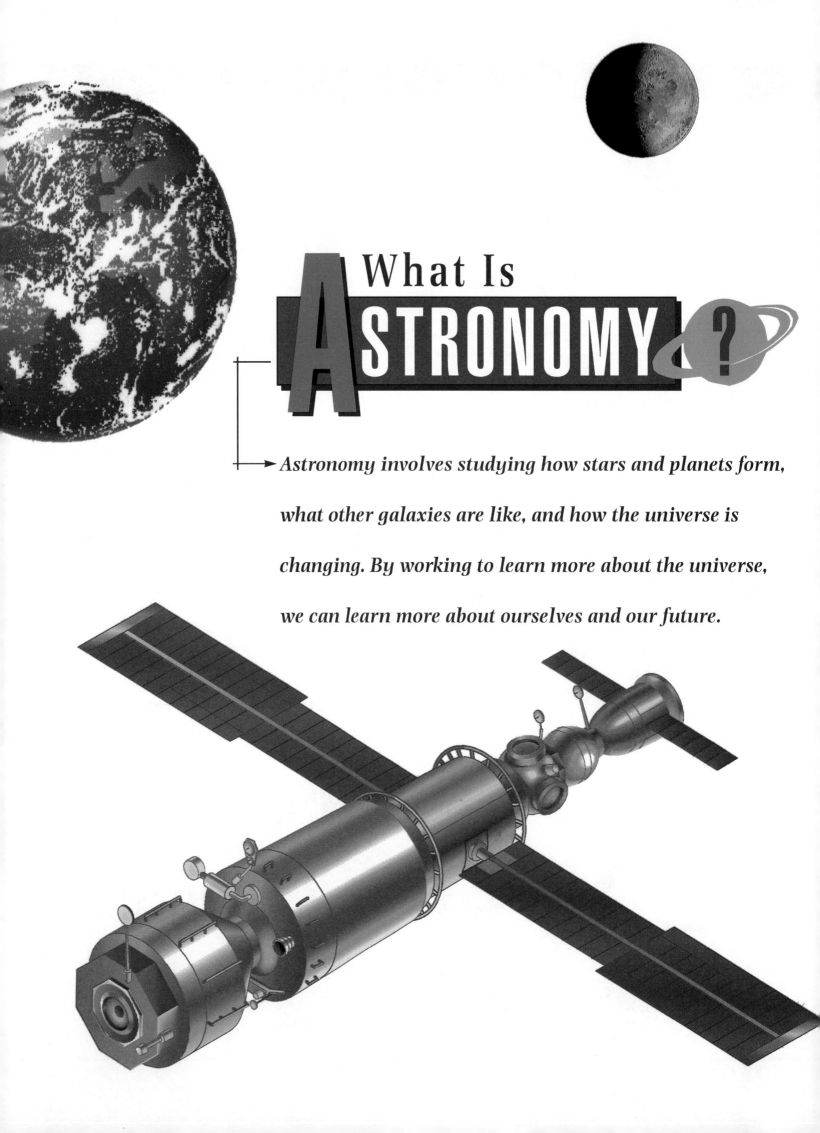

Astronomy involves studying how stars and planets form, what other galaxies are like, and how the universe is changing. By working to learn more about the universe, we can learn more about ourselves and our future.

Big Bang

Q. What is the universe?

A. The universe is everything. It includes you, the book you are looking at, the air you are breathing, and every other thing you've ever encountered. The universe also includes the Earth and everything on it, the sun and planets in our solar system, the Milky Way galaxy, the billions of other stars and galaxies beyond, and all the space in between.

Q. How big is the universe?

A. No one knows exactly how big the universe is, but we do know that it is growing larger all the time. Scientists have learned that all the galaxies we know seem to be moving away from each other and that the more distant galaxies seem to be moving faster. Most scientists believe the universe started in a great explosion called the Big Bang and that it has been expanding ever since.

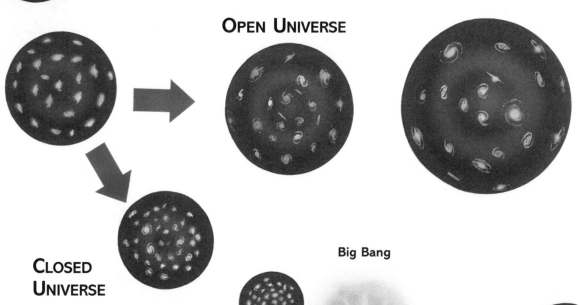

OPEN UNIVERSE

CLOSED UNIVERSE

Big Bang

Q. Will the universe continue to grow?

A. Astronomers have predicted two possible futures for the universe. One is that the galaxies will continue moving outward and the universe will expand until all of its energy is used up and it fizzles out. This is called an *open universe.* Another possibility is that we live in a *closed universe.* Some astronomers believe that gravitational attraction between galaxies will one day cause the galaxies to slow down. The universe will eventually stop expanding, and then gravity will begin to pull the galaxies back toward each other. All matter and energy will again come together at a single point in what is called the Big Crunch. After the Big Crunch, another Big Bang might happen, in which case a new universe would begin to form. Whether our universe is open or closed, its end will not come for many billions of years.

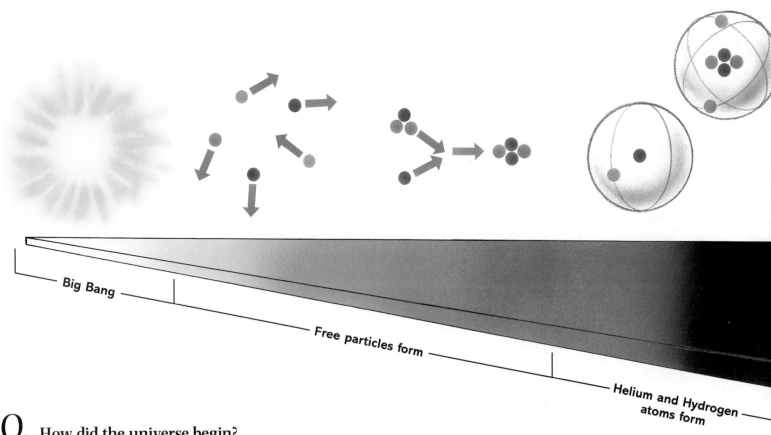

Big Bang

Free particles form

Helium and Hydrogen
atoms form

Q. How did the universe begin?

A. Astronomers and scientists do not know for sure how the universe began. However, most of them believe a theory that says the universe was formed between 10 billion and 15 billion years ago with a Big Bang. The Big Bang is thought to have been a huge, fiery explosion that brought time, space, energy, and matter into existence.

Q. What happened after the Big Bang?

A. Scientists theorize that after the Big Bang, the universe began to expand very rapidly. The entire universe started out smaller than the point of a needle and with a temperature of more than one billion billion degrees Fahrenheit. As the universe expanded, it also cooled. By the time it was 10 seconds old, the universe was about the size of our solar system, and its temperature had dropped to only about 10 billion degrees Fahrenheit. The universe continued to expand and cool, as it is still doing today.

Q. How long did it take for the universe to become as we now know it?

A. About 500,000 years after the Big Bang, the universe had cooled to about 5,000 degrees Fahrenheit. The lower temperature allowed swirling particles of matter to combine. First they formed free protons, neutrons, and electrons; then atomic nuclei; and finally hydrogen and helium atoms. As time went on, the universe continued to expand and cool, and small disturbances in gravity caused huge clouds of hydrogen and helium gas to form. In these gas clouds, stars began to form and galaxies began to take shape. Around one to two billion years after the Big Bang, galaxies began to cluster together. Within the galaxies, some stars had planetary bodies form and fall into orbit around them. In one such solar system, the planet Earth formed about five billion years ago, and life eventually appeared.

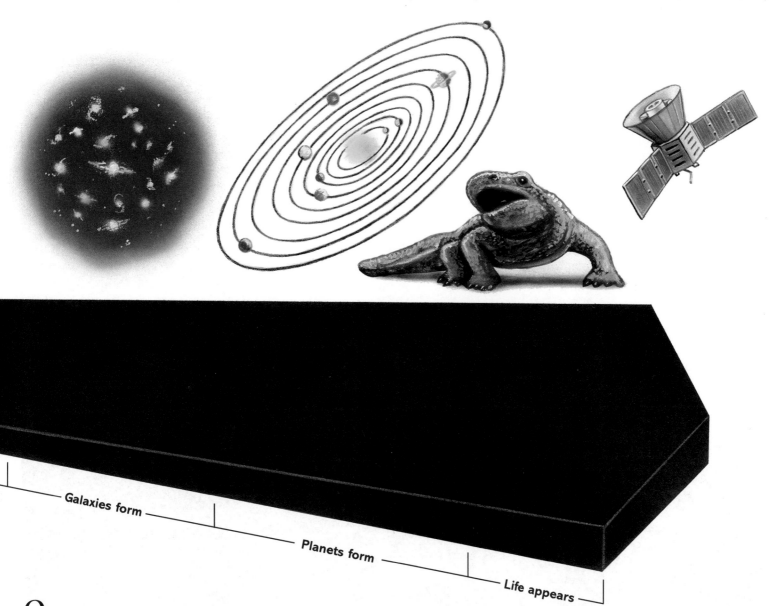

Galaxies form

Planets form

Life appears

Q. What is at the edge of the universe?

A. The universe has no true edge. Because the universe is so large, it can take a long time even for light to travel from one part of the universe to another. This means that when we look at the light of very distant objects, we are seeing them as they were many years ago. The farther away we look, the further back in time we are seeing. Recently, scientists used a telescope in orbit around Earth to look at the universe as it appeared when it was only about 500,000 years old. When the universe was younger than that, temperatures were too high for light to pass through, so we cannot see back any further than that.

Light-Year

The universe is so vast that the scientists who study it really can't use the measuring systems that we use for other things; miles and kilometers are just too small to be useful. Light travels at the amazing speed of about 186,000 miles per second. In a year's time, a ray of light will have traveled a bit less than six trillion miles. That distance is what we call a light-year, and scientists use it as a standard measure of distance for objects in space.

Q. **What is a galaxy?**

A. A galaxy is an enormous cluster of gas, dust, and stars. Astronomers believe that the universe contains more than 100 billion galaxies, and each galaxy contains billions of stars of its own.

Q. **Are all galaxies alike?**

A. There are four types of galaxies: spiral, barred spiral, elliptical, and irregular. A spiral galaxy looks something like a pinwheel. There are gigantic arms that seem to spiral out of a bright center. A barred spiral galaxy has a line or bar across the center that spirals out at each end. Elliptical galaxies vary in shape from flat disks to spheres; they contain old stars and very little gas and dust. Irregular galaxies have no definite shape. They are much less common than the other types.

About Andromeda

The Andromeda galaxy is one of the closest neighboring galaxies to our own Milky Way. On a clear night, it can be seen by the naked eye in the Northern Hemisphere. Close is a funny word when speaking about the universe. As close as Andromeda is, light from it takes more than two million years to reach Earth.

SPIRAL GALAXY FORMATION

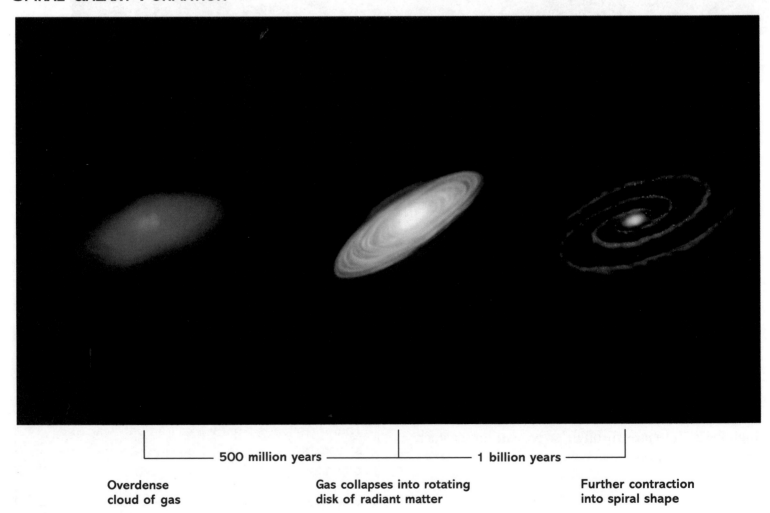

|— 500 million years —|— 1 billion years —|

Overdense cloud of gas

Gas collapses into rotating disk of radiant matter

Further contraction into spiral shape

TYPES OF GALAXIES

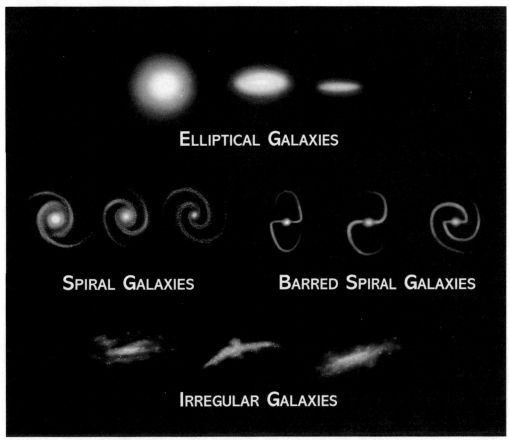

ELLIPTICAL GALAXIES

SPIRAL GALAXIES

BARRED SPIRAL GALAXIES

IRREGULAR GALAXIES

Q. Is Earth part of a galaxy?

A. Earth is part of a spiral galaxy called the Milky Way that contains billions of stars, and the Milky Way is part of the Local Group, which is a cluster of about 25 galaxies. The Milky Way is about 100,000 light-years across, and the Local Group is about three million light-years across.

Q. Are all galaxy clusters that large?

A. Some clusters contain thousands of galaxies and stretch across many millions of light-years. Very large galaxy clusters are called superclusters. Our Local Group is part of what is known as the Local Super-cluster, in which there are more than 100 galaxy clusters. Astronomers think that there may also be clusters of superclusters. The spaces between clusters are empty voids many times larger than the clusters themselves.

Q. What keeps the stars in a galaxy together?

A. The stars within a galaxy are kept together by gravity. This same force holds together stars, planets, and solar systems.

Star Gazers

Astronomers are people who study planets, stars, and other objects in space. In their work, astronomers use computers, telescopes, and other specialized instruments, and they also use various kinds of complex mathematics. They develop equations and theories to explain the origins and behavior of stars and other bodies in space.

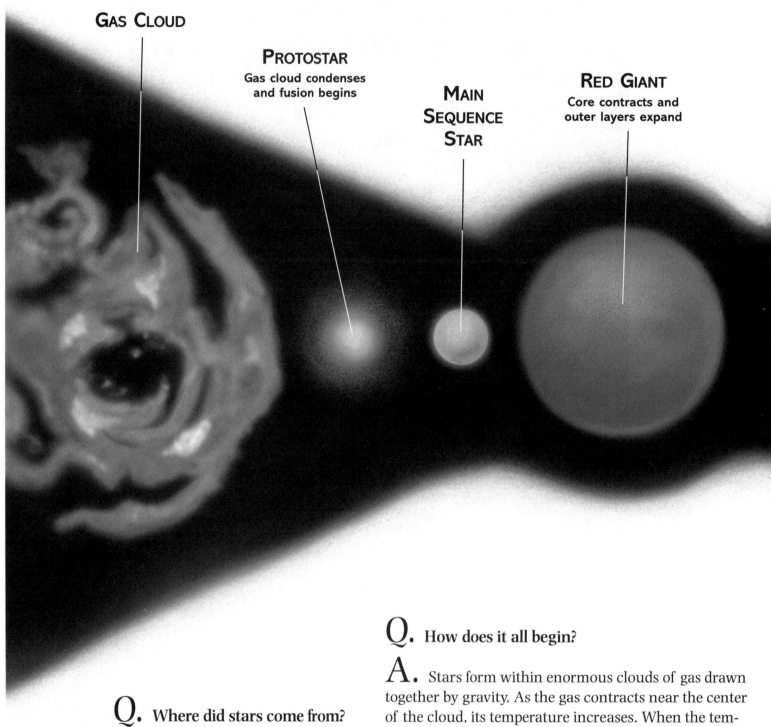

GAS CLOUD

PROTOSTAR
Gas cloud condenses
and fusion begins

**MAIN
SEQUENCE
STAR**

RED GIANT
Core contracts and
outer layers expand

Q. Where did stars come from?

A. Some stars have been in existence since early in the history of the universe. Others, like our sun, came from material produced by the first stars. Astronomers believe that stars have a specific life cycle in which they are born, grow, and die.

Q. How does it all begin?

A. Stars form within enormous clouds of gas drawn together by gravity. As the gas contracts near the center of the cloud, its temperature increases. When the temperature at the core reaches about four million degrees Fahrenheit, nuclear fusion begins, tremendous amounts of energy are produced, and the star begins to shine. Over a star's life, many changes in its appearance occur, mostly due to changes in the production of energy at its core.

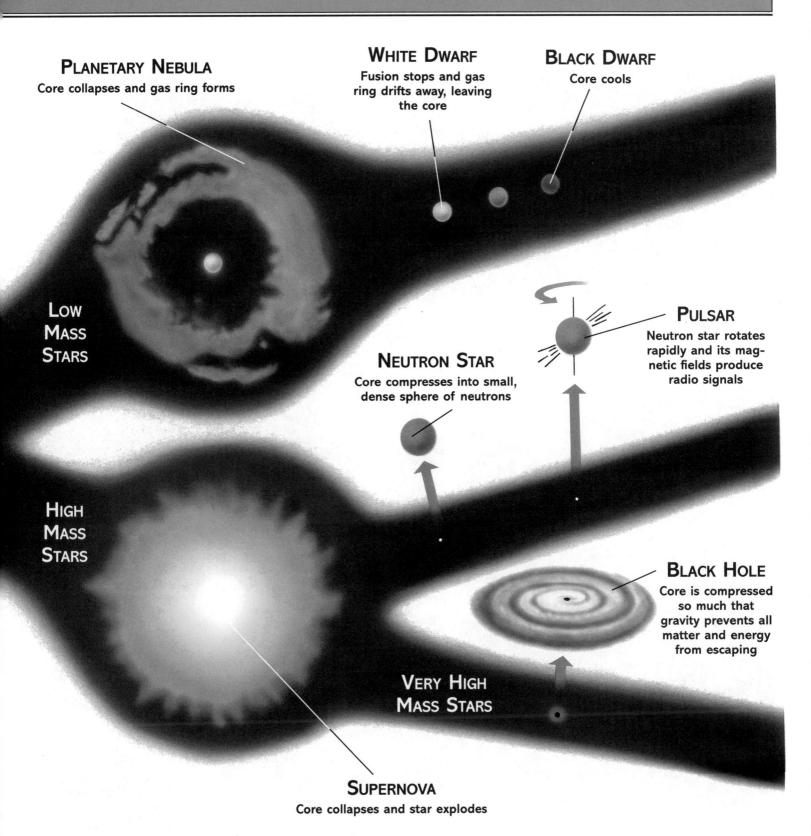

PLANETARY NEBULA
Core collapses and gas ring forms

WHITE DWARF
Fusion stops and gas ring drifts away, leaving the core

BLACK DWARF
Core cools

LOW MASS STARS

PULSAR
Neutron star rotates rapidly and its magnetic fields produce radio signals

NEUTRON STAR
Core compresses into small, dense sphere of neutrons

HIGH MASS STARS

BLACK HOLE
Core is compressed so much that gravity prevents all matter and energy from escaping

VERY HIGH MASS STARS

SUPERNOVA
Core collapses and star explodes

Q. **Are all stars the same?**

A. All stars form in pretty much the same way, but they are very different at different points in their life cycle. Also, the later stages of a star's life can take any of several paths depending on the *mass* of the star, or on how much matter it is made of.

Q. How did our solar system form?

A. Our solar system was born about five billion years ago. At that time, a gigantic, drifting cloud of dust and hydrogen gas began to condense to form a sphere. The particles packed together very tightly and became hotter and hotter. After a while, the terrific heat at the center of the sphere put into motion a chain of nuclear explosions. It was then that the sun began to shine. Nearby gases and dust particles were blasted away by the energy of the sun and formed a spinning oval ring. As the particles cooled, they clustered together, forming rocky or icy masses called planetesimals (pla nuh TEH suh mulz). These planetesimals formed the rest of the solar system, consisting of planets, moons, asteroids, meteoroids, and comets.

Q. What is a planet?

A. A planet is a spherical body of substantial size that is held in orbit by the gravitational pull of a star. Planets do not give off light of their own. They reflect the light of nearby stars.

Q. How many planets are in our solar system?

A. There are nine planets in our solar system. Four planets, known as inner planets, are rocky and much smaller than the enormous outer planets. The inner planets orbit close to the sun. They are Mercury, Venus, Earth, and Mars. In between the inner and outer planets is a band of rock and metal called an asteroid belt. The four large outer planets are Jupiter, Saturn, Uranus, and Neptune, which consist mainly of gases. Pluto, the ninth planet, is the smallest as well as the outermost planet.

What's the Matter?

The sun contains 99 percent of the matter in our solar system. The remaining one percent of the solar system is the nine planets, comets, moons, asteroids, and meteoroids. The great distances between the planets contain planetary dust and debris.

COMPARATIVE SIZES OF SUN AND PLANETS

Pluto   Neptune   Uranus   Saturn   Jupiter   Mars   Earth   Venus   Mercury   Sun

SUN

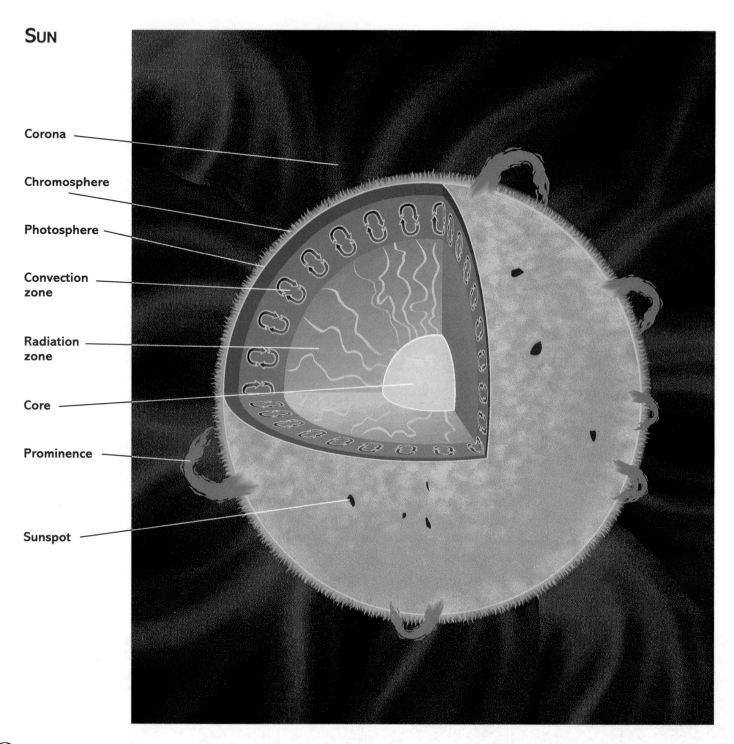

Corona

Chromosphere

Photosphere

Convection zone

Radiation zone

Core

Prominence

Sunspot

Q. **What is the sun?**

A. The sun is a small or medium-size star that is about 900 times wider than Earth. The sun is made of hydrogen and helium gases and has four layers called the *corona* (kuh RO nuh), the *chromosphere* (KRO muh sfere), the *photosphere* (FO tuh sfere), and the *core.* In between the core and the photosphere are two regions called the radiation zone and the convection zone. The churning gases at the sun's core reach extreme temperatures—about 25 million degrees Fahrenheit.

SUNSPOT

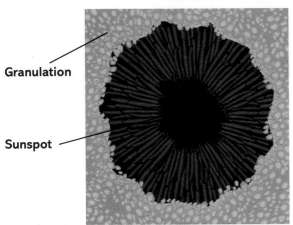

Granulation

Sunspot

MAGNETIC FIELD
LINES OF PROMINENCE

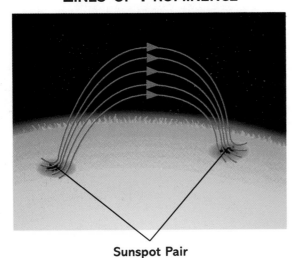

Sunspot Pair

PROMINENCE

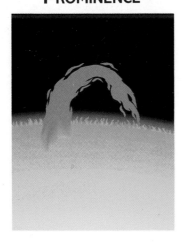

Q. **Why does the sun shine?**

A. At the sun's core, hydrogen atoms are constantly joining to form helium atoms. This process is called *nuclear fusion.* When fusion occurs, matter is turned into energy. When this energy is released, the sun shines, giving us heat and light. Our sun converts six million tons of hydrogen into helium every second and converts four million tons of matter into energy every second.

Q. **How long will the sun keep shining?**

A. Astronomers think that the sun is about halfway through its life. They estimate that the sun is now about 4.6 billion years old, so it would have enough energy to keep shining for another five billion years.

Q. **What is a sunspot?**

A. Astronomers studying the sun often see dark regions on its surface. These dark places are called *sunspots.* Sunspots appear dark because they are cooler than the rest of the sun's surface. Sunspots are actually magnetic storms on the sun's surface. The number of sunspots that appear on the sun always varies, but periods of great sunspot activity seem to occur every 11 years.

Warning: Dangerous to View

People should never look at the sun through binoculars or a telescope. The intense heat and light would be blinding. It is also dangerous to look directly at the sun with the naked eye. The sun's intense light can cause permanent damage to human eyes.

Q. **What is a planetary orbit?**

A. All of the nine planets circle, or orbit, the sun in the same direction. Except for Pluto, the orbits of the planets are almost circular. Scientists refer to planetary orbits as being elliptical—slightly flatter than a circle. Pluto's orbit extends from well beyond to just inside Neptune's orbit.

Q. **Aside from circling the sun, do the planets move?**

A. In addition to orbiting or revolving around the sun, the planets also rotate. You know that the Earth takes 365 days to orbit the sun and 24 hours to make one complete circle, or rotation, on its axis. Each of the planets moves around the sun and rotates on its axis.

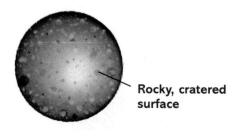

Rocky, cratered surface

MERCURY

Q. **What is the planet Mercury like?**

A. Mercury is the closest planet to the sun. It is terrestrial (tuh RES tree ul), meaning it has a solid surface like Earth does. Mercury has almost no atmosphere; it is so small and so close to the sun that its weak gravitational field can't hold on to any gases. A day on Mercury lasts 59 Earth days. The surface temperature reaches 800 degrees Fahrenheit during the day and -300 degrees Fahrenheit during its long night. Mercury has the greatest temperature change of any planet. A year on Mercury (the time it takes to orbit the sun) is equivalent to 88 Earth days.

The History of a Theory

In the second century, a scientist named Ptolemy developed a theory that Earth was the center of the universe. Ptolemy thought that all objects in the sky traveled in orbits around Earth as Earth remained still. It was not until the early sixteenth century that Ptolemy's theory was challenged. A Polish astronomer named Nicolaus Copernicus believed that the sun, not Earth, was at the center and the planets traveled in orbits around it. At the time, most people did not believe Copernicus's theories, but today we know that many of them are true.

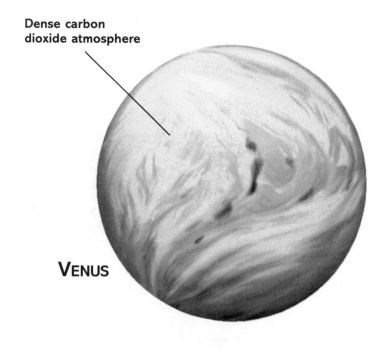

Dense carbon dioxide atmosphere

VENUS

Q. Can Mercury be seen from Earth?

A. It is difficult to spot Mercury from Earth because it is visible on some days only during twilight hours. The sun's brightness also makes Mercury difficult to see, since it is so close to the sun.

Q. What are conditions like on Venus?

A. Although Venus is approximately the same size as Earth and it is terrestrial, conditions on the Venusian surface are very harsh. Recently, two spacecraft, *Pioneer Venus 1* and *Magellan,* were able to penetrate the thick atmosphere of this planet. They learned that the atmosphere is mostly poisonous carbon dioxide and that fierce winds push yellow clouds of acid across the planet surface. During the day, temperatures reach 900 degrees Fahrenheit, making Venus the hottest planet in the solar system. The atmosphere on Venus is very thick; its air pressure is 90 times greater than Earth's. Life as we know it could surely never exist on Venus.

Q. Why is Venus hotter than Mercury?

A. Venus is almost twice as far from the sun as Mercury, so you might expect Mercury to be hotter. However, Venus has a thick atmosphere of gases while Mercury has no gases surrounding it. When energy from the sun strikes Mercury, much of it quickly bleeds off into space. Venus's thick atmosphere traps much of the energy from the sun and makes the planet hotter.

A Year and a Day

A day on Venus lasts longer than a year! It takes Venus 243 Earth-days to rotate once on its axis, but only 224 Earth-days to revolve once around the sun. Another peculiarity of this planet is that Venus rotates from west to east. On Venus, the sun rises in the west and sets in the east.

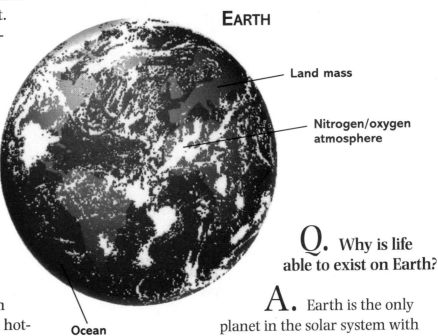

EARTH

Land mass

Nitrogen/oxygen atmosphere

Ocean

Q. Why is life able to exist on Earth?

A. Earth is the only planet in the solar system with large quantities of water in liquid form on its surface and in its atmosphere. The temperatures on Earth—which are determined in part by its distance from the sun—allow water to stay in liquid form. If Earth were closer to the sun, the oceans would boil away. If it were farther away, the oceans would freeze. All around the Earth is a sheltering layer of air called the atmosphere, which helps to keep the temperature fairly steady. Earth's atmosphere consists mostly of nitrogen and oxygen, with small amounts of carbon dioxide and water vapor. These conditions have allowed life as we know it to develop on Earth.

Q. **Why is Mars called the red planet?**

A. Mars shines with a red color because the surface soil of this planet is red. The Martian soil contains iron oxide; you may be familiar with a more common name for iron oxide—rust.

MARS

Martian Mountain

The largest volcano in the solar system is located on Mars. It's called Olympus Mons, which means Mt. Olympus, and it is one of four huge Martian volcanoes. This enormous mountain is 16 miles high and 370 miles wide, making it three times as tall as Earth's largest mountain, Mt. Everest. Olympus Mons was discovered by the United States spacecraft *Mariner 9*.

Q. **Does Mars have a moon?**

A. Actually, Mars has two moons. Both moons have an irregular shape, rather than being round. The smaller one, Deimos, is only about eight miles in diameter and orbits Mars from a distance of about 14,000 miles. Phobos is 14 miles in diameter and is about 6,000 miles from the planet. Their unusual shape and small size make some astronomers believe that the moons are actually asteroids that have been captured by Mars's gravitational pull.

Q. **Might there be life on Mars?**

A. Spacecraft sent to Mars have tested the soil there and found no signs of life. Many scientists feel this means no life exists there. Others think that life might have existed on Mars in the past. Still others feel that life might be present under the surface or in some unexplored region of the planet.

Scientists do have good reasons to wonder about the existence of life on this planet. There are many dormant volcanoes on Mars. Astronomers think that when these volcanoes were active, lava and steam poured from them. When the steam cooled, it fell as rain. It is thought that large moving rivers once crossed the surface of Mars. On Earth, life forms evolved in water, so it may have appeared at one time in the Martian rivers.

Those scientists who think there is no life on Mars point out that the planet has no liquid water today. Water seems to exist there only as ice, in the polar icecaps and perhaps under the Martian soil. Also, the Martian atmosphere is very thin, causing temperatures on Mars to average well below zero. Winds rage across the surface at very high speeds, causing dust storms that turn the Martian sky a deep pink.

Q. How big is Jupiter compared to the other planets?

A. Jupiter is more massive than all of the other planets in the solar system put together. More than 1,300 Earths could fit inside Jupiter if the planet were hollow.

Q. What is the large red spot on Jupiter?

A. The red spot on Jupiter is actually a giant windstorm called the Great Red Spot. This huge storm is almost three times the size of planet Earth.

Q. Could life exist on Jupiter?

A. Although we are only just beginning to explore Jupiter, scientists think that life as we know it could not exist there. The temperature is very cold, and the surface of this gigantic planet is an ocean of liquid hydrogen that could be as much as 10,000 miles deep.

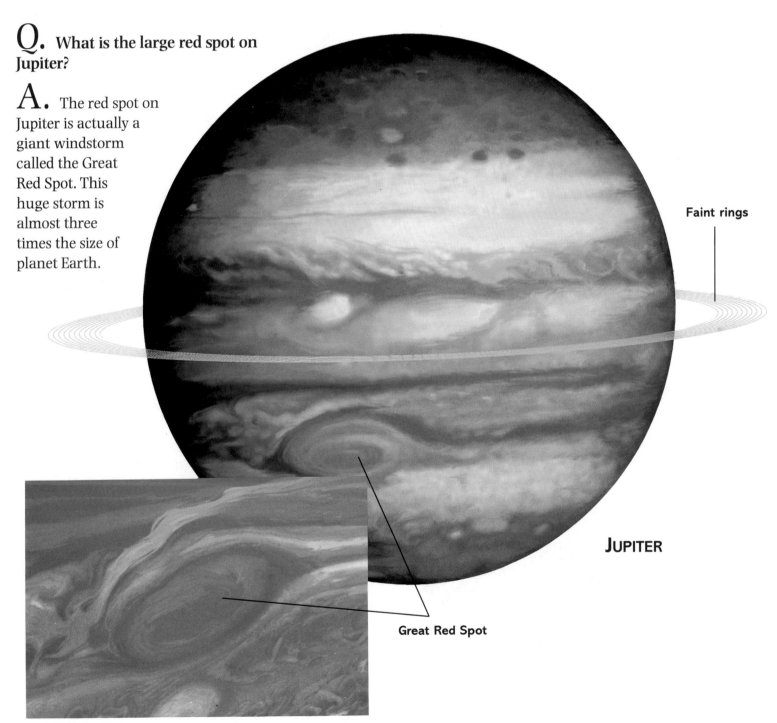

Faint rings

JUPITER

Great Red Spot

Q. What are Saturn's rings made of?

A. From Earth, Saturn seems to have only a few rings. After the *Voyager* spacecraft got a closer look, we learned that Saturn's large rings are made of thousands of smaller rings. Saturn's rings are made of ice fragments and small pieces of ice-covered rock.

Q. Is Saturn the only planet with rings?

A. For many years astronomers believed Saturn to be the only planet with rings. However, with great advances in space technology, it is now known that Jupiter, Uranus, and Neptune also have rings.

Q. How did Saturn's rings form?

A. Scientists do not really know for sure how the rings of Saturn formed. Some think that the rings contain materials left over from when Saturn first formed. Others think that the rings may be moons or asteroids that were broken to pieces.

SATURN

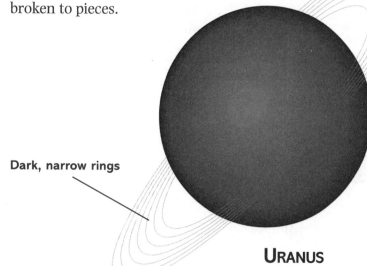

Dark, narrow rings

URANUS

Q. Why does Uranus appear to be lying on its side?

A. Uranus's axis is tilted at an angle of about 90 degrees. The planet rotates from south to north, rather than from east to west as Earth does. Scientists think Uranus was struck by a large object that knocked it on its side.

Q. What is Uranus made of?

A. Scientists have learned that this planet's surface seems to be an ocean of extremely hot water, methane, and ammonia surrounded by a thick atmosphere of hydrogen, helium, and methane. Beneath the ocean lies a rocky, molten core that is about the size of Earth.

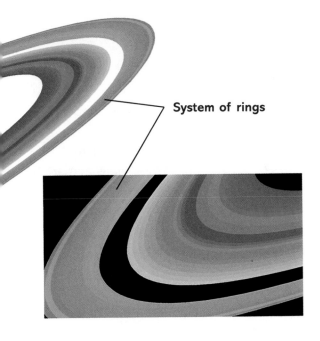

System of rings

A Special Moon

Titan is the name of Saturn's largest moon. It is one of the only moons in the solar system that has an atmosphere. Scientists were eager for the *Voyager* missions to send back information about this unique moon to learn if it could support life. The space probes found an atmosphere of nitrogen, which is similar to Earth. They also found that Titan's surface temperature of -280 degrees Fahrenheit keeps the moon frozen.

Great Dark Spot

Q. Why does Neptune look blue?

A. Like Uranus, Neptune has an atmosphere of helium, hydrogen, and methane. Methane absorbs red light and reflects blue and green light, which is why Neptune appears blue and Uranus appears blue-green. Neptune and Uranus are often called the twin giants because they are about the same size, mass, and temperature.

NEPTUNE

Faint rings

Q. When was Pluto discovered?

A. Pluto was the last planet in the solar system to be identified. The astronomer Clyde Tombaugh discovered it in February 1930.

Q. How big is Pluto?

A. Pluto is the smallest of all the planets in the solar system. It is smaller than Earth's moon. Because of its small size, scientists think that Pluto may actually be an escaped moon of Neptune. Another theory is that Pluto is actually an asteroid that drifted into a remote orbit around the sun.

PLUTO

Methane atmosphere

The Double Planet

Pluto has one large moon of its own called Charon. Because Charon is so large compared to Pluto, together they are sometimes referred to as a double planet. Charon is so large and so close that it revolves around Pluto in about six days, nine hours.

Q. What is a comet?

A. Comets make spectacular sights from Earth as they streak across the night sky. A comet is actually a chunk of rock, gas, and ice a few miles across that follows a very elongated orbit around the sun. Radiation from the sun strikes the comet's head and causes gas and dust particles to stream off of it and form two separate tails. As a comet nears the sun in its regular orbit, the size of its tails grows. As the comet moves away from the sun, the tails get smaller. The tails always stream off in the direction that the sun's radiation is moving—that is, away from the sun—no matter what direction the comet is traveling. This means that as a comet moves away from the sun, the tails actually form in front of the comet.

About Halley's Comet

Halley's comet is named for Edmond Halley, who was the first person to prove that comets have an elliptical orbit around the sun. Halley believed that comets seen in 1531, 1607, and 1682 were actually the same comet reappearing, and he predicted that it would again return in 1758. His prediction was correct and the comet was named in his honor. Halley's comet passes near Earth once every 76 years. It made its last appearance in 1986, and five space missions were sent to study it. They found a peanut-shaped nucleus at the head that covered an area of about ten by six miles.

COMET

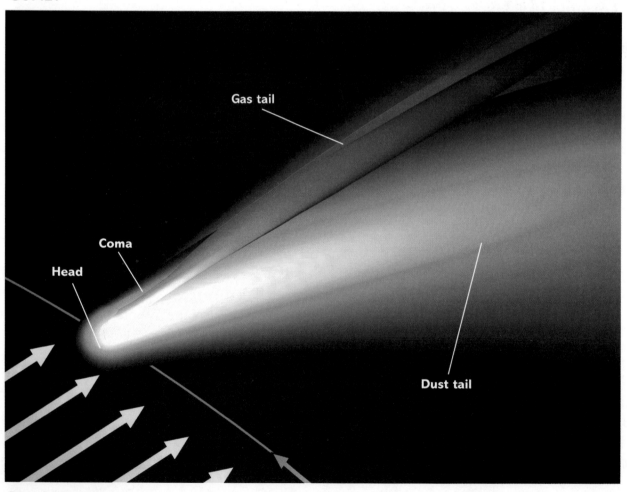

Gas tail

Coma

Head

Dust tail

Rays from sun

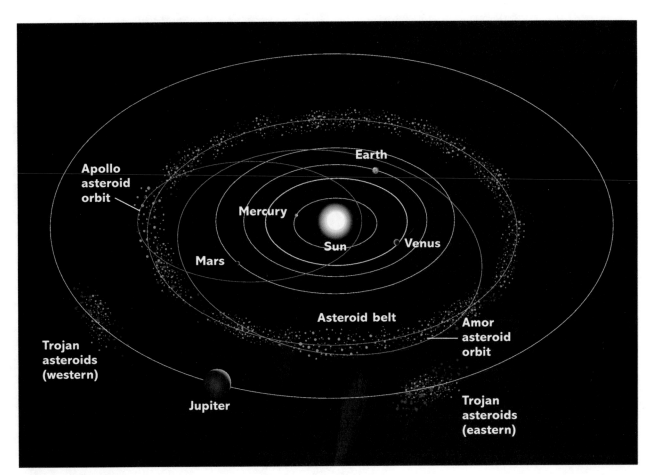

ASTEROID BELT

Q. What are asteroids?

A. Asteroids are rocky, metallic bodies that are much smaller than planets. Most asteroids in our solar system are scattered in a belt between the planets Mars and Jupiter. Within the belt, groups of asteroids follow different orbits around the sun. A few other groups of asteroids appear in other places in the solar system.

Q. What are the largest and smallest asteroids known to astronomers?

A. Ceres, the largest asteroid ever sighted, is 620 miles across—about one-quarter the size of Earth's moon. The smallest asteroids are only a few miles across.

Asteroids and Dinosaurs

Some scientists believe that an asteroid caused dinosaurs to become extinct about 65 million years ago. They believe that an asteroid struck Earth with a tremendous explosion and threw so much dust into the atmosphere that it changed the planet's climate. Dinosaurs, as well as 90 percent of all other life at the time, could not adapt to these changes, and they died out.

Q. **What does the surface of the moon look like?**

A. In 1969, humans first landed on the moon's surface, and we learned what the moon is like. It has a rocky, rough surface covered with thousands of scooped-out holes called craters. Scientists believe that the moon's craters were formed when meteors and other space debris crash-landed on the moon. There are also some large, smooth places on the moon. These smooth places are named oceans, seas, or lakes, depending on how big they are. They contain only rocks and soil, though—not water.

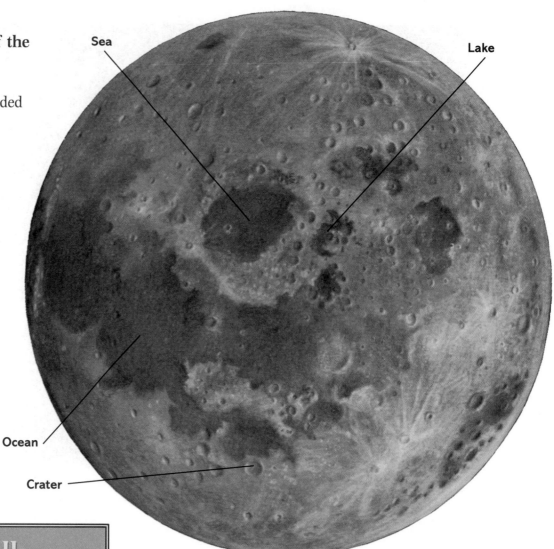

Sea

Lake

Ocean

Crater

LUNAR FEATURES

Moon Walk

The first human being ever to set foot on the moon was Neil Armstrong. Armstrong was part of the *Apollo 11* team that successfully landed a spacecraft on the moon's surface on July 20, 1969. Armstrong and the other members of his team took many photographs, performed several experiments, and brought home rock samples. Rock samples from *Apollo 11* as well as the five space missions to the moon that followed are still being studied by scientists all over the world. Some moon rocks are on public display in museums.

Q. **How big is the moon, and how far away is it?**

A. The moon is about one-quarter the size of Earth. It is our closest neighbor at about 230,000 miles. In space terms, that is considered quite close.

Q. **In what ways is the moon different from Earth?**

A. Aside from being much smaller, there are many other differences between Earth and the moon. First, the moon has no water or clouds—no atmosphere of any kind. There are no living things. There is also much less gravity on the moon—one-sixth that of Earth.

Waxing crescent

First quarter

Waxing gibbous

Full moon

Waning gibbous

Third quarter

Waning crescent

Q. **Why does the moon seem to change shape?**

A. We see the moon shine because light from the sun bounces off the moon's surface and is reflected toward Earth. As the moon revolves around Earth and Earth revolves around the sun, we see different parts of the moon's lit up surface. That's why the shape of the moon seems to change from a thin crescent to a full, fat circle. These shapes are called phases of the moon.

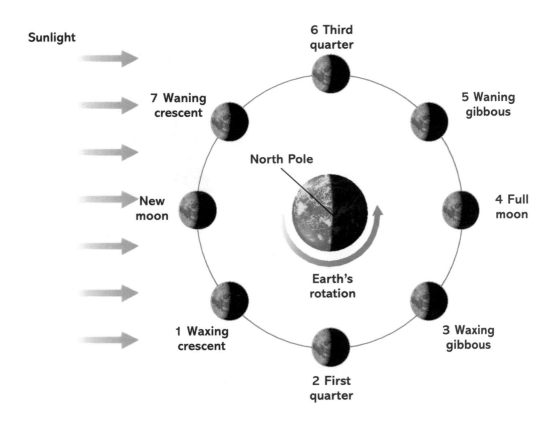

Big Black Sky

Did you ever wonder why all of the photographs taken on the moon show the sky to be black? It is very difficult to tell night from day on the moon. This is because there is no atmosphere on the moon to scatter light and make a blue sky.

Q. What is an eclipse?

A. Because the moon revolves around the Earth, and the moon and Earth together revolve around the sun, occasionally they block out some of the sun's light. During a solar eclipse, the moon comes directly between the sun and Earth. Slowly, the Earth moves into the moon's shadow, and sunlight is prevented from reaching the Earth.

There are two parts to this shadow. The smaller, inner shadow is called the *umbra* (UM bruh). The larger, outer shadow is the *penumbra* (puh NUM bruh). People standing directly in the path of the umbra see a total eclipse. People in the penumbra see a partial eclipse.

Q. What does it look like when a solar eclipse occurs?

A. Witnessing a total solar eclipse is quite an experience. The sky darkens, some animals think that evening has come, the air cools sharply, and for a few moments day turns into night. One very important rule to remember when viewing a solar eclipse is never to look directly at the sun.

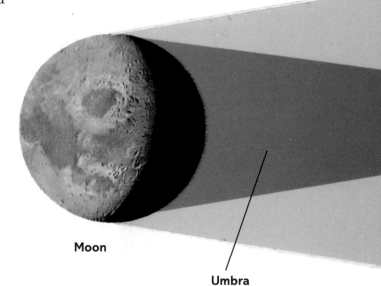

Moon

Umbra

SOLAR ECLIPSE

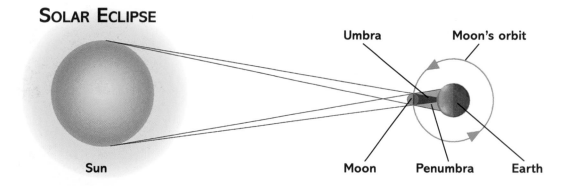

Sun

Umbra

Moon's orbit

Moon

Penumbra

Earth

LUNAR ECLIPSE

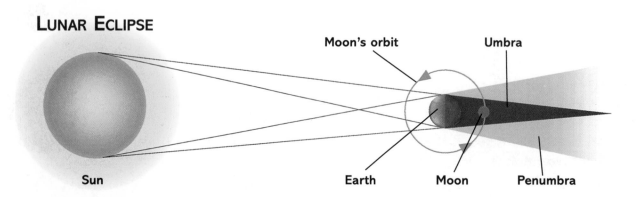

Sun

Moon's orbit

Umbra

Earth

Moon

Penumbra

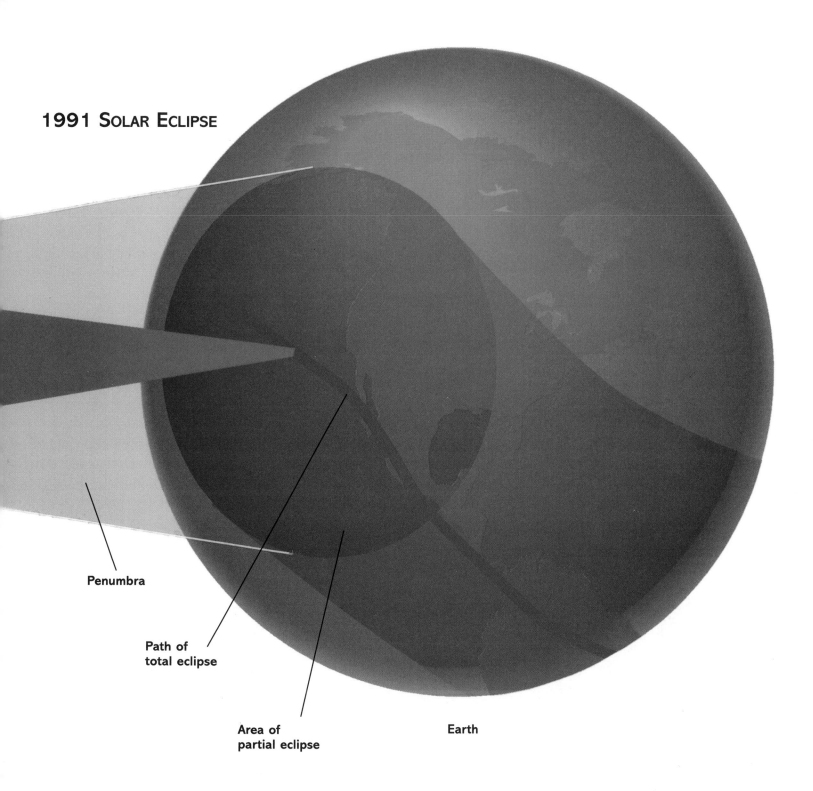

1991 SOLAR ECLIPSE

Penumbra

Path of
total eclipse

Area of
partial eclipse

Earth

Q. What is a lunar eclipse?

A. When the Earth comes directly between the sun and the full moon, a lunar eclipse occurs. This time, the moon is passing through the Earth's shadow. When the moon moves through the umbra, there is a total eclipse. If only part of it moves through the umbra, there is a partial eclipse. When Earth's shadow falls on the full moon, the moon's pale glow darkens to a deep, coppery color.

Q. How do telescopes help people study outer space?

A. The telescope has always been the main tool of astronomy. Telescopes magnify or enlarge images of faraway objects. There are two basic types of telescopes: *reflecting* telescopes and *refracting* telescopes. A reflecting telescope uses a concave mirror called the primary mirror to reflect light. The diameter of this mirror, called the aperture (AP ur chur), is used to talk about the size of the telescope. Generally, the larger the aperture, the more powerful the telescope. A refracting telescope uses a convex lens, called the objective, to collect light. Most astronomers today work with big reflecting telescopes.

Q. Where do astronomers store huge telescopes?

A. Telescopes are housed in enormous buildings called observatories. Most observatories are located atop tall mountains, above the thick clouds that might blur the images of celestial bodies.

Eyepiece

Light

Primary mirror

Secondary mirror

REFLECTING TELESCOPE

Giant Telescopes

Ten giant telescopes have been built in recent times. They are reflecting telescopes whose apertures range from 120 to 236 inches. The largest working single-mirror telescope in the world is on Mt. Semirodriki in Russia. Because it is so expensive to make huge single mirrors, astronomers are beginning to use multiple-mirror reflecting telescopes.

Light

Objective lens

Eyepiece

REFRACTING TELESCOPE

Q. Are there telescopes in space?

A. The largest telescope ever sent into space is the Hubble Space Telescope, launched in 1990. Although there were some technical problems with the Hubble, it still can record objects 10 times better than the best telescopes on Earth.

HUBBLE SPACE TELESCOPE

Ancient Astronomy

In ancient times, astronomers had nothing but their eyes with which to view the stars and the patterns they made. Yet, ancient astronomers were able to identify five planets and to chart lunar and solar eclipses. It wasn't until 1609 that Italian scientist Galileo Galilei made his own version of a telescope, using a concave and a convex lens mounted inside a lead tube. With his telescope, Galileo was able to view craters on the moon, sunspots on the sun, the rings of Saturn, and some of Jupiter's moons.

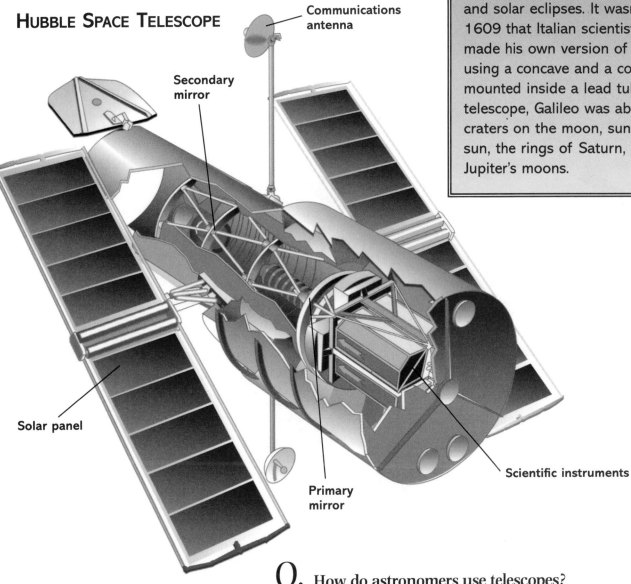

Communications antenna

Secondary mirror

Solar panel

Primary mirror

Scientific instruments

Q. How do astronomers use telescopes?

A. Surprisingly, most professional astronomers spend very little time looking through the eyepieces of telescopes. Instead, their telescopes are hooked up to complex instruments that allow the scientists to watch the image captured by the telescopes on video screens. They also use computers to control the telescopes and study the information the telescopes provide.

Q. How did astronauts go to the moon?

A. When the Apollo astronauts went to the moon in 1969, they got there in the Apollo Command Module. Before making the final landing on the moon, they moved into a smaller spacecraft, called the Apollo Lunar Excursion Module, which separated from the larger Command Module. This was the spacecraft that actually landed on the moon's surface while the Command Module continued to orbit the moon. You can see pictures of the Apollo Lunar Excursion Module, often nicknamed LEM, in many of the photographs of astronauts walking on the moon.

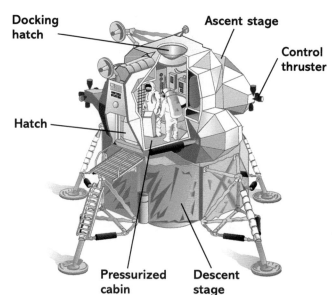

APOLLO LUNAR EXCURSION MODULE

MIR SPACE STATION

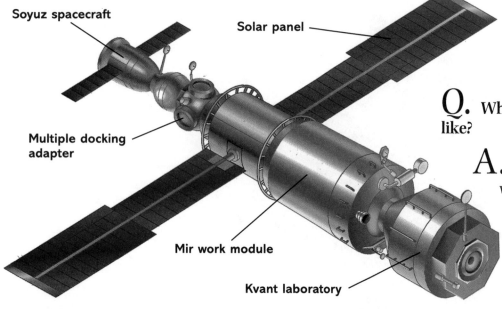

Q. What were the first trips into space like?

A. Soviet scientists amazed the whole world when they put the first satellite, *Sputnik 1*, into orbit around Earth in 1957. A few weeks later, they sent the first living creature into space—a female dog named Laika. In 1961, Soviet cosmonaut Yuri Gagarin became the first person to travel to outer space, and two years later, cosmonaut Valentina Tereshkova became the first woman space traveler. Today, the Russian space program's main project is the space station *Mir*. In Russian, the word *mir* means peace. Cosmonauts remain aboard the space station for several months at a time and perform many experiments. *Mir* is the largest and most complex space station ever to orbit Earth.

Travel to the Stars

Light from the closest star takes more than four years to reach the Earth. It would take a starship thousands of years to journey there, so people are not yet able to travel to the stars. One day, it is hoped that there will be new colonies of people on the moon, on space stations, and maybe on some of the planets in our solar system and beyond.

Q. Why do we send unpiloted craft into space?

A. We have sent many unpiloted space probes to study parts of our solar system. Three very special probes, however, were *Pioneer 10, Voyager 1,* and *Voyager 2,* which were sent to study the giant outer planets Jupiter, Saturn, Neptune, and Uranus. When they finished their assigned tasks of studying these planets, the probes continued out of our solar system into the vast reaches of space. The probes contain information about us and our planet in case they are ever found by alien life forms. *Voyager* carries photographs, drawings, and a recording that offers peaceful greetings in 53 languages and sounds of a baby crying, a human heartbeat, the roar of ocean waves, and birds, crickets, whales, and elephants calling.

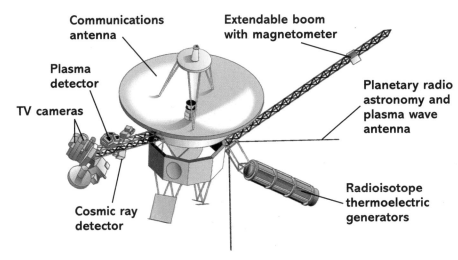

Communications antenna

Extendable boom with magnetometer

Plasma detector

TV cameras

Planetary radio astronomy and plasma wave antenna

Cosmic ray detector

Radioisotope thermoelectric generators

VOYAGER SPACECRAFT (DEEP SPACE)

SPACE SHUTTLE AT TAKEOFF

Q. What is the Space Shuttle?

A. The Space Shuttle can travel into space, come back to Earth, and then go into space again at a later date. It is reusable, unlike any spacecraft before it. The Space Shuttle blasts off like a rocket, orbits the Earth while its crew carries out various scientific experiments, and then glides back down to Earth like an airplane. It is hoped that the Space Shuttle can launch probes to other planets for further exploration.

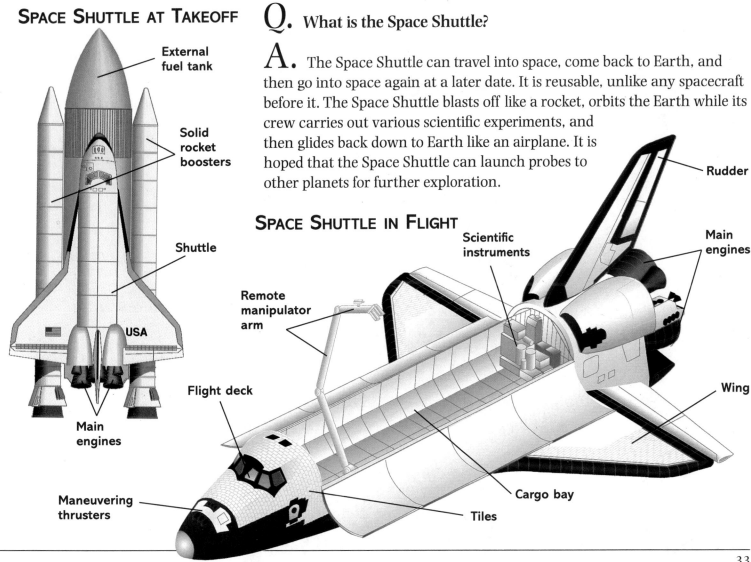

External fuel tank

Solid rocket boosters

Shuttle

USA

Main engines

SPACE SHUTTLE IN FLIGHT

Scientific instruments

Rudder

Main engines

Remote manipulator arm

Flight deck

Maneuvering thrusters

Cargo bay

Tiles

Wing

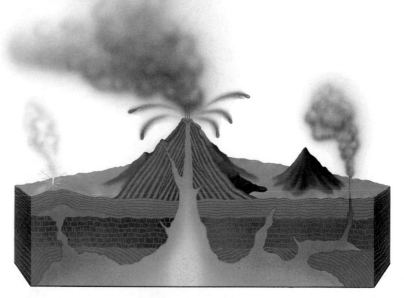

How Does the
EARTH CHANGE?

The Earth changes every day. Continents drift, mountains wear down, oceans rise and fall, and storms form and fade. Volcanoes, earthquakes, and hurricanes also cause sudden, violent changes in the Earth.

Q. What is the Earth made of?

A. The Earth has three main sections, or layers: the outer layer, or *crust;* the middle layer, or *mantle;* and the center layer, or *core.* Each layer has two different parts to it. The crust includes the continental crust, which is the part we call land, and the oceanic crust, or the ocean floor. The upper part of the mantle is solid; the upper mantle and the crust together are called the *lithosphere* (LIH thuh sfere). The lower mantle is a semi-molten layer called the *asthenosphere* (as THEE nuh sfere), which lies below the lithosphere. The outer core contains extremely hot liquid iron. The inner core, the hottest part of Earth, is a solid ball of iron and nickel.

Q. How old is the Earth?

A. Until the 1800s, scientists thought the Earth was only a few thousand years old. In recent times, geologists studied the structure of Earth's rocks and decided that the Earth was much, much older. By testing rocks to find their age, scientists estimated that the Earth first formed about 4.6 billion years ago as a mass of molten matter. Since then, the Earth has been slowly cooling.

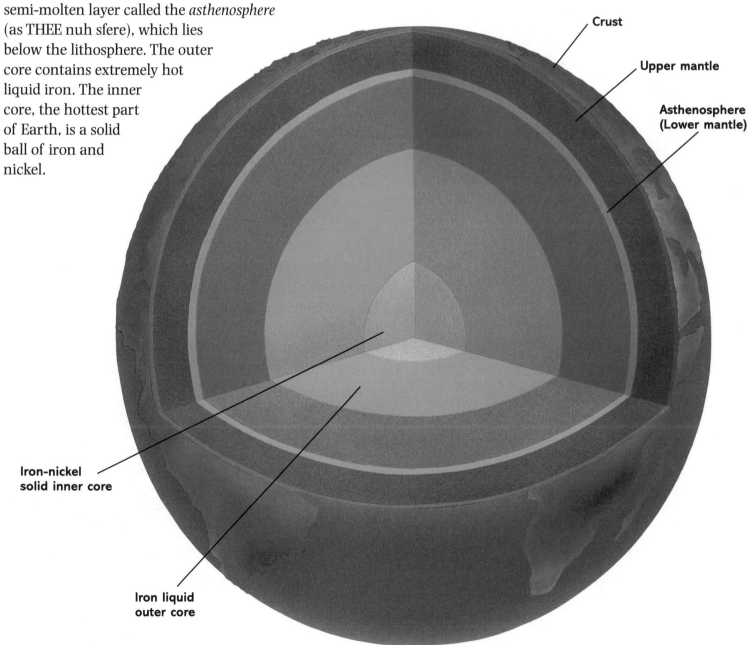

Crust

Upper mantle

Asthenosphere
(Lower mantle)

Iron-nickel
solid inner core

Iron liquid
outer core

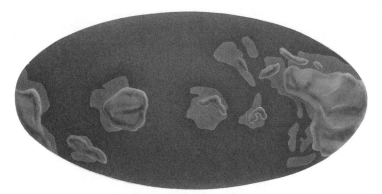

500 million years ago

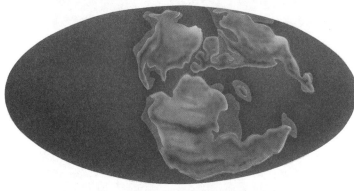

300 million years ago

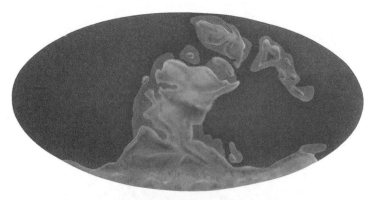

100 million years ago

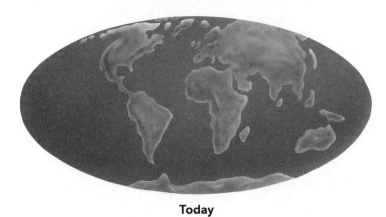

Today

Q. **Has Earth always looked the same as it does today?**

A. The surface of the Earth has been changing constantly since the Earth was first formed. Some of the changes are sudden and obvious, such as the ones caused by earthquakes and volcanoes. Others occur so gradually that they could hardly be noticed even over a person's lifetime. Probably the biggest of these slow changes is continental drift. The major landmasses, or continents, are actually moving at a very slow rate over the Earth's outer layer, some drifting toward each other and some away from each other. In fact, scientists believe that over millions of years the arrangement of the continents has changed a great deal.

When life first appeared on Earth over 500 million years ago, much of the land was covered by water, and the continents looked very different than they do today. About 300 million years ago, before dinosaurs first appeared, the continents had drifted together to form one huge landmass called Pangaea (pan JEE uh). By the time the dinosaurs disappeared 65 million years ago, Pangaea had broken up and the continents were drifting toward the positions they are in today.

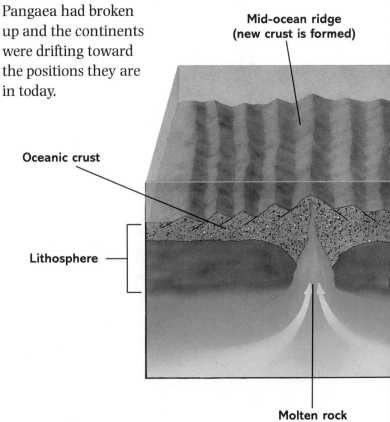

Mid-ocean ridge (new crust is formed)

Oceanic crust

Lithosphere

Molten rock

Q. What makes the continents drift?

A. The lithosphere (the Earth's crust and upper mantle) forms a shell around the planet, but it is broken into different sections called *plates*. The plates float on the semi-liquid lower mantle, or asthenosphere, kind of the same way your breakfast cereal floats on top of the milk in your bowl.

Of course, the plates cover the entire surface of the Earth, so the edges are right next to each other. In some places, heat within the Earth forces molten rock up between two plates; the edges of the plates are pushed apart and new crust is formed between them. In other places, this drifting forces the edges of two plates to collide, and one of them is forced under the other into the lower mantle, where it becomes molten. As new crust is formed in one place, old crust is destroyed in another, and the plates and continents gradually move.

Know Your Plates

Some scientists believe that the Earth's crust has six large plates, six small plates, and several fragments that are very small. Continental plates, such as the African plate, the Eurasian plate, the South American plate, and the North American plate, hold the landmasses we know today. Other plates, such as the Pacific plate and the Nazca plate, lie beneath the oceans and are known as oceanic plates.

THE EARTH'S CRUST

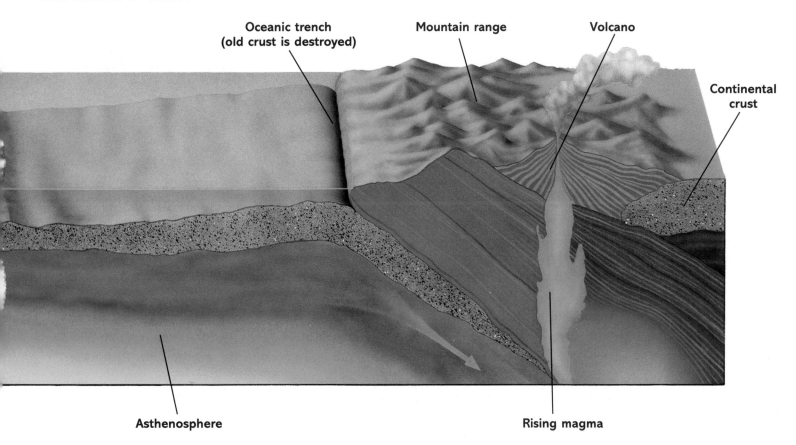

Oceanic trench (old crust is destroyed)   Mountain range   Volcano   Continental crust

Asthenosphere   Rising magma

Q. **What causes an earthquake?**

A. As the plates in the Earth's crust move, they create enormous amounts of tension and pressure. These forces can cause cracks, called faults, to appear in the rigid rock in the Earth's crust. After a fault forms, forces from the moving plates can cause the rock on either side of a fault to slide against each other, and this is what we call an earthquake. Faults are grouped according to whether the rock moves up, down, sideways, or in two directions at once.

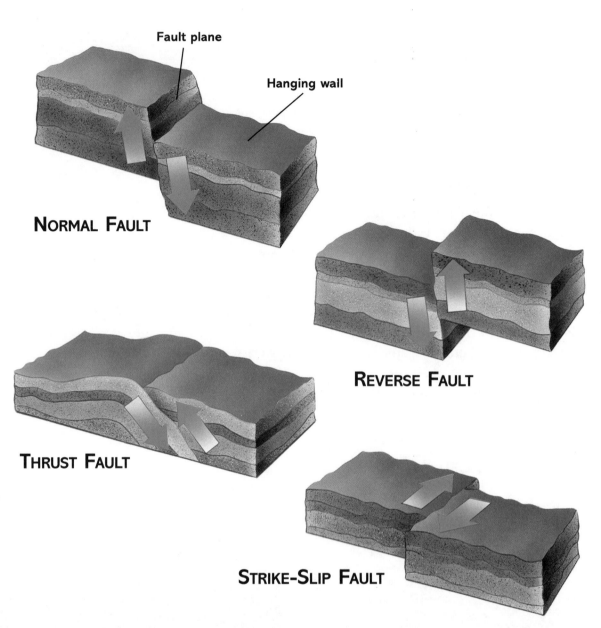

Fault plane

Hanging wall

NORMAL FAULT

REVERSE FAULT

THRUST FAULT

STRIKE-SLIP FAULT

How Strong Was That Quake?

One way to measure the intensity of an earthquake is the Mercalli Scale, which explains what is felt or seen by the people who observe the earthquake. A level I earthquake would not be noticed; a level III earthquake would make small objects tremble slightly or perhaps fall off shelves; a quake large enough to crack windows and move heavy furniture would be at level VI; at the top end of the scale, level XII, the ground would move in waves, great cracks would appear, and all buildings would be destroyed.

Another system of measuring earthquakes is the Richter Scale, which uses tools called seismographs (siz MUH grafs) to measure the energy released by an earthquake. A seismograph gives a number with a decimal point to rate the earthquake. Although there is no upper limit on a seismograph, no earthquake has ever registered higher than 8.9.

Q. Can an earthquake happen anywhere on Earth?

A. Most faults—and therefore most earthquakes—occur within a few hundred miles of a plate's edge. Earthquakes occur most often where plates are moving toward each other, but they also happen where plates are moving away from each other. Also, some faults have formed far from the edge of a plate, and they occasionally cause small earthquakes.

Q. Can people tell when an earthquake will happen?

A. Scientists have no way of accurately predicting earthquakes, but some stories indicate that animals might. For instance, preceding a large earthquake that occurred in 373 BC, in Helas, Greece, it was said that rats, snakes, weasels, centipedes, worms, and beetles left the city in droves. Residents of Messina, Italy, reported that dogs throughout the city howled uncontrollably just before an earthquake in 1783. One hour prior to an earthquake in Tashkent in the former Soviet Union in 1966, masses of ants carried their eggs out of anthills.

Scientists can tell where an earthquake has occurred, though. The point at which rock movement was greatest is called the *focus* and is usually underground. The *epicenter* (EH pih sen tur) is the spot on the surface directly above the focus. Scientists can identify these points by taking measurements of the quake from different locations and comparing them.

LOCATING AN EARTHQUAKE

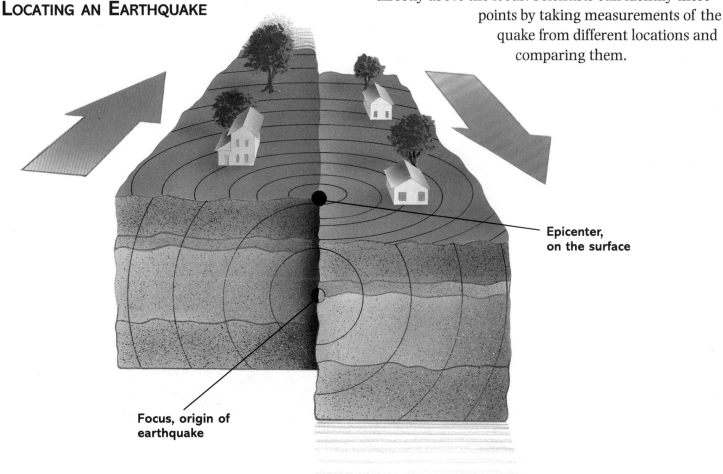

Epicenter, on the surface

Focus, origin of earthquake

Q. **What is a volcano?**

A. Sometimes the powerful forces within the Earth cause ruptures in the crust that release gases, ash, and molten rock from the mantle. These are volcanoes. When most people think of volcanoes, they think of cone-shaped mountains that suddenly and violently erupt; these volcanoes usually appear at places where two of the Earth's plates are grinding against each other. Other volcanoes are long fissures, or cracks, that form in spots where plates are moving apart. These volcanoes steadily spill out molten rock that cools slowly and forms a gentle slope on either side of the fissure. Volcanoes can also form away from plate edges, above unusually active parts of the Earth's mantle.

Q. **What was the largest volcanic eruption?**

A. The largest volcanic eruption in modern times happened in 1883 on the island of Krakatoa in Indonesia. Most of the island vanished in an extremely violent explosion that was heard 3,000 miles away. The eruption caused 36,000 deaths, created 120-foot waves, and threw a huge cloud of dust and ash 50 miles into the air.

Types of Volcanoes

Eruptions are put into groups based on how violent they are. Hawaiian eruptions produce slow-moving streams of thick lava that can flow great distances over the ground. These eruptions are seldom violent. Strombolian eruptions produce lava and send a steady stream of ash and small rock into the air. Vulcanian eruptions produce lava that is more fluid, and they hurl huge chunks of rock into the air. Peleean eruptions send a fast-moving river of rock and lava racing down the volcano. Plinian eruptions start with a huge explosion that destroys the top of the volcano and sends ash, lava, and rock streaming into the air.

VOLCANO

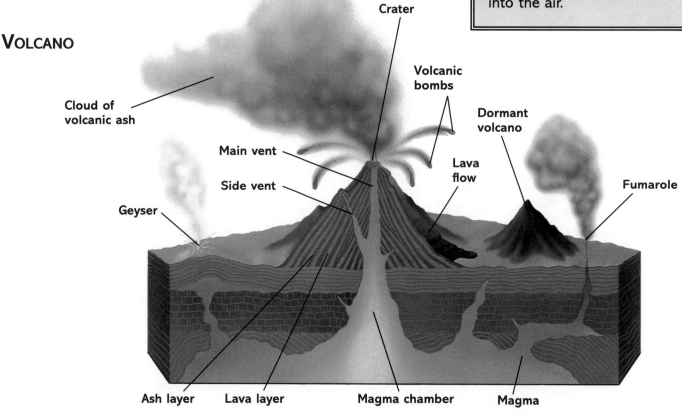

Crater

Volcanic bombs

Dormant volcano

Cloud of volcanic ash

Main vent

Side vent

Lava flow

Fumarole

Geyser

Ash layer   Lava layer   Magma chamber   Magma

UNDERWATER FORMATIONS

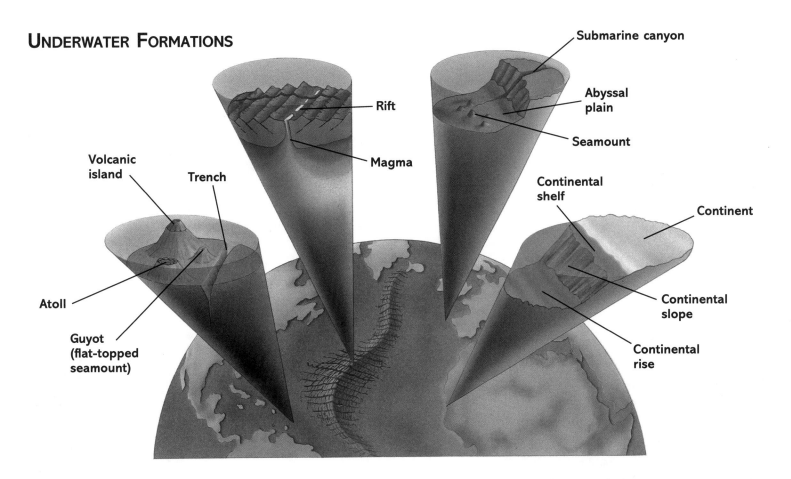

Q. What does the ocean floor look like?

A. People might think of the ocean floor as a flat, sandy plain dotted with a few rocks and caves. Parts of it, called abyssal plains, are long stretches of flatland, but much of the ocean floor contains towering seamounts, live volcanoes, flat-topped plateaus, twisting canyons, deep trenches, craggy ledges, and great slopes that lead up to the edges of the continents.

Q. Will the oceans always be the same size they are now?

A. The ocean floor changes over time just the way the land around us does. Underneath the ocean floor, magma from the mantle pours out of faults between the Earth's oceanic plates. New ocean floor spreads sideways, and the other ends of the plates collide with continental plates and plunge beneath them into the mantle. As these changes take place over many millions of years, new mountains are formed, old ones wear down, volcanoes build up to poke above the water as islands, and others collapse and fall back into the sea. These shifts slowly change the size, shape, and location of both land and sea.

Atlantic vs. Pacific

Today, the Atlantic Ocean is growing wider while the Pacific Ocean is shrinking. However, over the course of one year, an ocean's size may change by only an inch or so. In addition, the level of Earth's oceans is also changing. About a million years ago, great sheets of ice held so much of Earth's water that the ocean level fell. Over time, these sheets of ice began to melt and the level of the oceans rose. Changes such as this have occurred all through Earth's history.

Q. **Are all rocks the same?**

A. There are three different types of rock. *Igneous* (IG nee us) rock is formed from magma from deep within the Earth that is forced up and cooled. *Sedimentary* (sed ih MEN tuh ree) rock is formed from bits and pieces of other rocks and from the remains of once-living organisms. *Metamorphic* (met uh MOR fik) rock is rock that has been changed by intense heat or pressure.

Q. **Are all igneous rocks the same?**

A. When magma is extruded, or forced, to the Earth's surface as lava from volcanoes or fissures, it is called extrusive. The ocean floor and many oceanic islands are made up of basalt, which is an extrusive igneous rock. Andesite is another extrusive igneous rock; it is the most common volcanic rock in the Andes Mountains in South America, which is how the rock got its name. Rhyolite, obsidian, and pumice are other extrusive igneous rocks. Intrusive igneous rock is magma that never reaches the Earth's surface and becomes solid underground. Many intrusive igneous rocks form in large sheets called *dikes* that run through existing rock layers. Other sheets run parallel to existing rock layers and are called *sills*. Granite and gabbro are intrusive igneous rocks.

Q. **How do sedimentary rocks form?**

IGNEOUS ROCKS

Andesite · Rhyolite · Granite · Obsidian · Pumice · Basalt · Gabbro

SEDIMENTARY ROCKS

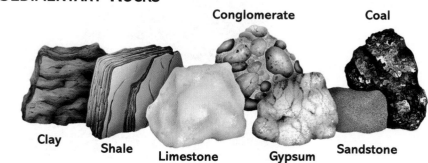

Conglomerate · Coal · Clay · Shale · Limestone · Gypsum · Sandstone

METAMORPHIC ROCKS

Skarn · Slate · Marble · Serpentinite · Schist · Gneiss

A. Wind, rain, and other forces wear away existing rock and produce pebbles, sand, silt, mud, and dust. All of these bits and pieces are moved around by wind, glaciers, or running water. When they finally come to rest, usually in water, the loose grains are gradually cemented together, forming rocks such as sandstone, gypsum, and shale. Other times, these pieces undergo natural chemical reactions that form sedimentary rocks such as limestone. Coal and some other sedimentary rocks come from organic matter—the remains of plants and animals—that have been chemically changed and then compressed. Sedimentary rocks form in layers called strata. Many sedimentary rocks hold fossils, which have helped scientists to learn much about how life evolved on Earth.

Q. How does metamorphic rock form?

A. Sometimes when energy is applied to a material, the material changes. When you put batter in the oven and apply energy in the form of heat, the batter changes into cake. When energy is applied to rocks in certain ways, they change and become metamorphic rocks. In regional metamorphism, energy from intense pressure within the Earth creates rocks such as schist, gneiss, serpentinite, and slate. In contact metamorphism, energy from heat creates small rocks such as marble and mineral deposits such as skarn.

The Rock Cycle

The Earth's moving plates cause changes in the crust that force all three types of rocks into the interior of the Earth. Some of this rock is forced down into the mantle, where the intense heat turns it back into magma. Eventually, some of this magma returns to the Earth's surface as lava. The lava forms igneous rocks, which in turn form metamorphic rocks and sedimentary rocks, each of which in turn forms more metamorphic rocks and sedimentary rocks. Again some of these new rocks are forced down into the mantle and become magma. This continuing complex process in which rocks are formed and reformed is called the rock cycle.

THE ROCK CYCLE

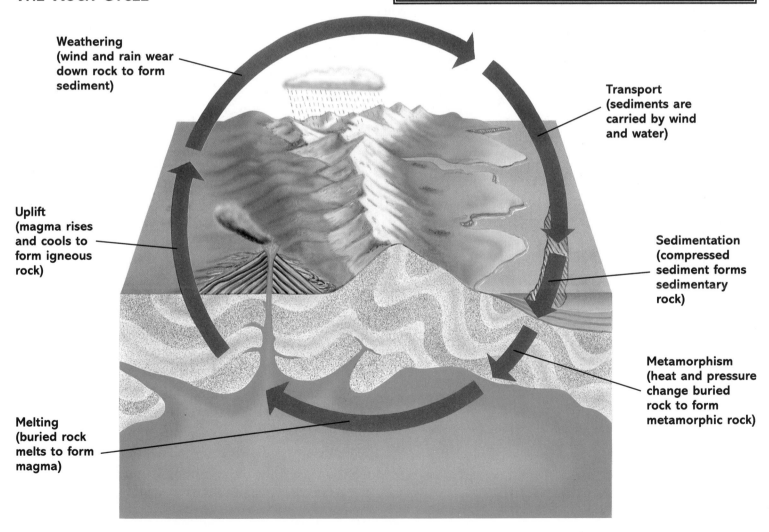

Weathering
(wind and rain wear down rock to form sediment)

Transport
(sediments are carried by wind and water)

Uplift
(magma rises and cools to form igneous rock)

Sedimentation
(compressed sediment forms sedimentary rock)

Metamorphism
(heat and pressure change buried rock to form metamorphic rock)

Melting
(buried rock melts to form magma)

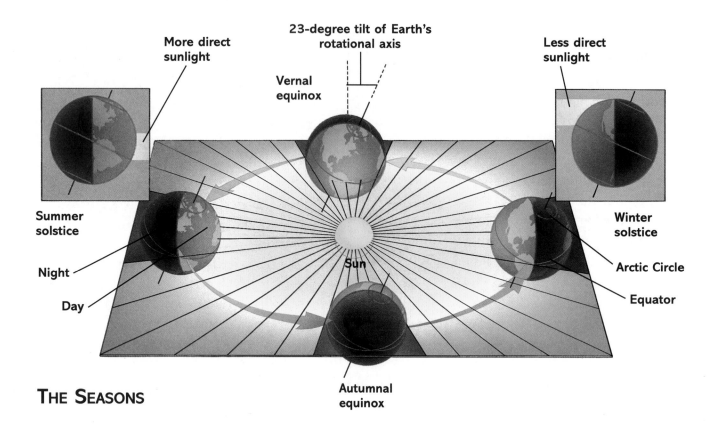

More direct sunlight

23-degree tilt of Earth's rotational axis

Vernal equinox

Less direct sunlight

Summer solstice

Night

Day

Sun

Autumnal equinox

Winter solstice

Arctic Circle

Equator

THE SEASONS

Q. What causes the seasons?

A. The Earth's axis is an imaginary line running through the Earth from the North Pole to the South Pole, and it's slightly tilted. At certain times during the year as the Earth travels around the sun, the northern half of the planet is tilted toward the sun and the southern half is tilted away from it. From June to September, the northern half gets more energy from the sun and experiences summer, and the southern half gets less energy from the sun and experiences winter. Between December and March, the Earth is on the other side of the sun and the situation is just the opposite: More sun means summer in the south, and less sun means winter in the north. The very longest day is called the summer solstice (SAHL stus). The very shortest day is the winter solstice.

Q. What causes autumn and spring?

A. In March and September, exactly halfway between the solstices, sunlight is received in equal amounts by both the Northern and Southern hemispheres. Days and nights are exactly the same lengths in both hemispheres. These positions are called the equinoxes (EE kwuh noks es). The vernal equinox marks the beginning of spring and the autumnal equinox signals the beginning of the fall season.

Q. Do all places on Earth go through these seasons?

A. No. The tilt of the Earth's axis doesn't really change the amount of sunlight that reaches the middle portion of the Earth, so those tropical areas have pretty much the same temperature year-round. Changes in the atmosphere all across the planet during the year do affect some of these areas, though, and give them wet seasons of heavy rains and dry seasons of clear skies.

Q. What is the atmosphere?

A. The atmosphere is a blanket of gases that surrounds the Earth, and the conditions in the atmosphere make Earth different than all the other planets in the solar system. The atmosphere makes life on Earth possible by providing us with the air we breathe. It also keeps out many of the sun's harmful rays and keeps in a constant amount of the sun's heat. Without it, temperatures would be over 150 degrees Fahrenheit during the day and would drop hundreds of degrees at night.

Q. What are the divisions of the atmosphere?

A. Earth's atmosphere is actually composed of several layers. The lowest layer, the troposphere (TRO puh sfere), is about five miles high at the poles and about ten miles high at the equator. It contains virtually all of the water in the atmosphere, and it is where weather occurs. The stratosphere (STRA tuh sfere), mesosphere (MEH zuh sfere), thermosphere (THUR muh sfere), and exosphere (EK so sfere) lie above the troposphere. Air begins to get very thin and finally disappears the higher up you go.

EARTH'S ATMOSPHERE

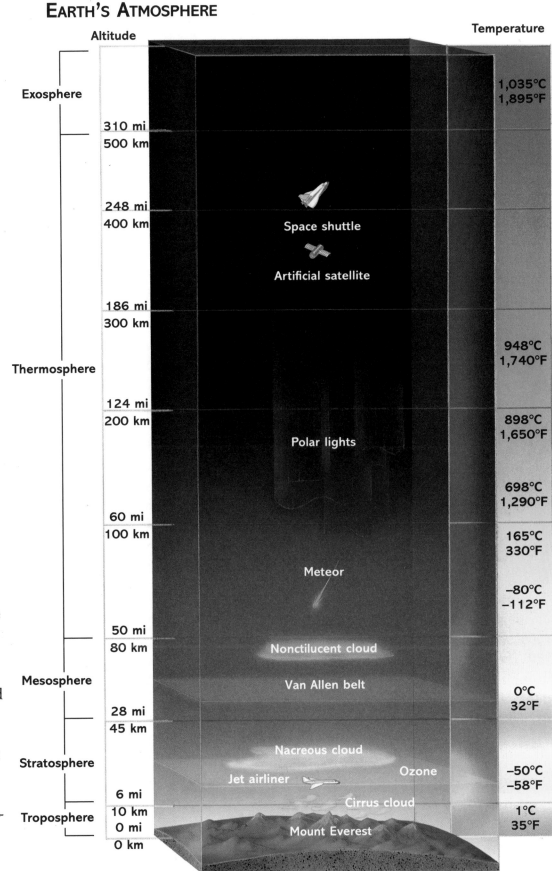

Altitude		Temperature
Exosphere		1,035°C 1,895°F
310 mi 500 km		
248 mi 400 km	Space shuttle	
	Artificial satellite	
186 mi 300 km		
Thermosphere		948°C 1,740°F
124 mi 200 km		898°C 1,650°F
	Polar lights	
		698°C 1,290°F
60 mi 100 km		165°C 330°F
	Meteor	−80°C −112°F
50 mi 80 km	Nonctilucent cloud	
Mesosphere	Van Allen belt	
		0°C 32°F
28 mi 45 km		
	Nacreous cloud	
Stratosphere	Jet airliner Ozone	−50°C −58°F
6 mi		
	Cirrus cloud	1°C 35°F
Troposphere 10 km 0 mi	Mount Everest	
0 km		

Q. **What is the water cycle?**

A. The sun's heat warms the Earth and lower atmosphere, causing some liquid water to *evaporate*, or turn into water vapor; living things, both plant and animal, also release water into the air as vapor. Warm air that contains water vapor rises and cools as it moves upward. The cooling vapor *condenses* back into liquid water in small droplets that cling to dust particles. Together, millions of these tiny droplets form clouds, and the clouds produce rain, hail, and snow that fall back to Earth. This *precipitation* collects in rivers, lakes, and, eventually, the oceans. Then, the whole thing begins all over again. This important process is called the water cycle.

Q. **Has there always been water on Earth?**

A. Earth's atmosphere has contained water for as long as it has existed. For millions of years, much of that same water has traveled around the world as it went through the stages of the water cycle over and over and over. Incredibly, the water you drink today might have been drunk millions of years ago by a dinosaur!

Q. **What forms can water take?**

A. Water is unusual because it is the only substance on Earth that commonly appears as a liquid (liquid water), a solid (ice), and a gas (water vapor) in nature. Any type of matter can take these three forms, depending on its temperature and the pressure around it, but natural conditions on Earth make it so other substances usually appear in only one or two of the forms.

Q. **Is steam the same as water vapor?**

A. Water vapor cannot be seen by the human eye. It is a gas. Steam is tiny droplets of water that have condensed, or cooled enough to return to liquid form.

Where Is the World's Water?

About three-quarters of Earth is covered by water, and more than 97 percent of all of the water on Earth is salt water. The Earth's largest bodies of water are the oceans, and most of the water that ends up there picks up salt and other minerals as it travels over land and through rivers on its way to the sea. That leaves less than 3 percent of Earth's water that is fresh, or without salt. About 2 percent of that fresh water is in the form of ice in the polar ice caps. That leaves less than 1 percent of fresh water for living things to use. Even though most of the Earth is covered with water, drinking water can still be difficult to find.

Approximate Percentage of Total Water Supply:	That Is Found in:
97.308	Oceans, seas, and salt lakes
2.04	Polar ice and glaciers
.61	Underground reservoirs
.009	Lakes
.005	Soil as moisture
.001	Atmosphere as vapor
.0001	Rivers

THE WATER CYCLE

Step 1. Energy from the sun warms the Earth's surface and air above it.

Step 3. Warm, moist air rises and cools as it moves upward. Water vapor condenses into clouds.

Step 2A. Water from the oceans, lakes, rivers, and the ground evaporates (becomes water vapor) into the air.

Step 2B. Water from living things transpires (is released as water vapor) into the air.

Step 4. Precipitation forms and falls.

Step 5. Runoff precipitation flows into rivers, lakes, and underground reservoirs and back to oceans

Q. **What are clouds?**

A. You already know that water evaporates and becomes water vapor. As water vapor rises in the air, it cools and condenses into tiny droplets of water. Many of these droplets together form clouds. Most of us think of clouds as things in the sky, but they can also form right near the ground. When that happens, we call it fog.

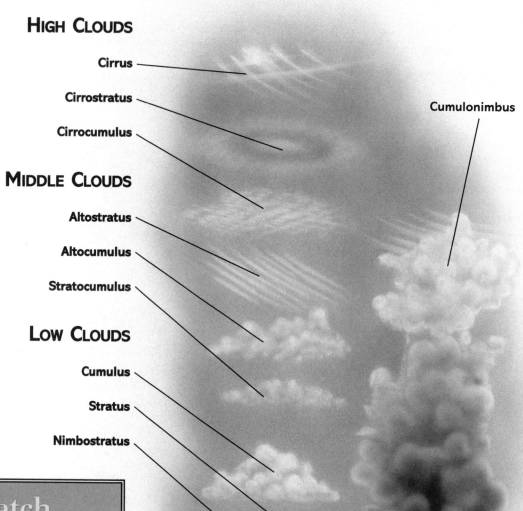

HIGH CLOUDS
- Cirrus
- Cirrostratus
- Cirrocumulus

MIDDLE CLOUDS
- Altostratus
- Altocumulus
- Stratocumulus

LOW CLOUDS
- Cumulus
- Stratus
- Nimbostratus

Cumulonimbus

Mix and Match Cloud Names

Scientists classify clouds according to their altitude (how high they are in the sky) and their shape. They use different Latin words to describe the altitude and shape and combine them to describe a particular type of cloud. Another Latin word is used in the name if a cloud causes precipitation.

High altitude cloud	Cirro
Mid altitude cloud	Alto
Low altitude cloud	NO PREFIX
Feathery, ice crystal clouds	Cirrus
Heaped, puffy clouds	Cumulus
Layered, flat sheets of clouds	Stratus
Rain, snow, or hail clouds	Nimbus

Q. **What do clouds do?**

A. Clouds play a big part in weather. The most obvious thing that clouds do is create precipitation, returning water back to Earth. Clouds also affect weather by keeping in some of the heat that reaches the Earth from the sun.

FORMATION OF RAIN

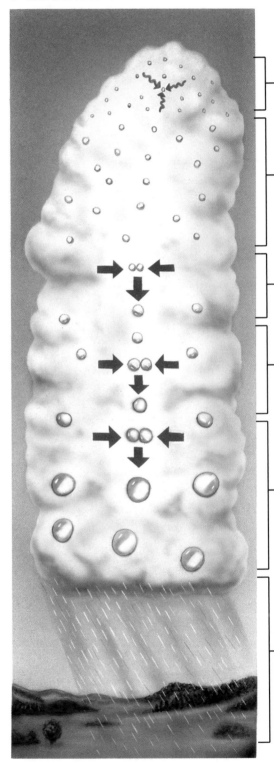

Step 1. Water vapor condenses into a cloud droplet.

Step 2. The cloud droplet grows as more water vapor condenses on it.

Step 3. Cloud droplets collide and water vapor condenses on them to form large cloud drops.

Step 4. Large cloud drops collide and water vapor condenses on them to form drizzle.

Step 5. Drizzle drops collide to form raindrop.

Step 6. Rain falls.

Q. What is rain?

A. Rain is the most common form of precipitation. The tiny water droplets that make up a cloud are so light in weight that the air holds them up. Inside a cloud, these tiny drops often collide and join together. They also grow when water vapor condenses on them as liquid water. If they become heavy enough, the air can no longer hold them up, and they fall to the ground as rain.

Q. Are there different kinds of rain?

A. Storytellers and poets have coined many names for different types of rain. We know terms such as drizzle, mist, downpour, rain falling in sheets, steady rain, showers, thunderstorms, and so on. Each of these terms describes a type of rainfall from extremely gentle to almost violent.

Q. What kind of clouds produce rain?

A. The cloud formations of most rainstorms are usually tall, puffy cumulus clouds. Sometimes there is so much moisture in the air, the huge cumulus clouds billow upward for thousands of feet, forming cumulonimbus rain clouds that cause violent, usually brief thunderstorms. Wide, low sheets of nimbostratus clouds produce steady rain that sometimes lasts for days.

Over the Rainbow

It takes two things to make a rainbow: sunlight and raindrops. When sunlight shines through raindrops, the light is bent and beautiful colors are seen against the clouds. Each color of the rainbow is made by many raindrops bending the light at a certain angle.

Q. Why are there different kinds of precipitation?

A. All precipitation begins with the cooling and condensing of water vapor in clouds. Different air currents, temperature, and humidity within clouds produce different kinds of precipitation.

Q. What is hail?

A. Hail is small pellets of ice that form from water droplets in clouds. In a tall cloud where air currents are strong enough and the temperature at the top of the cloud is cold enough, air currents can carry water droplets to the top of the cloud, where they freeze. The strong air currents can move these frozen drops up and down inside the cloud many times, and each time they rise up to the cooler air, a layer of ice freezes around them. Finally, these hailstones become too heavy for the air currents to hold up, and they fall to Earth.

Q. Why does it hail in the summer?

A. The conditions that form hail occur most often in the tall cumulonimbus clouds. These clouds stretch upward in the sky, sometimes for several miles, and they have cold temperatures at the top and strong air currents inside. We see hail more often in the summer because cumulonimbus clouds are more common and usually larger in the summer. These clouds form when large amounts of warm, moist air rise quickly and summer temperatures create large pockets of warm, moist air near the ground.

FORMATION OF HAIL

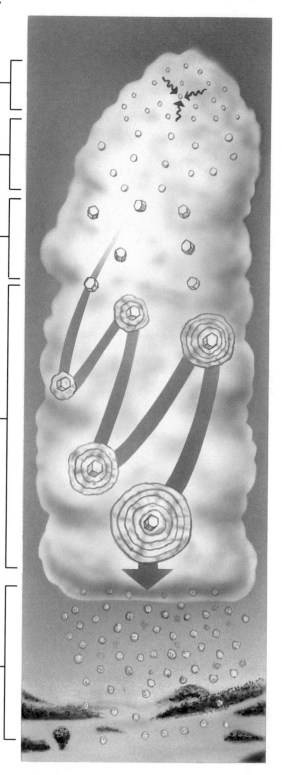

Step 1. Water vapor condenses into a cloud droplet.

Step 2. The cloud droplet grows as more water vapor condenses on it.

Step 3. Droplet freezes into an ice crystal.

Step 4. Air currents carry the crystal up, down, and horizontally through the cloud; droplets freeze around crystal in layers to form hail.

Step 5. Hail falls.

Q. What is lightning?

A. Lightning is electricity generated by the movement of particles in a cloud. Temperature differences within huge thunderheads cause air currents, which cause dust, water droplets, and hail to move around. The friction from this movement creates static electricity in the same way you do when you rub a balloon against your hair. Positively charged particles build up in the top of the cloud, and negatively charged particles build up in the bottom. The negatively charged particles in the bottom of the cloud attract positively charged particles from the ground, and they move toward each other. When they meet, lightning flashes.

Q. Does lightning only strike objects on the ground?

A. No. Lightning can also strike between two clouds or even within a cloud. It just takes a large build-up of positive charge in one place and negative charge in another.

Q. What is thunder?

A. The intense energy in a bolt of lightning generates heat. In fact, lightning heats the air around it to several thousand degrees Fahrenheit—perhaps as hot as the surface of the sun! The heat energy added to the air makes it expand quickly, and the air molecules move faster than the speed of sound. This very fast movement of air causes the noise we call thunder.

FORMATION OF LIGHTNING

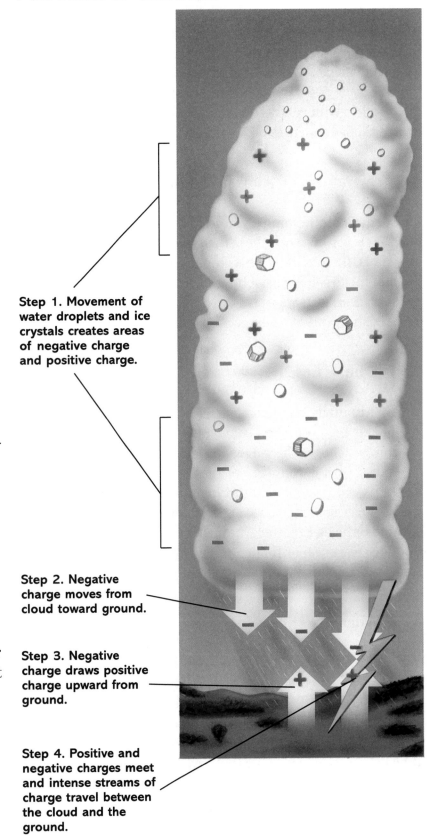

Step 1. Movement of water droplets and ice crystals creates areas of negative charge and positive charge.

Step 2. Negative charge moves from cloud toward ground.

Step 3. Negative charge draws positive charge upward from ground.

Step 4. Positive and negative charges meet and intense streams of charge travel between the cloud and the ground.

Q. **Why does it snow?**

A. Snow forms when the air temperature drops below freezing. The tiny water droplets in a cloud freeze and form ice crystals. These crystals grow into snowflakes as they collide with each other and as more water vapor condenses on them.

Q. **Why doesn't it snow in summer?**

A. Even in the summer, snow can form within clouds high up where the air is cold. As it falls, though, it passes through warm air and melts before it reaches the ground. If falling rain feels very cold to you, it may have been snow just a few seconds earlier.

Q. **What is frost?**

A. Although frost may look like snow as it blankets the ground on cold winter mornings, it is not snow. Frost does not fall from the sky; it appears out of the air. Air contains water vapor, and the vapor will freeze if it becomes cold enough. When the ground or objects on the ground are cold enough, water vapor that contacts them freezes right on them and forms frost.

Q. **What is frostbite?**

A. Frostbite occurs when part of the body gets so cold that blood cannot flow through the body tissues. If this happens for a long time, the tissue dies and can wither away. However, it takes quite a long time for frostbite to become that severe. Fingers and toes are the most easily "bitten" parts of the body.

FORMATION OF SNOW

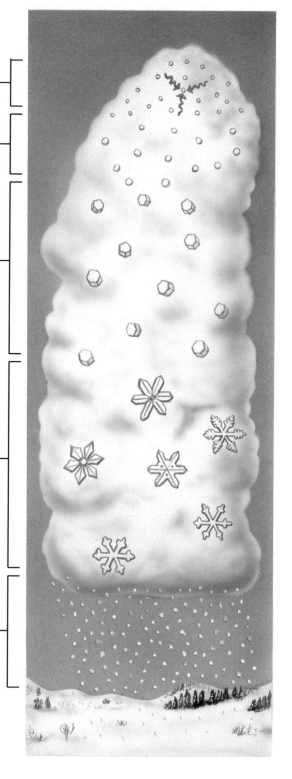

Step 1. Water vapor condenses into a cloud droplet.

Step 2. The cloud droplet grows as more water vapor condenses on it.

Step 3. Droplet freezes into an ice crystal.

Step 4. Ice crystal grows as water vapor condenses on it, water droplets freeze on it, and it collides with other ice crystals.

Step 5. Snow falls.

SNOW CRYSTALS

Column	Plate crystal	Needle	Irregular crystal	Sleet

Capped column	Stellar crystal	Spatial dendrite	Snow pellet	Hail

Q. **Why are no two snowflakes alike?**

A. Each snowflake is a collection of many ice crystals, and ice crystals come in a great many shapes. They can look like long columns, flat plates, thin needles, and many other things. The way a snow crystal looks depends on the temperature, height and amount of water of the cloud it forms in. Because flakes are made from so many different shapes, each one has a unique design. Snowflakes are dry when they form in air that is very cold and has less moisture. Dry flakes are very small and blow easily into snowdrifts. Wet snow occurs when the air is extremely humid and warm enough for many crystals to join together.

Rainbow Snow

Did you know that snow can come in colors? Pink and red snow are somewhat common in the arctic and mountainous regions of the world. This is because algae living among the ice crystals color whole patches of snow.

Q. What is a hurricane?

A. Hurricanes are very severe storms that form over warm tropical seas. There, warm temperatures mean that the air has much evaporated moisture and energy from heat. Huge amounts of these two things create enormous, violent storms that can stretch over hundreds of miles. The storms produce heavy rains, high winds, and enormous waves. Hurricanes can arise in the Atlantic Ocean, the Pacific Ocean, the Indian Ocean, and the China Sea.

HURRICANE

Wind speed of more than 190 mph

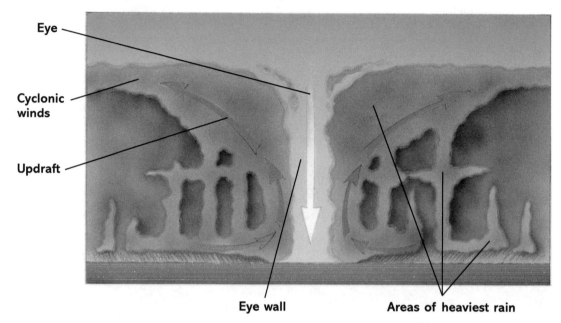

Eye

Cyclonic winds

Updraft

Eye wall

Areas of heaviest rain

Q. What is the eye of a hurricane?

A. The eye of a hurricane is a calm area at the very center of the swirling, spiraling mass of clouds. Cooler, heavier air at the center of the storm moves downward toward the Earth. In the rest of the storm, warm, moist air rises upward and produces rain. When a large tropical storm starts, the eye can be over 100 miles across. As the eye gets smaller and smaller, the storm becomes more and more violent.

Q. Can a hurricane travel across land?

A. Hurricanes are fueled by the heat and humidity that they suck up from the surface of tropical seas. As soon as they lose this power supply, they weaken and disappear. Hurricanes do reach land and cause damage there, but they die out soon afterward. Hurricanes also fade when they pass over cooler waters that don't supply the heat energy they need to keep going.

Hurricane Facts

• A hurricane can be 500 miles wide and 40,000 feet high. The entire storm moves at about 10 miles per hour.

• In one hour, a powerful hurricane can release the same amount of energy as sixteen 20-megaton nuclear bombs.

• Hurricanes in the Pacific are called typhoons.

• An Australian named Clement Wragge suggested giving names to hurricanes. At first they were given only female names. Now, an alphabetical list is made every year of alternating male and female names, and a new hurricane is given the next name on the list.

Q. **What is the difference between a tornado and a hurricane?**

A. Hurricanes are violent storms hundreds of miles across that form over the ocean in tropical climates. A tornado is a swirling column of air that can be between a few feet and a few thousand feet across. Hurricanes can last for days and travel thousands of miles. Tornadoes usually last for a few minutes and rarely travel more than a hundred miles.

Q. **Where do tornadoes come from?**

A. Tornadoes are always associated with thunderstorms. Sometimes, during a thunderstorm, a column of swiftly swirling air is produced. This column looks like a narrow, funnel-shaped cloud that extends from the clouds in the sky to the ground. Within this speeding cloud funnel are winds that can blow at hundreds of miles per hour. Scientists believe that tornadoes form when a pocket of warm, humid air near the ground rises quickly to meet cool, dry air in a passing cloud.

Q. **Do tornadoes occur only on land?**

A. Thunderstorms and tornadoes take place at sea as well as on land. When a tornado occurs at sea, it is called a waterspout.

Q. **What happens inside the funnel cloud of a tornado?**

A. Although they have tried, scientists cannot test the inside of a tornado. Tornadoes are so violent that any equipment in their path is destroyed. There have been some eyewitness accounts given by victims of tornadoes. They describe something similar to the eye of a hurricane, although much smaller.

TORNADO

- Updraft
- Vortex
- Rising air swirls clockwise
- Center of tornado
- Base of tornado

CLIMATE AND ECOSYSTEMS

Q. What is the difference between climate and weather?

A. Weather refers to the conditions in a particular place at a particular time, and it changes from one day to the next or even from one hour to the next. Climate refers to the kind of weather that a large region has over the course of a year. A region's climate stays the same for many years or decades, although it can change gradually.

Q. What determines a region's climate?

A. A region's climate is determined largely by where it is in the world. The amount of sunlight an area gets at any given time is important. Geographic features such as mountains and valleys make a difference, as do large lakes, oceans, and other bodies of water.

Q. How many different kinds of climates can be found on Earth?

A. There are three main types of climates: polar, temperate, and tropical. These three main climates each can be divided into three types based on the amount of rain that falls and the average temperature. The map shows you these nine climate types and where they occur throughout the world.

Q. What is an ecosystem?

A. An ecosystem consists of all of the living and nonliving things that interact with each other in a particular area. For example, a forest ecosystem is composed of birds and squirrels that live in the trees; rabbits and skunks that live in the bushes; insects that inhabit the region; all of the trees, bushes, and flowers that spring from the ground; and the soil, rocks, sunlight, rainwater, and air that make up the region. Ecosystems can be found in all of the environments on Earth, from polar regions to the equator to the depths of the ocean. The climate of a region is a part of the ecosystem and plays a large part in determining what kinds of organisms live there.

Q. How big is an ecosystem?

A. An ecosystem can be as big as an ocean, a forest, or even a planet. It can be as small as a drop of water in a pond. The boundaries of an ecosystem are determined by the person who is studying the ecosystem. People who study ecosystems are known as ecologists.

CLIMATES OF THE WORLD

North America

South America

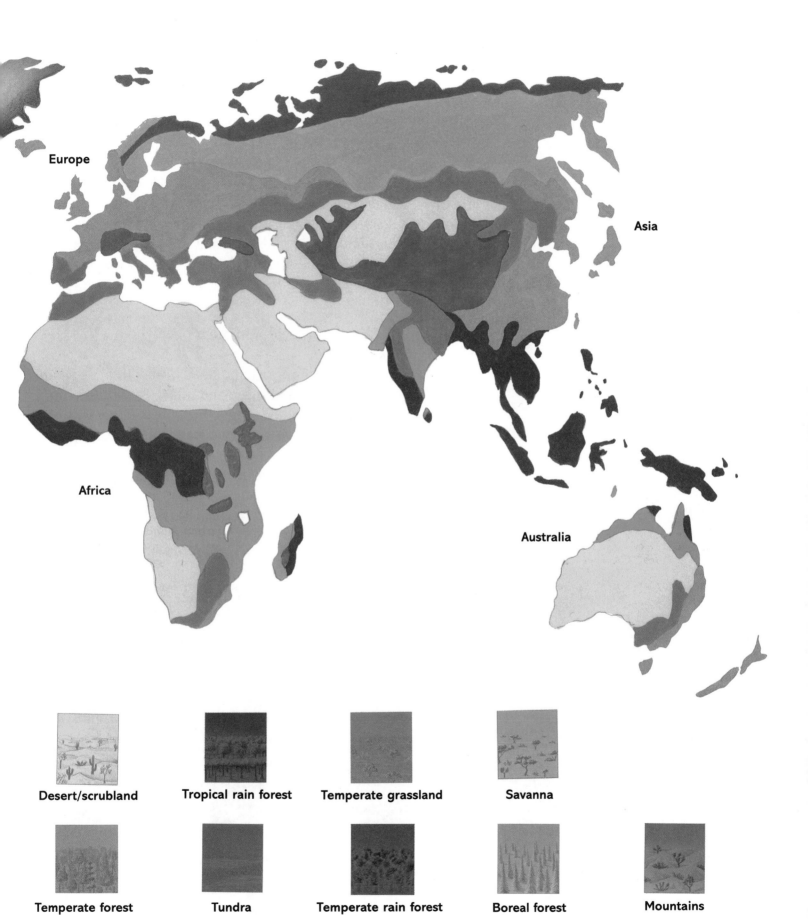

Europe

Asia

Africa

Australia

Desert/scrubland **Tropical rain forest** **Temperate grassland** **Savanna**

Temperate forest **Tundra** **Temperate rain forest** **Boreal forest** **Mountains**

Q. **What is pollution?**

A. Pollution occurs when people add unwanted materials to the natural environment in any of several ways. Sewage, oil, household wastes, chemicals from industry, and fertilizers and pesticides from farms can pollute the water. Paper, plastics, and items such as discarded batteries, old shoes, refrigerators, and so on are solid wastes that can pollute the land. Different gases produced by burning fuel in cars, by factories, and sometimes by household items such as spray cans can pollute the air when they are released into the atmosphere. Once pollutants get into the environment, it can take years or decades for them to go away.

Q. **Why is pollution harmful?**

A. Different pollutants can cause problems in different ways. Often, they contain chemicals that can be harmful to living things. Sometimes pollutants can alter conditions in the environment in ways that make it difficult for plants and animals to survive. Because plants and animals depend on each other for so many things, pollution that affects one kind of creature can often harm other creatures indirectly. If pollutants destroy a particular kind of plant, for instance, any animals that use that plant for food or shelter will be affected.

Q. **What is acid rain?**

A. Some of the pollutants we release into the air are gases containing nitrogen and sulfur. These gases can form acid compounds when they mix together with moisture in the air as the moisture condenses to form rain. This acid rain can damage buildings, harm plants, kill animals such as fish, and get into drinking water.

ATMOSPHERIC POLLUTION

Carbon dioxide, Sulfur dioxide, Carbon monoxide, Nitrous oxides, and other gases

Acid rain

Moisture in air

Sources of pollution:
Burning fossil fuels: Motor vehicles, industry, home

GREENHOUSE EFFECT

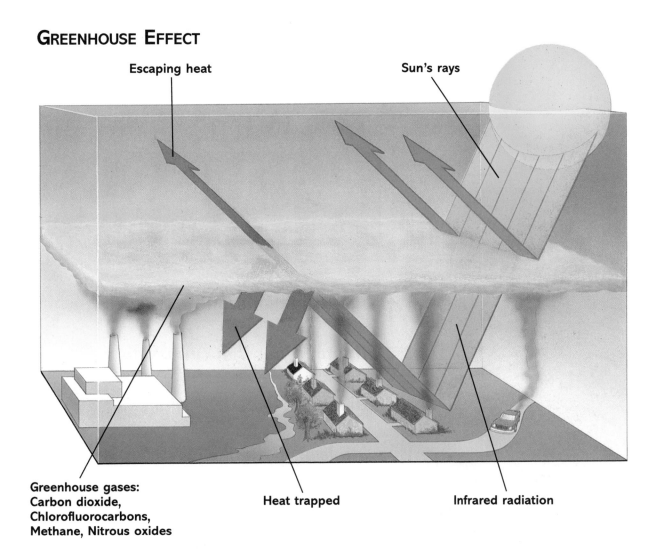

Escaping heat

Sun's rays

Greenhouse gases:
Carbon dioxide,
Chlorofluorocarbons,
Methane, Nitrous oxides

Heat trapped

Infrared radiation

Q. What is the greenhouse effect?

A. A greenhouse is a small glass building that traps heat from the sun. The sunlight can pass easily through the glass panes of the structure. Once inside, some of the energy in sunlight changes to heat, and the heat cannot easily pass through the glass, so it becomes warm inside the building.

The atmosphere that surrounds the Earth acts in many ways like the glass in a greenhouse. It permits sunlight to pass through it and warm the land and water on Earth. A portion of this heat will return to space, but much of the heat is trapped by water vapor and other gases in the atmosphere. The gases reflect some of this heat back to Earth, allowing the air in the lower atmosphere to stay warm enough for life to exist.

Q. Why are people worried about this?

A. The greenhouse effect is a natural part of the way the Earth works, and it's one of the things that creates conditions suitable for life. However, some of the pollutants people release in the air are gases that trap heat. As more of these gases are added to the atmosphere, the amount of heat being trapped increases and the planet's temperature goes up. This could cause major changes in climates and living conditions all over the world.

What Are PLANTS ?

Plants are a unique group of living things that can produce their own food. Different kinds of plants live all over the world, and they play an important role in shaping life on our planet.

Q. **What is a plant?**

A. Some people might describe plants as green living things other than animals. However, not all plants are green. All plants are alive, though, and most can do something that no animal can. They can use sunlight, water, and carbon dioxide to produce their own food.

Q. **Do all plants have the same parts?**

A. Not all plants are the same, but the kinds we are most familiar with have some similar parts. *Roots* anchor them to the ground and absorb nutrients and water from the soil. *Stems* of some sort spring up from the ground. *Leaves* soak up energy from the sun, and *seeds* or *spores* help to make new plants. Many have *flowers* and *fruit* that produce the seeds that become new plants.

Natural Recyclers

Fungi (FUN ji) include all the different kinds of mushrooms and the greenish mold you sometimes find on forgotten food in the refrigerator. More than 50,000 species have been identified, and they are grouped in the plant kingdom mainly because it's obvious that they are not animals. However, fungi really aren't like most plants either. They cannot produce their own food and so must

FUNGUS

ingest or take in food from their environment. Fungi break down dead animals and plants, releasing materials back into the air, water, and soil. In a way, they are natural recyclers.

PLANT

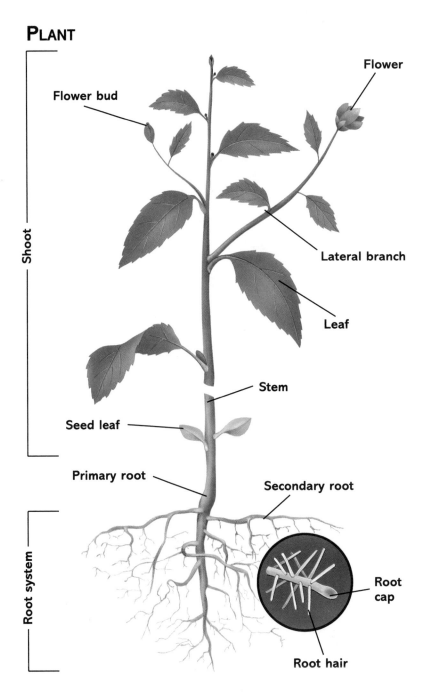

Flower bud
Flower
Shoot
Lateral branch
Leaf
Stem
Seed leaf
Primary root
Secondary root
Root system
Root cap
Root hair

ALGA

Q. **How many different kinds of plants are there?**

A. Most scientists divide plants into five major groups. *Algae* (AL gee) are the simplest plants, and many live in water. *Mosses* and *liverworts* have no true roots to take water from the soil, so they usually live in moist environments. *Ferns* and their relatives reproduce using spores. The seed plants separate into two main groups. The *gymnosperms* (JIM nuh spurmz), or "naked seeds," produce seeds with no covering on them. Flowering plants, such as the sunflower, are called *angiosperms* (AN jee uh spurmz), which means "encased seeds." They always produce some kind of protective covering around their seeds.

Q. **What are the smallest and the largest groups?**

A. Scientists group plants into about 400,000 different species. Only 500 of these are gymnosperms, and more than 250,000 of them are angiosperms. There are as many as 25,000 species of algae, 10,000 species of ferns, and 16,000 species of mosses.

FERN

MOSS

Q. **What is the difference between plants and trees?**

A. A tree is actually a very tall plant with a woody stem. Long ago, some plants developed lignin (LIG nuhn), a substance that made their stems tough and better able to support the plant. As a result, they could grow taller. Taller plants could gather more sunlight and so had a better chance of survival. Eventually, plants appeared with the woody trunks that modern trees have.

GYMNOSPERM

ANGIOSPERM

Plant Partners

Lichens (LI kunz) are actually two organisms—algae and fungi—that live as partners, growing together on a rock, tree, or other surface. The algae create food for themselves and for the fungus. The fungus provides protection from intense light and other elements that can harm algae, and it also supplies the algae with water. Together, these partners can grow in deserts and in the arctic. They are among the first forms of life to appear after a volcanic eruption. Lichens are slow growing and long lived.

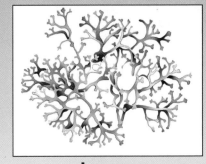

LICHEN

Q. **How are trees divided into groups?**

A. Trees fall into two of the plant groups mentioned earlier: gymnosperms and angiosperms. These divisions are based on how plants reproduce. Many people also separate trees into two main groups based on their type of leaves: *deciduous* (di SI juh wus) and *coniferous* (ko NI fuh rus).

Q. **What is a deciduous tree?**

A. A deciduous tree has broad leaves that it sheds every year, usually in the fall. Dropping its leaves is one way a deciduous tree prepares for winter; it helps the tree keep water, which is less available during the cold winter. Most deciduous trees live in temperate climates. In tropical regions, which have wet and dry seasons rather than warm and cold seasons, deciduous trees lose their leaves as the dry season approaches.

STRUCTURE OF A DECIDUOUS TREE

Foliage

Top

Branch

Twig

Limb

Crown

Trunk

Secondary root

Fibrous root

Taproot

WILLOW

MAPLE

OAK

BEECH

Q. Are all deciduous trees alike?

A. Deciduous trees come in many different varieties that can be separated by leaf type. The leaves of the willow, maple, oak, and beech are called *simple* leaves. This means that each leaf stem produces a single leaf. The ash and horse chestnut have *compound* leaves, which means that several small leaflets grow out of each leaf stem.

WHITE ASH

HORSE CHESTNUT

Q. Why do leaves change color in the fall?

A. Before many deciduous trees shed their leaves, the leaves turn from green to brilliant reds, oranges, and yellows. These colors, as well as green, are always present in the leaves. However, the green color covers the other colors. Before the leaves fall, chlorophyll (KLOR uh fil), a substance in the leaves that makes them green, drains away, leaving the other colors.

Q. How do trees know when it's time to grow new leaves?

A. As spring approaches in temperate climates, the day lengthens and the plants receive more sunlight. More sunlight also means that the air becomes warmer. Trees sense these changes and become more active. Soon buds form, and tiny new leaves push out from the twigs and branches. Once this process starts, it doesn't seem to take very long before the trees are again clothed in bright green leaves.

Living Fossils

The ginkgo (GING ko) trees are called living fossils. They are very similar to trees that lived 200 million years ago. Few if any ginkgoes remain in the wild. However, the custom of planting these trees in Chinese and Japanese temple gardens has helped them to survive. Ginkgoes are extremely tough trees, able to survive in cold weather and polluted air. Most ornamental ginkgoes are male trees. The female tree produces a fleshy fruit whose seeds smell like spoiled butter.

SCOTCH PINE

Q. **What kind of trees grow in cold places?**

A. Coniferous (ko NI fuh rus) trees, or conifers (KA nuh furz), are most common in cold areas, such as Canada, Scandinavia, and Siberia. Conifers also grow in high mountains where the temperatures are lower.

Q. **Why do conifers have such sharp, thin needles?**

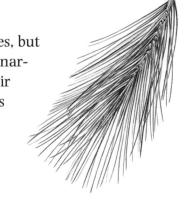

A. Not all conifers have needles, but many do. These needles are long, narrow leaves that end in points. Their shape and a waxy coating reduces water loss, which helps the trees survive in cold climates where water is often in short supply. Needles are also flexible so that snow slips right off instead of breaking the leaf or the branch.

PINE NEEDLES

Q. **Do any conifers shed their leaves in the winter?**

A. Almost all conifers keep their leaves year-round, which is why they are also called evergreens. Although conifers do shed their leaves and grow new ones, they do so gradually instead of all at once.

Q. **Do evergreens grow from seeds like leafy trees do?**

A. Evergreens do grow from seeds, but the seeds don't come from flowers or fruit as they do on many leafy trees. The seeds of conifers are contained in cones. Male cones release pollen that fertilizes the seeds in the female cones. The seeds are tucked up under the hard scales of the cone. As the cone matures, the scales open and separate, releasing the seeds.

Male

Female

PINE CONES

Q. **How tall can conifers grow?**

A. Conifers are among the tallest trees in the world. The Douglas fir can grow 200 feet tall or higher. The giant sequoia (si KWOI uh) in California can reach as high as 325 feet. Their trunks may measure up to 100 feet across. The wood contained in one of these trees can weigh up to 6,000 tons, making them the heaviest living things on Earth.

Q. **How long do trees live?**

A. The giant sequoias also enter the record books when it comes to age. Some are believed to be between 3,000 and 4,000 years old. However, the bristlecone pines are the oldest trees of all. Some of them live for more than 4,000 years. The oldest ever recorded is about 4,600 years old. Scientists determine the age of a tree by looking at the rings of wood in the trunk. A tree normally grows one ring per year.

DOUGLAS FIR

COASTAL REDWOOD

Q. **Why do some plants produce flowers?**

A. Plants produce flowers to make seeds that will grow into new plants. The male parts of a flower are the pollen-producing *stamens* (STA munz), which include the *anther* held up by the *filament*. The female parts are the *stigma*, the *style*, the *ovary*, and the *ovule* (AHV yool). The reproductive process starts when pollen from the male stamen reaches the female stigma. In many plants, the male and female parts mature at different times so a flower won't pollinate itself. Instead, the pollen from one flower gets transferred to another flower.

FLOWER

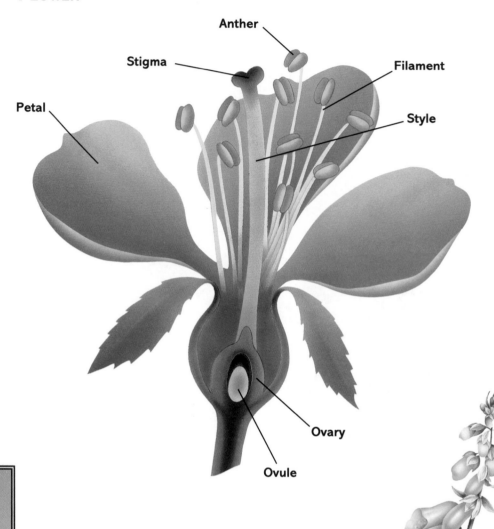

Anther

Stigma

Filament

Petal

Style

Ovary

Ovule

Smelly Flowers

The largest flowers of any plant belong to the rafflesia (ruh FLEE zhuh). They measure up to three feet across and weigh up to 15 pounds. They have a rotten smell, like meat left out too long without cooking, that attracts pollinating flies.

Q. **Why are flowers so colorful?**

A. Flowers are brightly colored in order to attract birds or insects to help pollinate the plants so seeds can grow. Birds are able to see and distinguish colors, and they are often attracted to particular colors of flowers. Petals with spots on them may attract insects. The smells many flowers produce also attract insects.

FOXGLOVE

Q. How do bees spread flower pollen?

A. Bees visit a flower to feed on the nectar, which is sweet liquid the flower produces to attract them. While it's getting the nectar, the bee may rub up against the stamens. The loose pollen grains stick to the insect's body and feet. When the insect flies to the next flower, it carries the pollen grains with it. The grains stick to the stigma and then fertilize the plant.

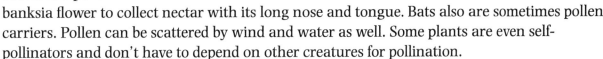

Q. In what other ways do plants spread pollen?

A. Some plants use other animals to spread pollen. The tiny Australian honey possum becomes a pollen carrier when it visits the banksia flower to collect nectar with its long nose and tongue. Bats also are sometimes pollen carriers. Pollen can be scattered by wind and water as well. Some plants are even self-pollinators and don't have to depend on other creatures for pollination.

PEAR

Q. What happens after pollination?

A. After a pollen grain lands on a stigma, it produces a pollen tube that grows through the stigma and down the style to the ovary. A cell from the pollen combines with a cell from the ovule to produce a fertilized seed. Usually, the plant then produces some kind of fruit covering to protect the seed.

Q. How are plant seeds scattered?

A. Seeds are scattered from parent plants in several ways. Animals attracted to juicy, brightly colored fruits will eat the seeds along with the fruit. Later, the hard, undigested seeds are ejected in the animal's wastes. Some fruits have spines that stick to the fur of animals that pass by, and the animals rub or scratch them off later. Other seeds have wing shapes that help them travel on the wind or float on the water. Some seed cases literally pop open, flinging the seeds in all directions.

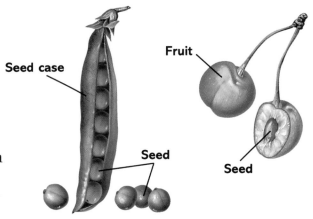

Q. What is the difference between plants that live on land and plants that live in the water?

WATER LETTUCE

A. Many plants that live in the water don't need a stiff stem to hold them up. They can just float on the water. Some water plants have special air bladders that help to keep the plants upright in water.

Q. Do water plants grow under or on top of water?

A. Some water plants grow along the edges of ponds and streams, while others grow in deeper water. Some grow completely under the water, while other plants float on the water's surface.

WHITE WATER LILY

Q. Did land plants appear before water plants?

A. Plant life began in the sea, where temperatures are more constant and the plants are surrounded by nutrients. Types of algae were the first plants. Slowly, the plants began to grow along the water's edge and develop the structures they needed for living on land. Some of the first land plants were mosses and ferns.

The flowering water plants, like the water hyacinth, actually evolved from plants that left the water, adapted to living on land, and then returned to the water.

WATER HYACINTH

Q. What would happen if you planted a water plant on land?

A. If you planted a water plant like the water lily on land, it would just flop over and lay along the ground. The slender stems of water plants lack the stiffness of land plants and cannot support the plant's weight. Water plants depend on the buoyant water to keep their leaves and flowers afloat. Since water plants are adapted to living in a liquid environment, they would probably dry out and die on land.

Q. Do people eat water plants or use them in any other way?

A. When you eat ice cream or travel in a vehicle with tires, you are using products made from giant kelp. Kelp produces a substance called algin (AL jin) that is used to keep ice cream from crystallizing and is useful in making tires. People also extract iodine from some forms of brown algae. A freshwater plant that many people enjoy eating is watercress.

Air bladder

GIANT KELP

A Plant by Any Other Name

All plants have scientific names, but they also have common names that are often quite descriptive. The water lettuce really does look a lot like a head of lettuce. The yellow skunk cabbage is also well named. It has a bad odor, like a skunk, that is intended to attract flies to pollinate the plant. It's easy to see how the American arrowhead got its name.

YELLOW SKUNK CABBAGE

AMERICAN ARROWHEAD

PHOTOSYNTHESIS

Q. **Why are leaves usually green?**

A. Leaves get their green color from a pigment called *chlorophyll* (KLOR uh fil). Plants use their chlorophyll to produce food in a process called *photosynthesis* (FO to SIN thuh sus).

Q. **How does photosynthesis work?**

A. The chlorophyll in a plant is able to absorb energy from sunlight. The plant also uses its leaves to absorb carbon dioxide from the air and uses its roots to absorb water from the soil. The plant then combines these elements to produce sugars and starches, which it uses as food. As a plant makes this food, it also produces oxygen as a waste product and releases it through its leaves.

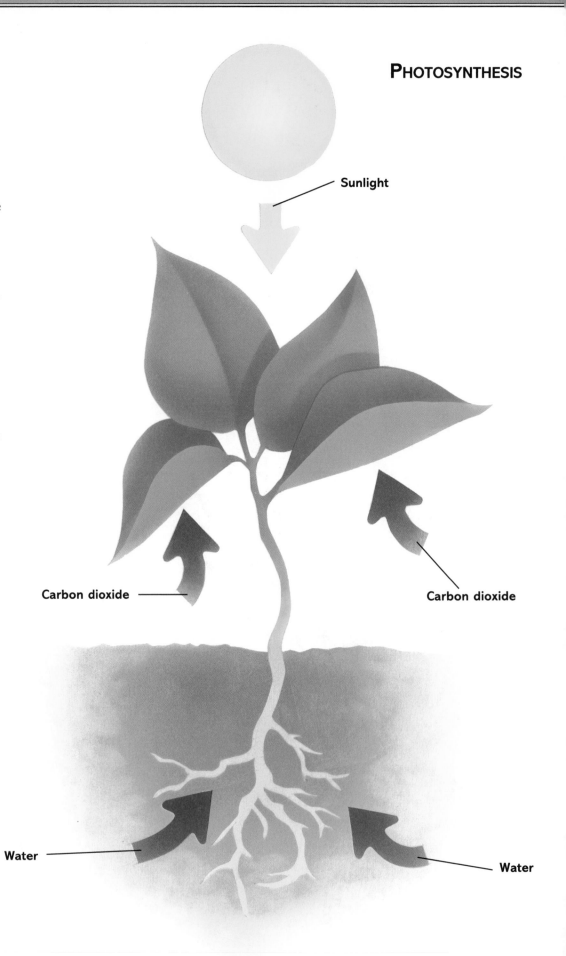

PHOTOSYNTHESIS

Sunlight

Carbon dioxide

Carbon dioxide

Water

Water

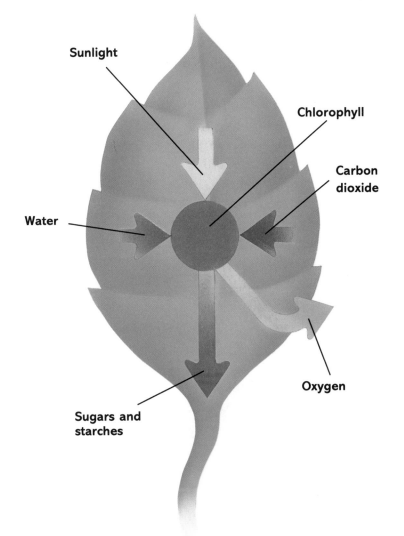

Sunlight

Chlorophyll

Carbon dioxide

Water

Oxygen

Sugars and starches

Q. Does the food stay in the leaves?

A. From the leaves, the sugars flow to other parts of the plant that do not carry out photosynthesis. These parts include the roots and the stem. The plant takes what it needs at the moment, then stores the rest. The stored sugars are later used to help the plant grow.

Q. What happens in plants that don't have green leaves?

A. Some plants don't have green leaves. The leaves of some Japanese maple trees are almost purple, for instance. These leaves do still have green chlorophyll, though. The green color is hidden by other pigments in the leaves.

Q. What if a plant doesn't get enough light for photosynthesis?

A. Some plants, such as those living on the dark floor of a rain forest, have adapted so they need less light to carry out photosynthesis. Every plant does need some sunlight to make its food, though. If a plant doesn't have the light it needs, its leaves appear pale and underdeveloped. If a plant is kept from light long enough, it will usually wither and die.

Q. What happens to trees after they lose their leaves?

A. Trees that lose their leaves in the winter are in a dormant state, as if they were asleep. They become less active and so require less energy, which allows them to survive the winter without their food-producing leaves.

Q. How do plants get their food?

A. Most plants can produce their own food in a process called photosynthesis. However, some plants supplement their diet with additional food. These plants are meat-eaters, or carnivorous plants. Many meat-eating plants grow in wetland areas, such as the bladderwort, sundew, pitcher plant, and Venus flytrap.

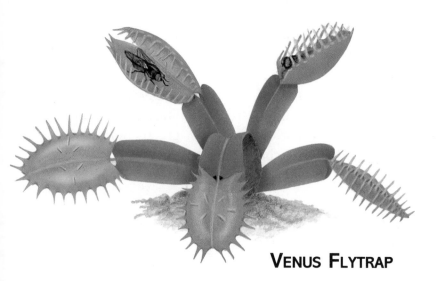

VENUS FLYTRAP

Q. How does the Venus flytrap catch flies?

A. Each half of the trap part of a Venus flytrap has three trigger hairs inside it. If an insect looking for nectar or a place to rest lands on the trap and touches two of the trigger hairs, the trap quickly snaps shut. Spines along the edges of the leaf form a cage. Unless it is very small, the insect cannot climb through to escape.

Q. What happens to the insect after the trap closes?

A. If the Venus flytrap leaf senses that it has caught something containing protein, it closes completely and begins digestion. Special glands produce enzymes that dissolve the soft parts of the insect in about two weeks. Then the leaves open and any undigested parts of the insect are blown away by the wind.

Q. How does the pitcher plant catch insects?

A. The leaves of a pitcher plant look very much like pitchers that hold liquid. Insects are attracted to the nectar around the rim of the pitcher, but the rim is very slippery. When insects land on the plant, they often fall into the pitcher. Many pitcher plants have stiff fibers like hair in the neck of the pitcher that grow downward and make it so the insects can't climb back up. Eventually, the insects end up at the bottom of the pitcher, where they are digested by enzymes from the plant.

PITCHER PLANT

Q. Why do some plants eat insects?

A. Boggy soils are often poor in nutrients, especially nitrogen. To make up for this problem, plants such as the Venus flytrap and the pitcher plant became meat-eaters. The insects provide the plant with nutrients it can't get elsewhere.

Q. Do all plants make their own food?

A. Some plants do not make their own food. Instead, these *parasites* cheat by stealing food from other plants. They attach themselves to the stems or roots of host plants and then burrow into the food channels and absorb the sugars and minerals the host plant would normally use for itself.

Q. How does mistletoe use the host plant?

A. Mistletoe is semiparasitic. It does have green leaves and can make some food for itself, but it also takes food from a host tree, such as an oak, walnut, or conifer. Its rootlike fibers reach into the tree, taking water and nutrients from the host.

MISTLETOE

Q. Are all plants that live in trees parasites?

A. Many plants grow on larger plants without damaging them. These plants are *epiphytes* (EH puh fights). By using a larger plant to support them and hold them up to the light, epiphytes have no need to develop strong stems. Many orchids are epiphytes that live on the bark of trees.

GRAPES

Q. How are plants helpful?

A. Plants are extremely important to life on Earth. In one way or another, virtually every living thing on the planet depends on plants for food. Even if an animal is a meat-eater, the animals it eats get their energy from eating plants.

People use a variety of plants in their regular diets. Corn and wheat are two of the most important food sources for people all over the world. We also eat a great many other plant products, such as carrots, peas, potatoes, grapes, oranges, and nuts.

CARROT

CORN

ORANGE

TOMATO

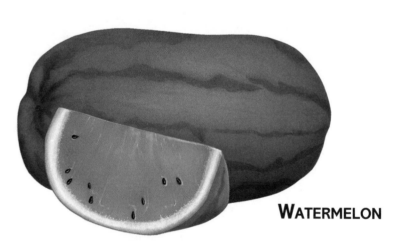

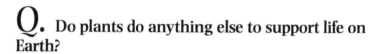

WATERMELON

Q. Do plants do anything else to support life on Earth?

A. Much of the oxygen you breathe was put into the air by plants. Plants absorb carbon dioxide and release oxygen. Air-breathing animals do the opposite; they take in oxygen from the air and release carbon dioxide when they breathe. In this way, plants and animals help each other to survive.

CINCHONA LEAVES

ALOE VERA

BELLADONNA

$Q.$ **How else do people rely on plants?**

$A.$ People produce fabric to make clothes from cotton plants. Many of the medicines we use also come from chemical compounds in plants. Quinine, taken from cinchona tree bark, is used to treat deadly malaria. The aloe vera plant produces an oil that soothes burns and is useful in cosmetics. Atropine, a drug used in eye surgery and to treat stomach problems, comes from belladonna.

$Q.$ **What about wood?**

$A.$ People use wood and the fiber from plants to make homes, furniture, hammers, rope, musical instruments, and beautiful sculptures. Pencils and papers are also made from wood. Cellulose from the cell walls of trees is found in carpeting, fabrics, photographic film, and toothbrush handles. Bark from the cork oak tree turns up as bottle cap liners and bottle stoppers. Tree saps are used in mouthwash, soap, and solvents.

$Q.$ **Are any plants harmful to people?**

$A.$ Anyone who has suffered the painful poke of a cactus spine or spent two weeks trying not to scratch a rash caused by poison ivy knows that plants can be harmful. If eaten, several kinds of plants can poison people or other animals and even kill them.

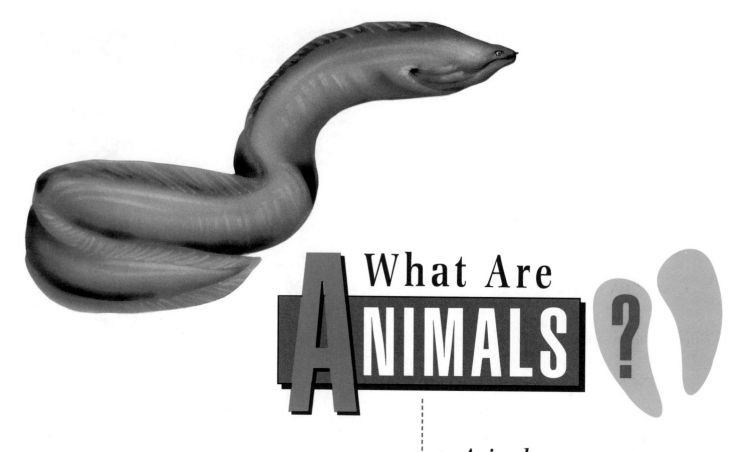

What Are ANIMALS ?

Animals are living things that consume other living things for food. More than a million different species of animals inhabit the Earth today, and many more species lived in the past but have become extinct.

Q. **When did the dinosaurs live on Earth?**

A. Many people think all dinosaurs lived on the Earth at the same time. However, dinosaurs roamed the Earth for nearly 150 million years. Take a look at the geologic time line on this page. The time of the dinosaurs stretches from a point in the Triassic Period to a point near the end of the Cretaceous Period. During that time, many different species of dinosaurs appeared, died out, and evolved or changed. Different dinosaurs lived at different times, and even some that look very much alike were actually separated by millions of years. The two ankylosaurs you see on this page look similar. However, the sauropelta lived over 100 million years ago, and the euoplocephalus did not appear until about 75 million years ago.

SAUROPELTA

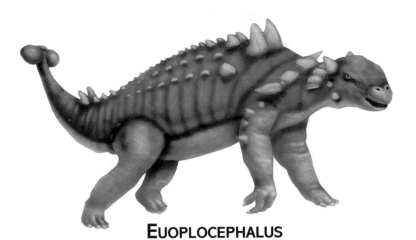

EUOPLOCEPHALUS

GEOLOGIC TIME LINE

YEARS AGO	ERA	PERIOD	EPOCH
10,000	CENOZOIC	QUATER-NARY	HOLOCENE
2.5 MILLION			PLEISTOCENE
7 MILLION		TERTIARY	PLIOCENE
26 MILLION			MIOCENE
38 MILLION			OLIGOCENE
54 MILLION			EOCENE
65 MILLION			PALEOCENE
136 MILLION	MESOZOIC	CRETACEOUS	
190 MILLION		JURASSIC	
225 MILLION		TRIASSIC	
280 MILLION	UPPER PALEOZOIC	PERMIAN	
345 MILLION		CARBONIFEROUS	
395 MILLION		DEVONIAN	
430 MILLION	LOWER PALEOZOIC	SILURIAN	
500 MILLION		ORDOVICIAN	
570 MILLION		CAMBRIAN	
PRECAMBRIAN FROM 4.6 BILLION YEARS AGO			

Q. How are dinosaurs named?

A. No matter what language you speak, a dinosaur's name is the same. In this way, paleontologists (scientists who study life forms that existed in prehistoric times) around the world can share information. Often, they name a new dinosaur by examining its most outstanding feature and using a Latin or Greek name that describes this feature. For example, think about the triceratops. You may know that tri means "three." Ceratops means "horned face." Do you think that "three-horned face" is a good description of triceratops?

TRICERATOPS

Q. Why do so many people think of Tyrannosaurus rex when they think of dinosaurs?

A. Even people who know very little about dinosaurs have heard of Tyrannosaurus rex. The huge, frightening T. rex was an early dinosaur discovery. The first nearly complete skeleton surfaced in Montana in 1902. Even with all the discoveries of meat-eating dinosaurs since that time, T. rex still remains the most famous and popular. Although most people think of T. rex as a fearsome hunter, some scientists think it may have been a scavenger, but no one knows for sure.

TYRANNOSAURUS REX

DILOPHOSAURUS

Q. What other predatory dinosaurs were there besides T. rex?

A. The dilophosaurus is one example of a carnivorous, or meat-eating, dinosaur. The crest on its head was made of two thin ridges of bone. The structure of its skull and the type of teeth it had make it seem more like a scavenger than a predator. The T. rex was about 45 feet long; the dilophosaurus was about 20 feet long.

Q. Why did some dinosaurs grow so big?

A. The diplodocus is one of the longest and largest dinosaurs found so far. Dinosaurs may have grown so large that their size may have discouraged predators from attacking them, the way that an elephant's size today keeps other animals from hunting it. Also, a tall dinosaur could reach high up into a tree to eat the leaves. If the big dinosaurs were cold-blooded, their large bodies also would cool much more slowly, so they would be able to retain more heat during the night.

Q. Were there any small dinosaurs?

A. You may be surprised, but some dinosaurs were no larger than chickens or people. One of the smallest was the compsognathus. Because most of its three-foot-long body was made up of a thin tail, this little animal may have weighed no more than a hen. The compsognathus evidently ran fast, and scientists could tell it was a meat-eater from the kind of teeth it had.

COMPSOGNATHUS

Q. What advantages did small dinosaurs have?

A. The six-foot yandusaurus ate plants. Because of its small size, you might think it would be easy prey for meat-eating dinosaurs. However, you can tell from its structure that it could run. Also, its small size would allow it to hide in tiny places where other dinosaurs would not see it.

YANDUSAURUS

Craning Their Necks

Just like the animals that share our world today, dinosaurs came in all shapes and sizes. Long-necked dinosaurs used their extra reach to get to tasty leaves in treetops like giraffes do today. Dinosaurs like the diplodocus had tremendously long necks. The long, thin neck was structured like a crane and had strong bones that could support the neck and head.

DIPLODOCUS

Q. How do scientists figure out what dinosaurs looked like?

A. When a paleontologist uncovers a dinosaur skeleton, the bones are often scattered and jumbled. Putting them together to see what the animal looked like is like a complicated jigsaw puzzle. Once the bones are assembled, scientists can tell a great deal from the shape of the skeleton. However, when stegosaurus was found, the plates along its back were a mystery. No one was sure whether to arrange them in a single row or two alternating rows. Finally, a stegosaurus skeleton was found that clearly showed the plates were in two staggered rows.

STEGOSAUR

Q. How do scientists know how dinosaurs lived?

A. The bones and other remains of dinosaurs tell stories about how they lived as well as what they looked like. The prenocephale had a thick, domed skull. Scientists believe the males would compete with each other during mating season by butting their heads together as many

PRENOCEPHALE

horned animals do today. A dinosaur's teeth also tell a story. Flat teeth suggest a dinosaur that ate plants. Meat-eaters had sharp teeth. The remains of eggs and nests also tell a story. One nest had several eggs and the remains of young animals, which suggests that the mother took care of the babies after they hatched.

Q. How do scientists know where to look for the remains of dinosaurs?

A. At first, dinosaur skeletons were found by accident. Then paleontologists began to realize that most remains were found in certain types of ground. Bones become fossilized after being buried in sand or mud. So scientists look in sedimentary rock that has been laid down in layers over millions of years.

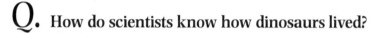

Dinosaur Sounds

Many hadrosaurs had unusual bony head ornaments. The parasaurolophus had a great bony crest that stretched out about six feet behind its head. Because the crest had two hollow channels running through it, scientists thought it might be used to breathe while the head was underwater. However, there was no breathing hole. Then they figured the crest may have been an amplifier to increase sound.

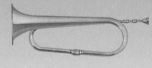

The dinosaur may have used its crest like a big horn or bugle to sound an alarm.

Q. When did the dinosaurs disappear from the Earth?

A. No one really knows for sure. However, many scientists now believe that the Earth was hit by a huge meteorite toward the end of the Cretaceous Period. Dust from the impact shot into the atmosphere and cooled the planet considerably, killing first the dinosaurs' food and then the dinosaurs. Sediments from this era show high amounts of a rare element called iridium, which is common in meteorites. Fossils are numerous above and below this layer, but very few are found within it. There is also evidence of a meteorite crater in the Gulf of Mexico. Other scientists believe the dinosaurs were slowly dying out anyway as Earth's climate and land changed. What do you think?

LAMBEOSAURUS

Q. Are there any descendants of dinosaurs living on Earth today?

A. Many people believe that modern birds are dinosaur descendants. Dinosaurs and birds may have had a common ancestor over 200 million years ago. Crocodiles are considered among dinosaurs' closest living relatives. Crocodiles have changed little since the Triassic Period.

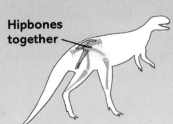

CROCODILE

The Hip-Bone Connection

From looking at fossil remains, paleontologists have found that dinosaurs can be divided into two main groups according to the structure of their pelvis, or hip bones. Study the small pictures here to see the differences between ornithischian, or "bird-hipped," dinosaurs and saurischian, or "lizard-hipped," dinosaurs. Dinosaurs stood with their legs directly under their bodies,

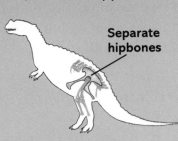

Separate hipbones

SAURISCHIANS (LIZARD-HIPPED)

unlike reptiles we know today. In fact, dinosaurs may be more closely related to birds than to reptiles as shown by their skeleton structure. They also may not have all been cold-blooded as reptiles are. (A cold-blooded animal depends on the sun to warm it rather than producing its own heat as mammals and birds do.) Some dinosaur bones show evidence of having passageways for blood vessels, just like the bones of warm-blooded mammals.

Hipbones together

ORNITHISCHIANS (BIRD-HIPPED)

Q. How many different kinds of animals are there on the Earth today?

A. You may be surprised to learn that no one knows for sure. Scientists are still discovering new species, and they think that every day several existing species become extinct. To give you some idea of the diversity, there are about one million known species of insects, arachnids, and crustaceans; about 8,600 species of birds; nearly 6,000 species of reptiles; and about 4,500 species of mammals (including humans). There are thousands more species in other groups.

Q. Why are animals put in groups?

A. With more than a million animal species alive on Earth, scientists had to figure out some way of grouping them in order to study them. They started with two main categories: animals without backbones (invertebrates) and animals with backbones (vertebrates). These groups are then further divided into smaller groups. The invertebrates include sponges, worms, insects, arachnids, crustaceans, and mollusks. The vertebrates include fish, amphibians, reptiles, birds, and mammals. All together, there are 33 major groups, or phyla (FI luh), of animals.

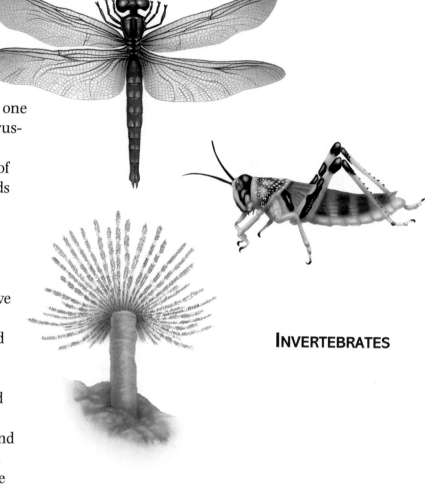

INVERTEBRATES

VERTEBRATES

Q. Which animal group is the largest?

A. The insects are the largest group. There may be as many as 900,000 different species. That's more than the number of species in all the other groups combined.

Q. What groups of animals live in water?

A. Of the 33 major groups of animals, 32 of them have members that live in the ocean, and 15 of the groups live only in the ocean. Fish are the most common group of animals that live in water. Fish include sharks, eels, trout, and cod. Fish are able to live in water because they have gills, which they use to take oxygen from the water. Other groups that live in water include whales and dolphins. These animals are mammals. They must come to the surface regularly to breathe air. Some birds and amphibians spend part of their time in water.

FISH

STAG BEETLE

Q. How are the bodies of animals without backbones supported?

A. Many animals that have no backbone or internal skeleton live in water, which supports their bodies. Other invertebrates have what is called an exoskeleton, which means "outside skeleton." An exoskeleton is a flexible, hard covering that protects the body like a suit of armor. Insects like the stag beetle have an exoskeleton.

Animal, Mineral, or Vegetable?

Scientists use certain rules to decide if a living thing is an animal, a plant, or neither. All plants and animals have cells, and all are able to reproduce. Plants are usually stationary, but animals are able to move. Animals must get their energy by eating other organisms, whereas most plants make their own energy.

Viruses are a group that raises some interesting questions. You probably know them as things that cause certain diseases, from the common cold to AIDS. They do reproduce, but only inside a host cell. While they don't seem to produce or consume energy and they don't have all the components of a cell, viruses do seem to be alive.

PROTOZOANS

Q. Are protozoans animals?

A. Most protozoans consist of only one cell, but they are able to move, they do reproduce, and they must get their energy source by eating or absorbing other organisms. These characteristics identify them as animals. There are four major groups of protozoans: flagellates (FLA juh lutz), sarcodines (SAR co dinz), ciliates (SIH lee utz), and sporozoans (spor uh ZO unz).

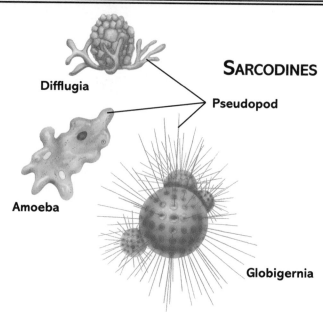

SARCODINES

Difflugia

Pseudopod

Amoeba

Globigernia

FLAGELLATES

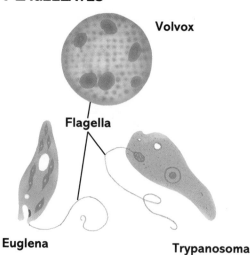

Volvox

Flagella

Euglena

Trypanosoma

Q. How do protozoans move around?

A. The different types of protozoans have different ways to move. The flagellates travel by moving their flagella, a long stringlike piece attached to the body. The sarcodines extend a pseudopod, or "false foot," to pull themselves along. The ciliates move little hairlike cilia that cover their bodies, which propel them forward at a high rate of speed for a protozoan—about a millimeter per second. Adult sporozoans have no such structures and are unable to move.

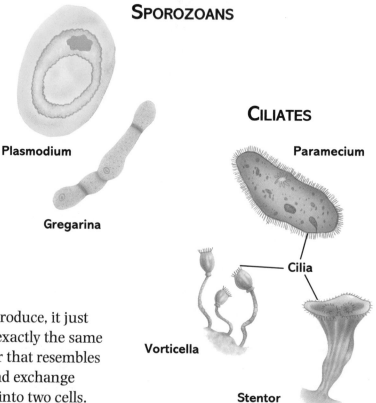

SPOROZOANS

Plasmodium

Gregarina

CILIATES

Paramecium

Cilia

Vorticella

Stentor

Q. How do sporozoans get food if they can't move around?

A. Sporozoans are all parasites. They live inside the bodies of other animals and feed on them. Some sporozoans can cause their hosts to become quite sick. Malaria is caused by a sporozoan called plasmodium.

Q. How do protozoans reproduce?

A. When an amoeba or other protozoan is ready to reproduce, it just divides right down the middle. The two daughter cells are exactly the same as the parent cell. Some protozoans reproduce in a manner that resembles sexual reproduction. Ciliates reproduce when they meet and exchange genetic material. Then they separate and each one divides into two cells.

SPONGE

Q. **Are sponges alive?**

A. Sponges look much like plants. Some even look like rocks. However, scientists have found that sponges do grow and reproduce. Their bodies have no nervous system. Instead, different kinds of cells provide support, gather food, and digest food. Sponges permanently attach themselves to rocks or other underwater surfaces.

Q. **Is a sea anemone a flower?**

A. Sea anemones are soft-bodied animals that live in the ocean. They attach themselves to rocks or other objects and use their stinging tentacles to catch tiny fish and other organisms. The waving, brightly colored tentacles remind people of flowers. In fact, that's why they were named after the anemone flower, which they resemble. Sea anemones can grow to about one foot across.

SEA ANEMONE

JELLYFISH

Q. **Are jellyfish really made of jelly?**

A. Jellyfish are not really made of jelly. Their bodies, though, have no bones or outside skeleton as support, and they might seem like jelly-filled sacks. Long stinging tentacles hang down from their bodies and catch any prey that wanders into them.

Q. **How do jellyfish move through the water?**

A. Jellyfish can move a little by pumping water from their bell-shaped bodies. However, for the most part they drift on ocean currents as they trail their tentacles like fishing lines in the hope of capturing something to eat.

Q. Why do crabs move sideways?

A. Crabs' walking legs are jointed and end in points. Crabs move on the tips of these points. They can move in any direction, but because of the position and structure of their legs, they always seem to be moving sideways. As most people know, crabs also have large claws. These claws are actually the crabs' front legs, which have been modified for a special purpose. Crabs use their claws for defense and to capture prey. Lobsters, shrimp, and other close relatives of crabs also have modified front legs, most often in the form of claws.

CRAB

Q. Are all lobsters red?

A. Lobsters are not really red. In fact some lobsters are dark blue, and some are even multi-colored. Lobsters only turn bright red when they are dropped in a pot of hot water.

Q. What group do crabs and lobsters belong to?

A. Crabs, lobsters, and shrimp are crustaceans, which is a group related to both spiders and insects. All of these animals are invertebrates with segmented bodies protected by external skeletons. Insects have bodies divided into three segments, and they always have six legs. Like crustaceans, spiders have bodies with two segments, but spiders always have eight legs and they have no antennae. Crustaceans usually have ten legs and two pairs of antennae on their head. Also, most crustaceans have gills and live in water, while spiders and insects are air breathers. Crustaceans also go through many growth stages where they shed their outer skeleton as their body outgrows it, and then they produce a new one.

Q. Are any other animals crustaceans?

A. Barnacles are an unusual kind of crustacean. Unlike their relatives, they spend much of their lives in one place, attached to rocks, driftwood, ships, or other animals. Their bodies' are almost entirely covered by a hard outer shell, and they feed by reaching their special arms into the water to capture small food particles floating past.

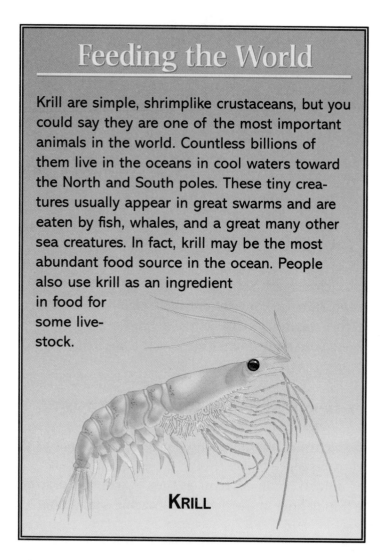

Feeding the World

Krill are simple, shrimplike crustaceans, but you could say they are one of the most important animals in the world. Countless billions of them live in the oceans in cool waters toward the North and South poles. These tiny creatures usually appear in great swarms and are eaten by fish, whales, and a great many other sea creatures. In fact, krill may be the most abundant food source in the ocean. People also use krill as an ingredient in food for some livestock.

KRILL

SNAIL

Q. **How do snails get their shells?**

A. All snails have soft, moist bodies that make them very vulnerable. In fact the name of the group they are a part of, mollusks, comes from a Latin word meaning "soft." Snails are able to protect themselves by forming a shell made of calcium carbonate, which they extract from the soil and from the food they eat. Newly hatched snails have tiny, nearly transparent shells that grow larger and stronger as the snail grows.

Q. **Why don't slugs have shells?**

A. Slugs are related to snails, but they don't have shells. For protection, slugs curl into a tight ball when touched and secrete a slippery slime that makes it difficult to grab them.

Q. **How big can an octopus get?**

A. The octopus is distantly related to snails and slugs. The giant octopus can weigh up to 600 pounds and have a tentacle span of almost 30 feet. However, because its body is soft, the giant octopus can squeeze into quite small places. If caught away from its hiding places, an octopus may defend itself by biting, by changing color to look more threatening, or by squirting a cloud of ink. The ink cloud forms a shape similar to the octopus, acting somewhat like a decoy, and it interferes with a predator's sense of smell, which many ocean hunters rely on. The octopus is thought to be the smartest of all the invertebrates.

How To Be a Mollusk

Mollusks include many creatures that might seem to have little in common—clams, oysters, snails, squid, and octopi. Scientists recognize that these animals do all share some features. They all have soft, unsegmented bodies and complex sense organs. Many are able to produce some kind of shell for protection, and they all have a type of foot used for moving or for digging.

OCTOPUS

SEA STAR

Q. Is a starfish really a fish?

A. A starfish, or sea star, is actually a member of a group of animals called echinoderms. Other members of this groups are sand dollars, sea urchins, sea cucumbers, and sea lilies. Nearly 1,600 different species of sea stars have been identified. Not all of them have the familiar star shape; some can have 20 or more arms.

Q. A sea star doesn't have a head, so how does it eat?

A. Some sea stars are scavengers, but most are relentless predators. They eat small fish, sponges, corals, worms, mollusks, and crustaceans. To dine on a clam, a sea star uses the suction pads on its tube feet to pry open the shell slightly. The sea star extends its stomach outward through its mouth, which is located on the underside of its body. Its stomach slips in through the opening in the clam's shell and releases digestive juices that break down the meat of the clam. The stomach then absorbs the liquid.

Q. Why are sea urchins so prickly?

A. Some sea urchins have sharp spines all over their bodies. These spines protect them from animals that think they would make a tasty snack. Some sea urchins cover themselves with seaweed or other bits of debris to hide from predators. If a small animal manages to get between a sea urchin's spines, the sea urchin has little stalks with pincers on the end that can remove invaders. If a predator tries to reach between the spines, the stalks can also release a venom to sting the enemy.

SEA URCHIN

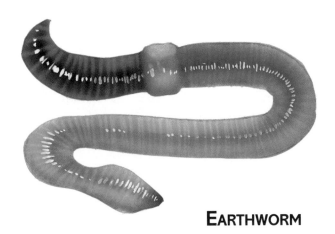

EARTHWORM

Q. How do earthworms travel underground?

A. The earthworm tunnels through the ground eating the soil. It travels by stretching its front end forward and then pulling its rear half up. The common earthworm seen in backyards can grow up to a foot long. However, some Australian earthworms can measure up to ten feet long.

Q. Where else do worms live?

A. Earthworms belong to a group of segmented worms called *annelids* (A nuh lidz). About 12,000 species make up this group, the largest of which live mainly in the ocean. Annelids come in many different shapes and sizes. Fan worms have fanlike tentacles called *radioles* (RA dee olz) that they use to breathe and to gather food. Most live on the bottom of the ocean in tubes made of mud and sand. They come out to feed, but if they sense danger, they quickly retreat into their tubes.

Q. How can some worms live so deep in the ocean?

A. The bottom of the ocean is a dark, forbidding place. The sun's rays cannot reach this deep, and the pressure of the water is immense. However, the bodies of some tube worms are adapted to this strange world. Many of them live on any organic bits and plankton that float by. Some huge tube worms cluster around hot spring vents where they absorb minerals spouting from the vents. If you were able to bring a live tube worm to the surface, it would not be likely to survive.

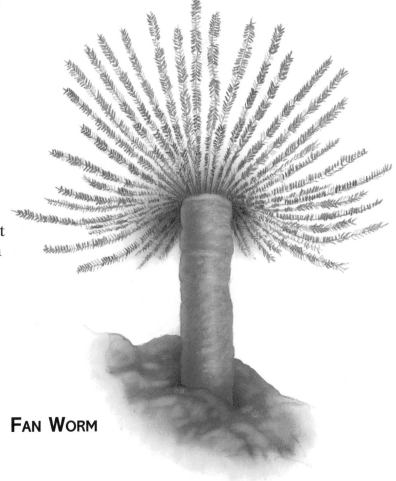

FAN WORM

Q. How many different kinds of spiders are there?

A. About 70,000 species of arachnids have been identified, including spiders, mites, ticks, and scorpions. To belong to this group, an animal must have eight walking legs. Most spiders have eight eyes that are very sensitive to movement. As predators, arachnids rely on their keen eyes for spotting potential meals.

Q. Where do spiders get the silk they use to make webs?

A. Spider silk comes from a liquid protein produced by glands in a spider's abdomen. As the liquid comes out of the four to eight spinnerets on the back of the spider, it dries into a strong thread.

SPIDER

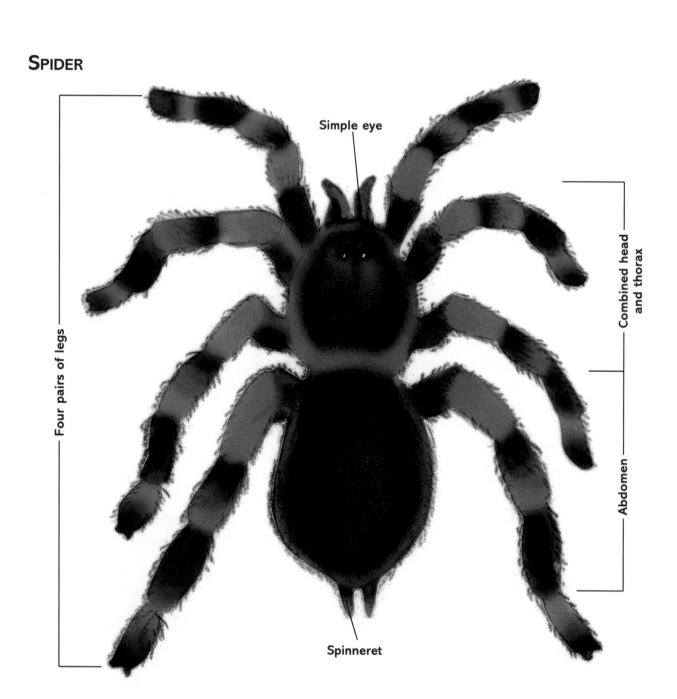

Four pairs of legs

Simple eye

Combined head and thorax

Abdomen

Spinneret

Q. **Which spiders are poisonous?**

A. All spiders have some form of poison they use to kill their prey. However, most spiders are harmless to humans, even though their bite might be painful. The spiders most poisonous to humans are the brown recluse, the black widow, the Sydney funnel-web, and some species of tarantulas in Africa and South America.

Q. **How do spiders catch their prey?**

A. Most people know that spiders spin webs. Some of the threads in a web are sticky and some are not. When an insect touches the web, the sticky threads hold it fast, and the spider feels the vibrations of the struggling insect. The spider runs down the nonsticky threads and bites the prey or wraps it in silk. Spiders cannot chew; they only drink liquids. They pump digestive juices onto their prey, then wait until the juices turn the insect into a soup. Some spiders hunt in other ways. The trap door spider makes a hole in the ground, and waits inside. When an insect passes by, the spider runs out and grabs it. Like the trap door spider, the wolf spider hunts for and pounces on its food instead of using a web.

Q. **Are all scorpions poisonous?**

A. Scorpions are much more dangerous than spiders. Scorpions have a stinger on the end of their curved tails, which they carry high over their backs. They grab their prey with their clawlike pincers and then sting it. They usually hunt insects, spiders, and other scorpions.

A Spider Story

Arachnids got their name from a Greek myth. The story tells of a young woman named Arachne who boasted that she could weave anything, including rugs or cloth, better than the goddess Athena. Angrily, the goddess challenged the woman to a weaving contest. When the goddess saw that Arachne's work did rival her own, she furiously destroyed Arachne's thread. In despair and anger, Arachne killed herself. Feeling remorse for what she had done, Athena took the woman's body and changed it into a spider who still had the skill to weave fine silken threads.

SCORPION

INSECT

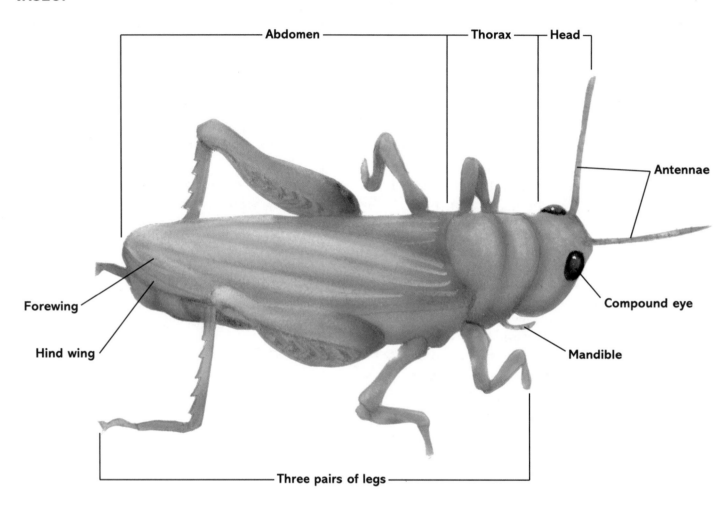

Abdomen — Thorax — Head

Antennae

Compound eye

Mandible

Forewing

Hind wing

Three pairs of legs

Q. **What makes an animal an insect?**

A. Many people believe that anything that crawls and looks like a bug is an insect, including spiders. Insects and spiders are related, but they are different in some basic ways. Instead of the eight legs (four on a side) that spiders have, insects have six (three on a side). Insects also have three parts to their bodies: a head, thorax, and abdomen. You can see these parts on the diagram of the grasshopper. Finally, insects have a compound eye instead of the simple eye that spiders have.

Q. **What are social insects?**

A. Social insects live in large groups or colonies in which every member has a specific job to do. Ants are the most common social insects. An ant colony is made up mostly of worker ants that are responsible for gathering food, building and maintaining nest tunnels, taking care of ant eggs before and after they hatch, and guarding the nest. The largest ant in a colony is the queen. She is the only ant who lays eggs. Now and then, mating males and queen ants are born. They have wings and leave the nest when they are ready to mate.

Q. **What is an ant nest like?**

A. Many ant nests are underground. They consist of several tunnels and chambers or rooms. The rooms serve different purposes. Some are places for workers to rest, some are food storage areas, and others are nurseries where the ant eggs are hatched and the larvae raised.

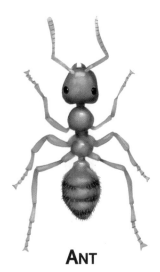

ANT

Ant Farmers

Some kinds of ants actually keep other insects, just like people keep cows. Ants love sweet things, and the honeydew produced by aphids is a favorite of certain ants. The ants protect the aphids from predators such as ladybugs and even help take care of the aphids' eggs. In exchange, the ants collect the honeydew secreted by the aphids' bodies.

Q. **How are bees like ants?**

A. Some bees are social insects. Honey bees live in large colonies with specific jobs for the queen, drones (males), and workers. Instead of tunnels and rooms, they build hives with honeycombs, where they store food and raise baby bees. The queen may live up to nine years, but two to three years is more common.

QUEEN BEE

Q. **How do bees make honey?**

A. Bees swallow nectar that they gather from flowers. Special enzymes combine with the nectar in a bee's crop, or honey stomach, and produce honey. The bees then store the honey in the hive in cells made of wax, which their bodies also produce.

DRONE

Q. **How do the bees know where to find nectar?**

A. Bees are attracted to the bright colors and scents of flowers. Scout bees fly around the area of the hive looking for sources of nectar. When they find a source, they fly back to the hive. They perform a special dance for the other workers that tells them where the nectar is, including the direction and distance. A group of workers then takes off to gather the nectar.

WORKER

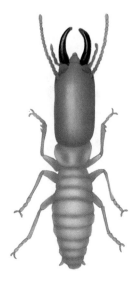

TERMITE

Q. Why don't people like many insects?

A. Many different insects create problems for humans. Termites, which live in large colonies, can be a threat to people's homes. Some types of termite eat wood. Even though the cellulose in wood is hard to digest, termites have special organisms in their stomachs that can digest cellulose. When termites get into a house, they chew up the wood, leaving mostly sawdust behind. This can be a problem if the supports of a house are made of wood.

Q. In what other ways are insects harmful to people?

A. Many kinds of insects carry diseases. Houseflies can spread germs by picking up harmful bacteria from decayed material. Cockroaches will eat almost anything in a house. Grasshoppers, locusts, and many other insects can destroy crops. Mosquitoes, of course, inflict itchy, sometimes painful bites on people, and they can also spread diseases such as malaria.

MOSQUITO

Q. Are any insects helpful to people?

A. Ladybugs are one kind of insect that people consider friendly and helpful. They feed on aphids and other plant-eating insects. Ladybugs provide a natural way to reduce garden and crop pests without the use of harmful chemicals.

A Big Pest

Fleas plague people and animals more than almost any other type of insect. Fleas live on the blood of other animals. Their bite causes intense itching. Some types of flea can also carry deadly diseases, such as the bubonic plague. The flea itself is an incredible animal. It can jump more than a foot, which is like a person being able to jump over a 360-foot-high building. Fleas can live up to four months without eating, and their tiny claws and bristly bodies make them extremely difficult to remove from an animal's fur.

FLEA

CICADA

Q. How do caterpillars turn into butterflies?

A. The caterpillars you see on plants and trees are nothing but feeding machines. After several weeks, a caterpillar suddenly stops eating and begins spinning. It surrounds itself with silk threads that harden into a cocoon. Within the cocoon, the body of the insect begins to change. After several weeks, the cocoon splits and the insect, now a butterfly, breaks free. At first, its wings are crumpled. They slowly harden and spread until the butterfly is ready to fly.

Q. How long do butterflies live?

A. Compared to us, butterflies have very brief lives. Adult monarch butterflies live for about 10 months, but most butterflies have a much shorter life span. Many live only long enough to find a mate and lay their eggs before they die.

Q. How do insects reproduce?

A. Insects reproduce in a variety of ways. Most lay eggs. After hatching, insects go through various stages of change before they become adults. Many insects, such as butterflies, experience a metamorphosis, in which they go through four stages: egg, larva, pupa, and adult. Metamorphosis in some insects, like cicadas, is incomplete. Instead of a larval and pupal stage, the newly hatched insects go through a nymph stage, in which they shed their skin periodically as they grow. One type of cicada nymph burrows in the ground where it stays for up to 17 years until it develop into an adult and emerges to mate.

BUTTERFLY

Q. How are fish divided into groups?

A. The thousands of different kinds of fish fall into three different groups. The bony fish have skeletons made of bones. About 20,000 different bony species have been identified, although scientists believe twice as many remain unknown. These are the animals you usually think of when you think about fish: perch, trout, angelfish, minnows, tuna, goldfish, and so on.

Another big group is the cartilaginous fish. This group has flexible cartilage in their skeletons instead of hard bones. Cartilage is the soft but strong material in your ears and nose that makes them flexible; you also have cartilage in between many of your joints, such as your knees or elbows. The cartilaginous fish include sharks and their relatives the rays.

The jawless fish are an unusual group. As you might guess, they have no jaws. Instead they have round mouths lined with sharp teeth that they use to attach to larger animals and feed on them. The jawless fish don't have scales, and their bodies are very slimy.

JAWLESS FISH (LAMPREY)

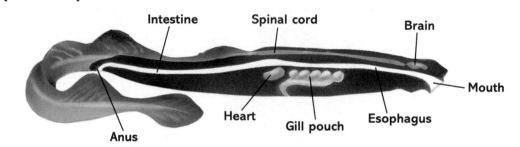

CARTILAGINOUS FISH (GREAT WHITE SHARK)

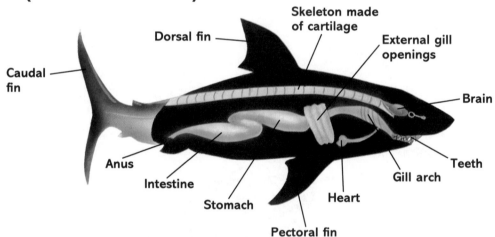

BONY FISH (PERCH)

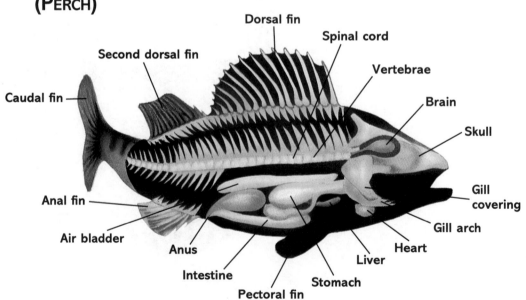

Q. Why are sharks always swimming?

A. Bony fish have an organ called a swim bladder that helps them to float. Like a balloon, the bladder contains air. By inflating or deflating the bladder, bony fish can rise, sink, or hover in the water. Because sharks don't have swim bladders, they need to keep swimming or else they will sink toward the bottom.

Q. How big do sharks get?

A. Most people have heard of the fierce great white shark of monster movie fame. These sharks can grow to 20 feet long and 2,500 pounds. However, the basking shark is bigger—up to 30 feet long and 10,000 pounds. This gentle shark feeds on tiny sea creatures that it filters through bristles in its mouth. The largest shark of all, which is also the largest fish, is the whale shark. Also gentle, the whale shark can weigh more than 30,000 pounds and grow 40 feet long. The whale shark feeds much like the basking shark.

Q. Why do salmon swim upstream?

A. Salmon are unusual because they are one of the few fish that spend their lives in both salt and fresh water. Salmon hatch in fresh-water rivers. As they grow, they swim downstream, finally ending up in the salty ocean. When it is time to lay their eggs, the females return to the rivers from which they came and begin to swim upstream. The males also return and swim upstream to fertilize the eggs. They can travel up to 25 miles in a day. After spawning, most salmon die.

Q. How is a trout like a salmon?

A. Trout are actually cousins to the salmon. However, most trout live their entire lives in fresh water. Trout fishing is a popular sport in many countries. The rainbow trout is one of the best known.

RAINBOW TROUT

Q. Why are fish dark on the top side and light on the bottom side?

A. Like many animals, fish have their own form of camouflage or protective coloring for protection. If you look down at a fish from the water's edge, you may have trouble seeing it because its dark color blends in with the bottom of the stream or lake. If you were under the fish in the water, you might also have trouble seeing it because its light belly blends with the light above and the sky.

CHINOOK SALMON

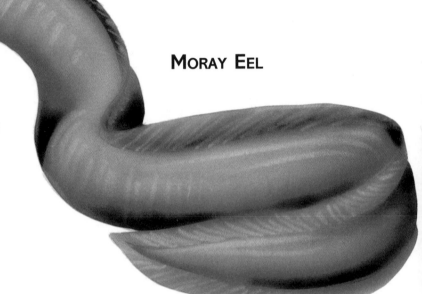

MORAY EEL

Q. Do eels really produce electricity?

A. Most eels do not produce electricity. However, there is a species of electric eel that lives in South America. Its body has thousands of special cells arranged like batteries that can produce hundreds of volts of electricity.

A Fish Story

Piranhas have a reputation for being fierce and deadly. Actually, many species of piranha are no more dangerous than other fish their size. There are, however, a few species of piranha that are remarkably effective hunters. These piranhas are equipped with razor-sharp teeth that can cut into prey like a saw. They also live in big groups that attack together with lightning speed. The combination of their teeth and their pack-hunting habits mean that they can quickly kill and consume animals that are much larger than an individual piranha.

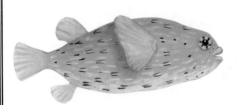

PIRANHA

Q. What is another way fish can protect themselves?

A. Some fish depend on looking scary in the hopes that predators will leave them alone. The porcupine fish raises its spines and blows up its body to nearly twice its size. A puffed-up porcupine fish is too much of a mouthful for most predators.

PORCUPINE FISH

PORCUPINE FISH INFLATED

Q. **Why are flounders flat?**

A. The flat flounders look very much like fish that have been stepped on or have been put together in the wrong way. The bodies of flatfish look like full-bodied fish on their sides. But both eyes are on one side of the fish's head, making it appear almost twisted. Flatfish like the flounder live on the bottom of the ocean. Their strange shape evolved so they could blend in with the sand and mud on the bottom and still be able to see. Young flounder are actually born with an eye on each side of their heads. Before they become adults and settle on the seafloor, one eye migrates to the other side of the head.

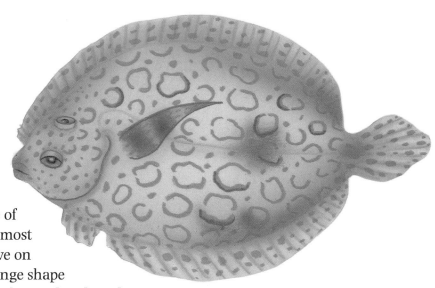

FLOUNDER

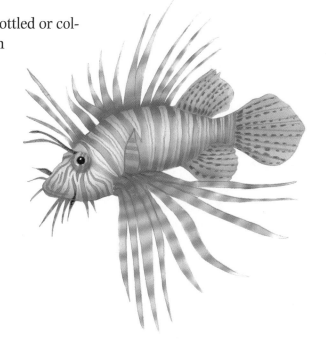

REGAL ANGELFISH

Q. **Why are some fish brightly colored or patterned?**

A. Many fish are mottled or colored so they blend in with sand and rocks. The lionfish has irregular stripes that help it blend in with seaweed. However, many tropical fish have bright colors. Their colors work as camouflage because they live among bright-colored corals. Stripes and spots also help to break up the outline of the fish's body as it swims, which confuses predators.

LIONFISH

Q. **Why do frogs live near water?**

A. Like all amphibians, frogs live part of their life cycle in water. A frog lays its eggs in the water. When the eggs hatch, little tadpoles emerge. Like fish, they have gills that allow them to breathe in the water. Through metamorphosis, they slowly turn into frogs. As the change takes place, each tadpole develops legs, its tail disappears, and lungs begin to form inside its body. When the process is complete, the frog hops out onto land.

Q. **Why are frogs always shiny?**

A. The skin of most frogs and amphibians must always remain moist. Because they have poorly developed lungs, the moist skin of amphibians helps them breathe by absorbing oxygen. If frogs dry out, they can't get enough oxygen and they die. That's another reason why they are never far from water.

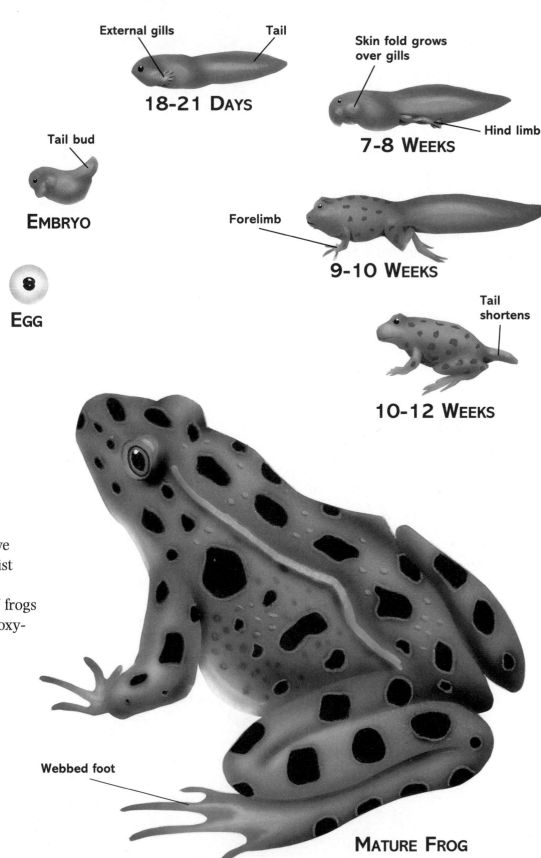

External gills Tail

18-21 DAYS

Skin fold grows over gills

Hind limb

7-8 WEEKS

Tail bud

EMBRYO

EGG

Forelimb

9-10 WEEKS

Tail shortens

10-12 WEEKS

Webbed foot

MATURE FROG

Q. **How are frogs and toads alike and different?**

A. Frogs and toads belong to the same family and have nearly identical lifestyles. Generally, toads have rougher, warty, drier skin, while frogs are smooth. Toads also tend to have shorter legs than frogs.

Q. **What do frogs and toads eat?**

A. Most frogs and toads eat insects. Many of them have an interesting way to capture their food. Frogs and toads have long sticky tongues that they use to grab flying insects in midair. Large species of frogs will also eat fish, snakes, other frogs, and even small mammals.

Q. **Why are salamanders hard to find?**

A. Salamanders love dark, wet places. You may never see one unless you go to a wet woodland and look around at night with a flashlight or turn over stones and logs during the day to find where they might be hiding. They look a little like lizards, but their skin is usually smooth and moist, and they have no claws. Some salamanders are brightly colored and others are plainer.

RED SALAMANDER

Q. **What is the difference between an amphibian and a reptile?**

A. Amphibians bridge the gap between animals that live just in water or just on land. Amphibians spend part of their lives in water and part on land. They have slick, moist skins that most of them must always keep wet. Most reptiles live completely on land, while some spend time in water and on land, like crocodiles and turtles. However, they have a rough, scaly skin that protects the body from water loss.

AMPHIBIAN

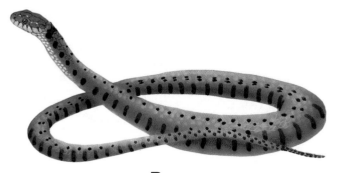

REPTILE

HORNED TOAD

Q. **Why do reptiles like to lie on rocks in the sun?**

A. Reptiles are cold-blooded, so their bodies do not produce and maintain warmth. Although a reptile's scaly skin is fine for keeping in moisture in the dry places where most of them live, it is not good at retaining warmth. Many reptiles, like snakes, lie in the sun during the day to soak up heat.

Q. **What happens when lizards lose their tails?**

A. Some lizards have a special form of protection. When grabbed by the tail, they can wiggle free and run, leaving their tail behind. The bones in the tail have cracks here and there where the tail can break off, and the muscles in the tail also separate. Usually, if a lizard loses its tail it will grow a new one after several weeks, although the new tail is often smaller.

Q. **Have there ever been any real dragons?**

A. The dragons you may have seen in storybooks are magical creatures that never existed, although some dinosaurs may look like dragons. However, there are animals alive today that we call dragons, although they are much smaller than their storybook cousins. The water dragon you see here lives in Asia. Another kind of dragon is the Komodo dragon, which is the world's largest lizard. The Komodo dragon can grow to 10 feet long and weigh 300 pounds.

WATER DRAGON

Q. How many kinds of snakes are poisonous?

A. Of the nearly 2,500 different species of snakes, only about 800 of them are poisonous. Of these, only about 250 are dangerous to people. One of the most poisonous is the African black mamba, which is also the fastest snake in the world. Over short distances, it can travel seven miles per hour, which is about twice as fast as most people can walk. The rattlesnake is also poisonous. It usually coils up when it is threatened and rattles its tail, making a buzzing noise as a warning to stay away. The rattles are made of old skin.

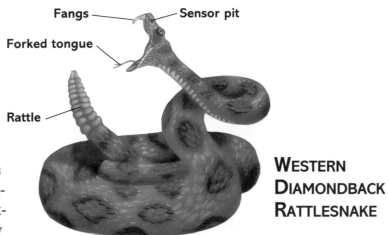

Fangs — Sensor pit

Forked tongue

Rattle

WESTERN DIAMONDBACK RATTLESNAKE

Q. How do snakes capture their prey?

A. Poisonous snakes use their venom to capture and kill prey. Boas and pythons squeeze their prey to death. They coil around an animal, then constrict their muscles until their victim suffocates.

RETICULATED PYTHON

Q. How do snakes swallow their prey?

A. Snakes often kill prey much larger than they are. They also swallow their prey whole rather than biting and chewing. A snake's jaws are made extremely flexible by a special bone that works like a hinge so the mouth can be opened wide. A flexible ligament connects the two halves of the jaw so the lower jaw can be moved sideways. The snake moves over the prey, pushing it down its throat with its muscles. Freshly swallowed prey leaves a big lump in the middle of the snake.

Snake Imposters

Some snakes are copycats. Harmless snakes often are colored almost exactly the same as poisonous snakes. For example, the Mexican milk snake and the scarlet kingsnake look a lot like the deadly coral snake. Predators who see a milk snake or a kingsnake will think it is poisonous and leave it alone.

KINGSNAKE

Q. Do turtles ever leave their shells?

A. A turtle's shell is part of its body and cannot be removed without killing the animal. Because turtles are slow-moving creatures on land, they shrink inside their shells when threatened instead of running. Most predators cannot bite through the shell, so they learn to leave turtles alone.

Q. Why is a turtle in danger when flipped on its back?

A. It is very difficult for a turtle to turn over when flipped on its back because its legs won't touch the ground. A turtle on its back may suffocate, dehydrate, or starve if not helped.

Q. What is the difference between turtles and tortoises?

A. Tortoises are "land turtles" and are generally found in dry areas. The largest tortoise is the giant tortoise found only on isolated islands. It can weigh up to 600 pounds. No one knows how long giant tortoises can live. They may survive over 100 years. Turtles live in or near water. The leatherback is the largest turtle on Earth today; it can reach a weight of 1,600 pounds.

EASTERN BOX TURTLE

HINGED TORTOISE

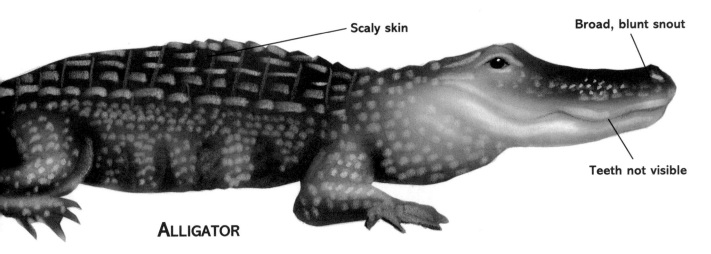

Scaly skin

Broad, blunt snout

Teeth not visible

ALLIGATOR

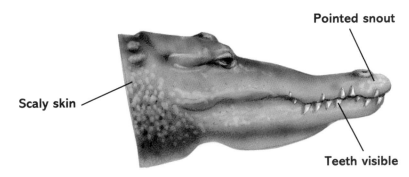

Pointed snout

Scaly skin

Teeth visible

CROCODILE

Q. **What is the difference between crocodiles and alligators?**

A. Crocodiles and alligators have differently shaped heads. The alligator has a short, blunt nose, while the crocodile's nose is longer and thinner. Both animals have extremely strong jaws that can grab prey in an instant. Another way to tell them apart is that some of a crocodile's teeth are visible even when its mouth is closed, but an alligator's are not.

Q. **What do crocodiles eat?**

A. Crocodiles are meat eaters. When young, alligators and crocodiles will eat small fish, frogs, and other animals. When grown, they can overpower animals as large as deer or antelope. Like many other predators, they will eat almost anything they can catch, including turtles and muskrats.

Raising an Alligator

Although alligators are fierce predators, they are gentle parents. The female American alligator builds a large, warm nest for her eggs and stays by them until they are ready to hatch. She helps the eggs hatch by rolling them gently against the roof of her mouth to crack them open. New-born alligators can be eaten by many animals, and their mothers are known to protect them. They sometimes even carry them to water in their mouths.

Q. How do birds fly?

A. If you look at the diagram of the bird's feather on this page, you can how see the barbules on a feather lock together. This structure makes the feather have a firm surface that pushes against the air. When a bird flaps its wings downward, the feathers push against the air and produce a force that lifts the bird up. When the bird pulls its wings back up, the feathers spread open and let the air pass through, which lessens resistance against the air that would push the bird downward.

BIRD'S FEATHER

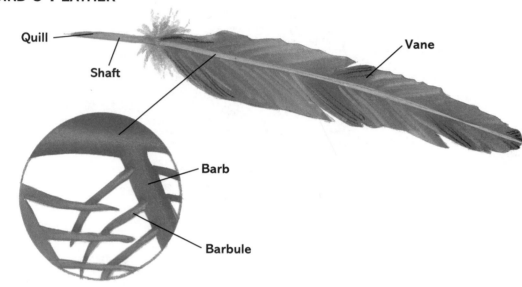

Quill · Shaft · Vane · Barb · Barbule

BIRD'S WING

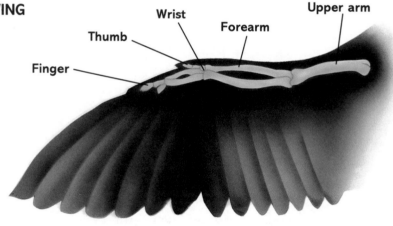

Thumb · Finger · Wrist · Forearm · Upper arm

EMPEROR PENGUIN

Q. Do all birds fly?

A. Not all birds fly. Ostriches, for example, have large, heavy bodies and tiny wings. Penguins also have small wings in proportion to their bodies. Their bodies and wings are better suited to swimming in the ocean.

Q. How do birds protect themselves if they can't fly?

A. With their long, powerful legs, ostriches can reach speeds of 35 miles per hour and outrun their predators. Penguins are streamlined, efficient swimmers in the water. Since most of their predators are in the water, penguins will swiftly swim and jump up on the land to escape.

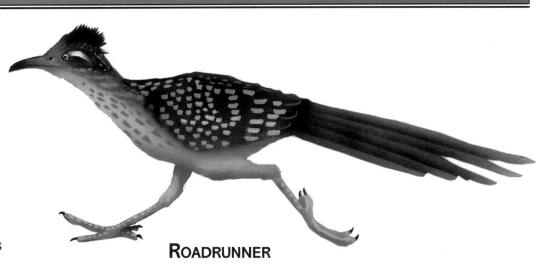

ROADRUNNER

Q. Is the roadrunner really as fast as it is in cartoons?

A. The roadrunner can fly, but it prefers to run. Some sources say it can run 24 miles per hour. As a predator, it uses its great speed to chase after insects and snakes.

Q. Why do birds sing?

A. Most birds make sounds and calls. However, a bird song is a pattern of sounds regularly repeated. The American goldfinch is a popular songbird in backyards. Birds have many reasons for singing and calling. Males may be marking their territory to warn other males away. They also sing for mates, in the hopes that females will be attracted to them. Calls can warn other birds about predators. Migrating birds often call to each other to stay together, especially at night.

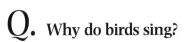

AMERICAN GOLDFINCH

Q. Why do some birds have colorful feathers, while other birds are dull colored?

A. The males and females of many species of birds are differently colored, with the males having much brighter feathers than the females do. The males use their bright feathers to attract mates, while the females use their dull feathers to blend into their surroundings while they sit on their nests. In some species of birds, there is no obvious color difference between male and female.

Male

Female

WOOD DUCKS

Bird Builders

Most birds lay their eggs in some kind of nest. These nests can be made of a wide variety of materials and take on unusual shapes. The rufous ovenbirds build large, ball-shaped nests of sand and cow dung that are strong enough to withstand being hit by a rock. Cliff swallows and house martins make nests of mud. These nests are as strong as adobe homes, which are also made of mud, straw, and water.

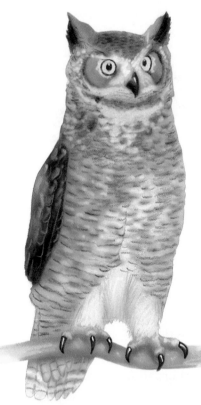

GREAT HORNED OWL

Q. **Why do owls have such big eyes?**

A. Owls are nocturnal birds, which means they are active at night. Owls must be able to see their prey in the dark, so their eyes are large to let in as much light as possible. Their eyes are positioned forward so that they can see moving prey.

Q. **How are birds of prey alike?**

A. Although birds of prey come in many sizes and shapes, they all have some features in common. They have feet with talons that can grab and hold prey. They also have sharp, strong beaks made for tearing meat and keen eyesight for spotting prey from a great distance. Many birds of prey, like the falcon, have powerful wings and tapered bodies that allow them to fly and dive quickly to catch their meals.

PEREGRINE FALCON

EUROPEAN KINGFISHER

Different Beaks, Different Diets

Birds' beaks are specially adapted to their diets. The crossbill's beak overlaps at the tips, which makes it a perfect tool for prying seeds out of pinecones. Some birds, like the sandpiper and the kingfisher, have bills shaped like pliers for picking up small creatures or grabbing fish in the water.

Q. **What do other birds eat?**

A. Birds eat a variety of foods, including fish, insects, snakes, seeds, fruit, and flower nectar. Robins eat worms, and flamingos eat algae. Some birds, such as vultures and condors, eat the remains of dead animals.

CALIFORNIA CONDOR

Q. **Why are some birds endangered?**

A. The population of many species of birds is so low that they may soon become extinct. Many of these birds have become endangered because people have destroyed their habitats or released chemicals into the environment that poison them or harm their eggs. One of the largest birds in the world, the California condor, once faced extinction. Because it seemed they could not survive on their own, the few remaining condors were brought in from the wild during the 1980s. A refuge was set aside for them to live in, and the first condors bred in captivity were released to live on their own in 1992.

Q. **Why do some birds have webbed feet?**

A. Just as birds have different beaks to match their diets, they also have different feet to match where they live. Birds with webbed feet, such as ducks and pelicans, are swimming birds. They use their feet like flippers to swim through the water.

AMERICAN WHITE PELICAN

Q. **Where do birds go in the winter?**

A. Some birds stay in one area year-round. Others, however, move toward the equator in the winter and then return to other areas in the spring. Many birds migrate long distances. The Canada goose travels the length of the North American continent. Groups of geese fly in a wedge-shaped pattern, honking as they go.

CANADA GOOSE

Q. How do you know if an animal is a mammal?

A. Mammals share many characteristics with other groups of animals. However, only one combination of characteristics makes a mammal. If an animal has fur or hair, is warm-blooded, and feeds its young with milk, then it is a mammal.

Q. How are mammals divided into groups?

A. Mammals come in several different groups. Many of them are familiar animals that fall into groups you would recognize: primates; bats; rodents; rabbits; baleen whales; toothed whales; insectivores; carnivores; odd-toed hoofed mammals; even-toed hoofed mammals; elephants; marsupials, or pouched mammals; and monotremes, or egg-laying mammals. The others are more unusual and include pangolins, which have scales made of dense hair; manatees or sea cows; aardvarks; flying lemurs; hyraxes, which are rodentlike animals related to elephants; and edentates, which are toothless mammals including sloths, anteaters, and armadillos. All of these divisions are based on physical features.

AMERICAN BISON

Q. Do all mammals live on land?

A. Many people think that all mammals live on land. However, many spend all or part of their lives in the ocean. These marine mammals include whales and dolphins, manatees, seals and sea lions, and the walrus.

WALRUS

CARNIVORE

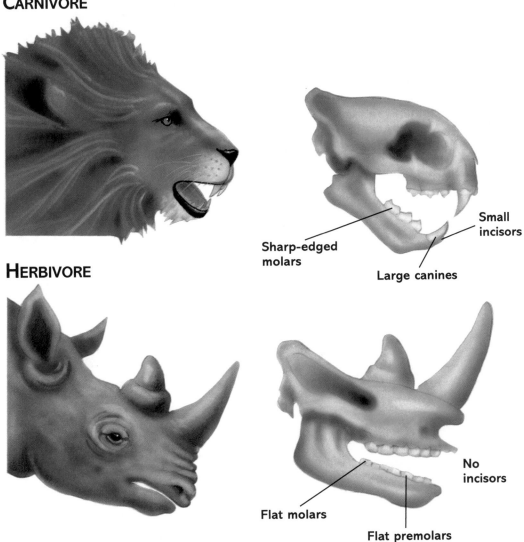

Sharp-edged molars

Small incisors

Large canines

HERBIVORE

No incisors

Flat molars

Flat premolars

Q. **What do mammals eat?**

A. You can generally tell what mammals eat by looking at their teeth. Flat, grinding teeth show that an animal eats plants. Plant eaters are called herbivores. Meat-eaters have sharp teeth for tearing and chewing meat. These animals are called carnivores.

Q. **Do any mammals eat both plants and other animals?**

A. Yes, many mammals do eat both plants and meat. They are called omnivores. Humans are omnivores, as are chimpanzees. Omnivores have a combination of sharp teeth and flat molars.

Prehensile tail

SPIDER MONKEY

Q. **How do monkeys stay in trees without falling?**

A. Monkeys are agile creatures that spend much of their time in trees. They are able to jump from branch to branch, grabbing on securely with their feet and hands. Many also have prehensile tails that they can use to grab branches.

Q. **Why do gorillas beat on their chests?**

A. Gorillas are often portrayed as fierce animals that scream, roar, and pound their chests. They put on a good show, mainly in hopes of appearing fierce so their enemies will back off and run away. However, gorillas are known to be gentle and intelligent animals.

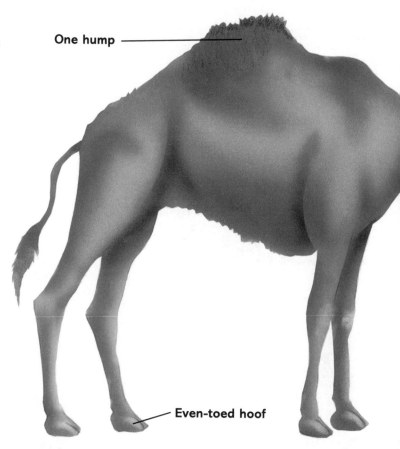

One hump

Even-toed hoof

DROMEDARY CAMEL

GORILLA

Q. **What is the difference between apes and monkeys?**

A. Apes and monkeys have several things in common. Both groups are primates, and they share certain behaviors and basic physical traits. One obvious difference, though, is that monkeys have tails and apes do not. Most apes are also much larger than monkeys. The gorilla, for instance, can stand as tall as five-and-a-half feet and weigh hundreds of pounds. Spider monkeys, marmosets, and baboons are monkeys; chimpanzees, gibbons, and orangutans are apes.

Q. Why does a camel have a hump?

A. Dromedaries, or one-humped camels, are mainly desert creatures. Their bodies are capable of storing fat in their humps and then using this hump for nourishment when nothing else is available. As these fat reserves are used, the hump shrinks and sags. Camels are also able to survive long periods without water. They obtain much of their water from desert plants. When they finally find water, they can drink much more at once than any other animal.

Q. Why does an elephant have a trunk?

A. The elephant's trunk is really its nose. This flexible, muscular appendage is handy for a number of things. An elephant can use its trunk to smell and examine all kinds of things. It can even pick up small objects with its trunk. The trunk is also useful for drinking and taking baths. The elephant sucks water into its nose, then squirts the water into its mouth or over its back. Elephants also take dust baths, using their trunks to throw dirt over their bodies as protection from the sun's rays.

Q. Is it true that elephants "never forget"?

A. Elephants have a reputation for remembering things a long time. In general, this is true. In the wild, 50-year-old elephants will remember feeding grounds they visited in their youth. Elephants also have close relationships with others of their kind that they seem to remember for all of their long lives. They even seem to remember locations where significant events happened; sometimes they will stop and linger at a spot where a fellow herd member died. Captive elephants that learned tricks when they were young can remember them decades later.

ASIAN ELEPHANT

Cat falls

Cat twists head around

Body follows

Legs stretch down

Q. How can cats land on their feet when they fall?

A. Cats don't land on their feet every single time they fall, but they do most of the time. Cats have been known to fall from great heights and survive. This may be one of the reasons people believe that cats have "nine lives." You can see from the diagram on this page how cats are able to twist themselves in midair so that their feet are pointing toward the ground.

Q. Why are there so many different kinds of cats?

A. Modern domestic cats, like dogs, are largely a result of selective breeding by humans. This means that people controlled which cats mated so that certain characteristics became dominant.

Some traits became dominant through mutation. The Manx cat has no tail, a trait which is probably the result of a mutation. The Rex has soft fur that is tightly curled and gives the Rex an unusual dense, velvety coat. This trait is the result of breeding.

No tail

MANX

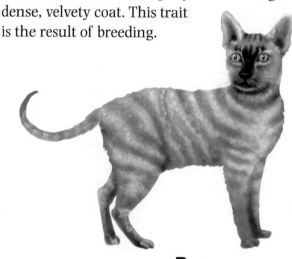

REX

Q. Were dogs ever wild?

A. The dog was one of the first wild animals to become linked with humans. Evidence shows dogs may have been living with humans for nearly 10,000 years. No one really knows how this partnership started, but dogs adopted humans rather than the other way around. Thousands of years ago, canine scavengers may have chosen to live alongside humans, who were skillful hunters that left scraps behind after their meals. Dogs have many wild relatives living today, including wolves and coyotes.

Q. Why do wolves live in packs?

A. Wolves live in packs or groups because they are social animals. A pack may contain as few as three or more than twenty wolves. Packs include adult males and females and their pups. The pack works together to hunt food. A few will chase an animal, such as a deer, while others circle and come in from the sides. After making a kill, the wolves share their food with each other.

LABRADOR RETRIEVER

RIVER OTTER

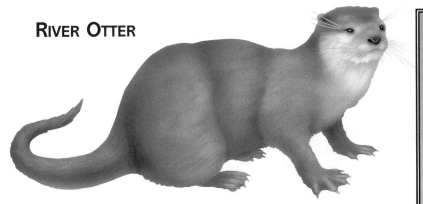

Q. Why are otters so playful?

A. River otters seem to be naturally playful and sociable. They enjoy romping and chasing each other, swimming, and sliding down river banks. In the winter, they will run and slide on ice. Otters will play for hours. Many animals use this kind of play as a way to learn the skills they need for survival.

Horse Toes

Like other animals, mammals have changed a great deal through evolution since they appeared on Earth. The horse is one example. A modern horse walks and runs on one toe. Early horse ancestors, however, were about the size of a dog and had five toes. Later, a slightly larger, three-toed animal evolved. Over many generations, the middle toe became larger, and the side toes eventually no longer touched the ground. The bones of the two side toes fused into the leg bone as the modern horse developed a hoof.

HORSE'S FOOT
One digit

BEAVER

Q. Why do people say "busy as a beaver"?

A. Beavers are very active animals. They spend a great deal of time gnawing down trees and using the logs, along with sticks and brush, to build dams across streams and lakes. These dams hold back enough water for the beavers to build lodges with underwater entrances. Because beavers work so hard and for such long hours, they are described as "busy."

Q. What happens when an opossum plays "dead"?

A. An opossum can't move very fast when it is on the ground. So when it is threatened by an enemy, it has an interesting defense. It drops to the ground and pretends to be dead. Its body is limp, its eyes are shut, and its tongue hangs out. Most hunters are designed to catch live, moving animals, and their instinctive hunting tactics don't respond to dead things. After a while, they leave the opossum alone. In a few minutes, the opossum recovers, gets up, and moves on. The opossum is the only American marsupial, which is an animal that raises its babies in a pouch.

Q. Where do other marsupials live?

A. Most marsupials live in Australia. These include honey glider possums, moles, bandicoots, sugar gliders, wombats, koalas, wallabies, and the kangaroos. Right after a baby kangaroo is born, it uses its strong forearms to crawl into its mother's pouch. Here the baby nurses for several months, until it has grown large enough to leave the pouch.

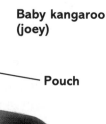

Baby kangaroo (joey)

Pouch

MARSUPIAL (KANGAROO)

Q. **Why do some mammals have horns?**

A. Many animals, such as the Arabian oryx, have horns. These horns are usually used for defense against enemies. During breeding season, males will use their horns to fight each other. The winning male is able to mate with the females. Other animals, such as deer, have antlers. Horns are permanent, while antlers are shed and regrown yearly.

ARABIAN ORYX

Q. **If a mammal has no horns, sharp claws, and can't run fast, how does it defend itself?**

A. Many animals have come up with interesting adaptations to protect themselves. The skunk, for example, sprays a terrible-smelling liquid in the face of its enemy, effectively chasing it away. Porcupines have a sharp way to protect themselves. Their bodies are covered with long, sharp quills that easily detach. When a porcupine is threatened, it raises these quills, and any predator that comes too close will get the barbed points stuck in its skin. The quills are difficult to remove, and the painful wounds they make can become infected and eventually kill the animal.

PORCUPINE

Q. **Why do zebras have stripes?**

A. Zebras live on the wide-open plains of Africa, so you may wonder why they have a coloring that would work as camouflage in shadowy wooded areas. One theory is that as zebras travel together in large groups, the stripes make them all blend together so predators at a distance can't pick out a single animal to chase. Another idea is that the stripe patterns allow zebras to identify each other.

ZEBRA

Baleen

WHALE

Q. **How does an animal as big as a whale find enough to eat?**

A. Baleen whales such as the blue whale and the humpback whale eat plankton, which they strain from the water with the baleen in their mouths. Plankton is made up of various tiny creatures that drift through the ocean in huge numbers. A blue whale's stomach may be able to hold up to two tons of food at one time.

Q. **How fast can animals run?**

A. The cheetah is the fastest land animal. It can run up to 70 miles per hour in short bursts. This high speed allows it to chase down and catch prey such as antelope. If a quick run doesn't result in a catch, the cheetah has to slow down and stop. It can't keep running for long periods of time.

Q. **Why do cheetahs have spots?**

A. Cheetahs, like many other wild cats, have spots to help hide them in the grasslands where they live. With camouflage, a cheetah can get close enough to its prey without being seen in order to lunge at it and hopefully catch it. Leopards also have spots, although they are much larger than the cheetah's small spots. Leopards spend a lot of time in trees, so their spots blend in with the dappled light filtered by leaves.

CHEETAH

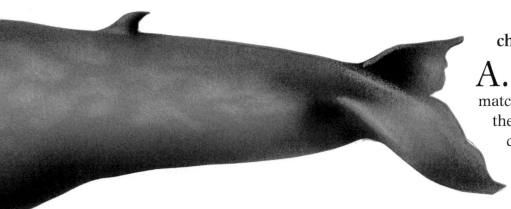

Q. Does a chameleon really change color?

A. A chameleon can change color to match its background. Special color cells in the chameleon's skin contain different color pigments. In each cell, the pigment is usually all collected at the center, but the chameleon can make it spread through the cell and become more prominent. By controlling the different color pigments this way, a chameleon can change its color to match its surroundings. It will also change color when stimulated by temperature and by emotion, such as fear.

Q. What other forms of camouflage do animals have?

A. Many animals, both predators and prey, are colored to match their surroundings. The ptarmigan has an even more specialized way to hide itself. Its plumage changes with the season. In the summer, when the ptarmigan walks across landscape that is mostly brown, the bird's feathers are brownish red. In the winter, when snow is on the ground, the ptarmigan's feathers turn white so that it blends into the snow.

PTARMIGAN

Alive with Color

Some species change their camouflage adaptations to match environmental conditions. The peppered moth is an example. The exact color of each individual peppered moth varies; some are darker and some are lighter. In the 1800s when factories became common, trees and other parts of the landscape became dark with soot. The light-colored peppered moths stood out against these new dark backgrounds, and birds and other predators were able to find them easily. The dark moths were found and eaten less often, so more of them survived and were able to breed. Their offspring tended to be dark, so there were few light-colored peppered moths left. Later, when factories were built that produced less soot, the color of the landscape changed again, and the dark moths were now easier for predators to find. Over time, the light moths became common again.

Q. **What is a duck-billed platypus?**

A. From the name, you might almost think a duck-billed platypus was a bird. However, it is really an unusual kind of mammal called a monotreme. Like all mammals, monotremes are warm-blooded and have fur; unlike other mammals, they lay eggs. The platypus has a leathery-looking bill that it uses to suck up food from the bottom of ponds, and it has front feet that look like flippers.

DUCK-BILLED PLATYPUS

Q. **Is a sea horse really a horse?**

A. A sea horse is really a fish, although its head looks like a horse's head. These little fish wrap their tails around vegetation to anchor themselves. They eat plankton and small fish. When threatened, sea horses can change color almost instantly, from gray or black to bright yellow or purple. Sea horses are unusual in another way, too. The female lays her eggs in a pouch on the male's abdomen. The male fertilizes the eggs then incubates them in his pouch.

Prehensile tail

SEA HORSE

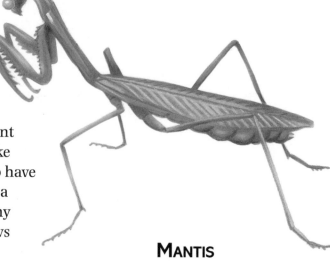

Q. **What is a mantis?**

A. The mantis is a large insect that is specially designed to hunt other insects. Many mantises have bodies that make them look like plant leaves, so other insects don't notice they are near. They also have long and powerful front legs that can quickly reach out and grab a meal. The legs also have ridges on them that help to hold on to any animals the mantis grabs. Finally, the mantises have powerful jaws that allow them to kill and eat the insects they catch.

MANTIS

Q. Do hummingbirds really hum?

A. Hummingbirds, among the tiniest birds on Earth, do not hum like people do. Instead, their wings, which move so fast they seem to be a blur, produce a faint humming sound as they hover in front of a flower or feeder to suck the nectar with their long, slender beaks. Hummingbirds are among the few fliers that can hover (some moths can), and to do so, they must flap their wings as fast as 50 times per second.

RUBY-THROATED HUMMINGBIRD

Q. Do bats really drink blood?

A. Vampire bats that live in Central America and South America do drink blood. They lightly land on cows and horses and make small cuts on them with their sharp teeth. The bats then lap up a small amount of blood and fly away. Most bats, however, have a very different diet. Some eat insects and some eat fruit. One species actually catches and eats fish.

BAT

Q. Why do skunks smell bad?

A. Skunks don't smell bad themselves, but they have a liquid stored in two anal glands at the base of their tails that does. When threatened, skunks will turn around, raise their tails, and shoot the liquid into the face of their enemy. The foul smell drives away any potential predator.

ANTEATER

Q. Do anteaters really eat ants?

A. Yes. Anteaters survive by eating ants and other insects. They have long tongues that allow them to slurp up insects, and they also have strong front claws for digging them out of the ground. Anteaters are different from most other mammals because they have no teeth.

SKUNK

Q. **How do dolphins use sounds?**

A. Dolphins, porpoises, and other toothed whales have no vocal chords, but scientists believe they are able to produce a variety of sounds with a special oil-filled organ in their foreheads called the melon. They use these sounds to communicate with each other and to analyze their environment. The sound waves they send out bounce off of objects around them. The animals sense the reflected sound waves and are able tell what kind of object reflected them. This skill, called echolocation, is so well developed in toothed whales that some of them can tell the difference between similar objects of only slightly different size, or between two objects that are the same shape and size but are made of different materials.

PORPOISE

HOWLER MONKEY

Q. **Why do dogs howl?**

A. Domestic dogs usually howl because they are lonely and want companionship from people or other dogs. Wild dogs howl, too. Wolves howl to let other wolves know where they are. The howl may mean "stay out of my territory," or "here I am, come find me." Sometimes wolves howl before they go hunting to prepare themselves for the job ahead.

Q. **What does a howler monkey sound like?**

A. The howler monkey's call sounds like a roar. It can be heard for more than a mile. The monkey makes this sound by forcing air through the hyoid bone in its throat. This amplifies the roar and makes it extremely loud.

GIANT PANDA

Q. Why are some animals endangered?

A. Animals are disappearing from the world for different reasons. Often, it's because humans have destroyed their homes and their source of food. The giant panda lives in central China, where it feeds mostly on bamboo. As people took over more and more land, there were fewer places where bamboo could grow, and pandas began to run out of food. Their range in the wild is now quite small. Since they breed poorly in captivity, efforts to help this popular animal have not been very successful.

Q. What are some examples of animals that have recently become extinct?

A. The passenger pigeon is one animal that is no longer a part of our world. The dodo bird is another. These are two obvious examples. However, scientists estimate that several species disappear from Earth every day, many of them before people even knew they existed.

Q. What are people doing to help?

A. The bald eagle is one species that people have been able to help. Pesticides in the environment almost drove them to extinction in many of their natural habitats. Laws controlling hunting and pesticides gave the eagles a chance to survive, and today they are increasing their numbers.

BALD EAGLE

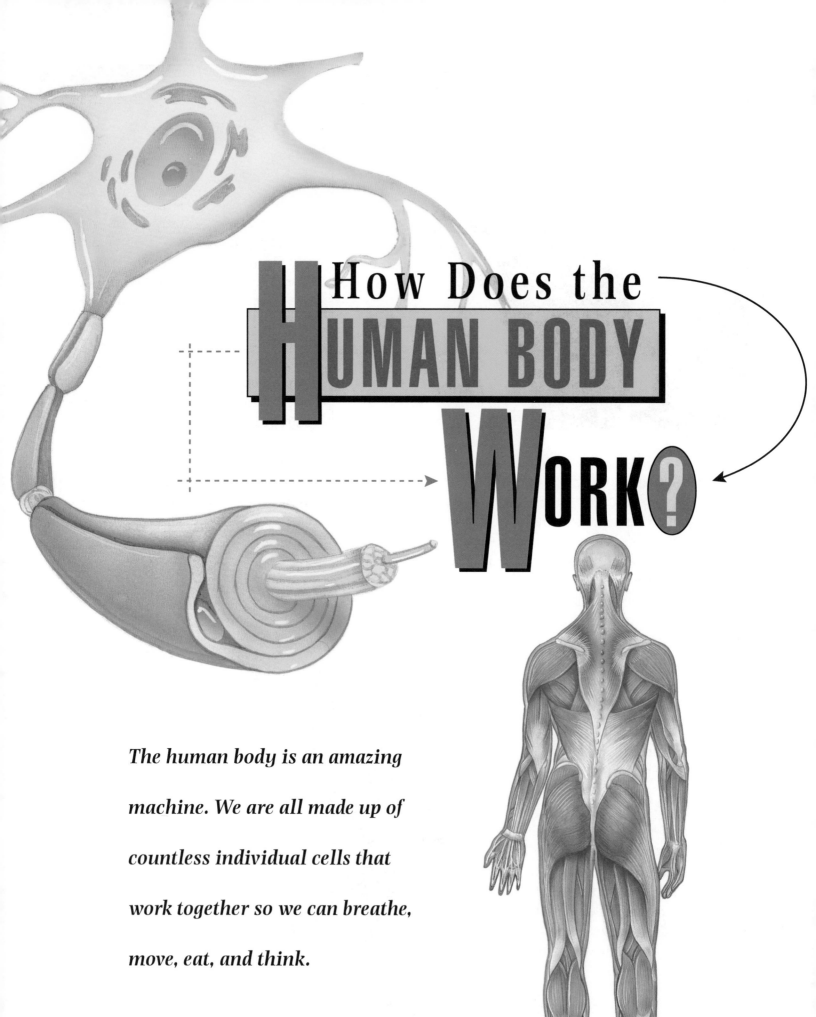

How Does the HUMAN BODY WORK?

The human body is an amazing machine. We are all made up of countless individual cells that work together so we can breathe, move, eat, and think.

Q. What is my body made of?

A. Every living thing, both plant and animal, is made of cells. A cell is a tiny particle of living matter so small that most cannot be seen without a microscope. Some organisms consist of only one cell. A human being has approximately 100,000,000,000,000 (100 trillion) cells in his or her body.

Q. What do cells do?

A. All cells take in food, get rid of waste, and do work. Cells work together in much the same way that members of a community do.

Q. What is a cell made of?

A. The outside of a cell is called the cell *membrane.* It holds the cell's shape, lets food in, and allows waste material to leave. The biggest part of a cell is called *cytoplasm* (SI tuh pla zum). Cytoplasm looks something like jelly, and it is made of water and protein. Within each cell is a *nucleus.* The nucleus is the "director" of the cell. It signals the other parts of the cell about what to do. Each cell's nucleus contains threads called *chromosomes.* Chromosomes have special instruction holders called *genes* that tell a cell what work it is to do.

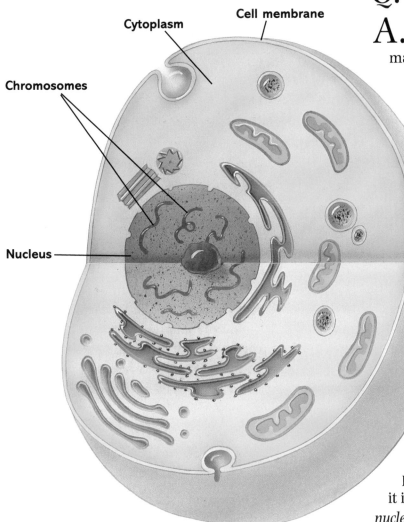

Cytoplasm

Cell membrane

Chromosomes

Nucleus

BASIC CELL STRUCTURE

Q. Are all cells the same?

A. The human body has many different types of cells, such as nerve cells, muscle cells, bone cells, and so on. Different types of cells look different from each other and perform different jobs. Similar types of cells work together to form the major organs of the body. For example, many nerve cells working together make up the brain.

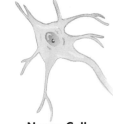

Bone Cell   **Striped Muscle Cells**   **Red Blood Cell**   **Nasal Cell**   **Nerve Cell**

Q. **What is skin made of?**

A. Skin contains two layers: the *epidermis* (eh pu DUR mus) and the *dermis* (DUR mus). The epidermis is the top layer of hardened dead skin cells. The body continually replaces this layer to repair daily wear and tear. The dermis is the skin's lower layer. It contains tiny nerve endings, hair follicles, and glands that produce sweat.

Q. **What does skin do?**

A. Skin is the body's protective coating. It keeps dust, germs, and the sun's harmful rays from entering the body. It also contains thousands of tiny nerve sensors. Each type of sensor detects a different type of feeling, such as touch, pressure, or heat, and sends messages about it to the brain. Since skin covers the entire body, sensors all over the body are constantly sending the brain the millions of messages that enable a person to feel. Skin also plays a role in regulating the body's temperature. When the body is too hot, the skin sweats; when the body is too cold, the skin gets goose bumps or shivers.

The Bare Facts

Skin is the body's largest organ. An adult's skin surface area is about 22 square feet. The skin of an adult weighs about 6 or 7 pounds.

Reading with Your Fingers

The skin of a person's fingertips is very sensitive. Louis Braille used that fact to come up with a way for people who are visually impaired to read. Braille is a system of reading by touch. Each number 0–9 and each letter of the alphabet is a pattern of raised dots. People with limited vision move their fingertips over the patterns in order to read. Louis Braille himself became blind at the age of three. He developed the Braille system of reading when he was 15 years old.

Q. **Why do people have different color skin?**

A. People come in colors ranging from the palest white to nearly black. A substance in the skin called *melanin* gives people their color. Since melanin is very dark in color, the more melanin a person has, the darker his or her skin is. Melanin helps to protect the skin from the sun's ultraviolet rays. That's why people who live closer to the equator—where the sun's rays are more direct—have more melanin in their skin.

Q. **What is a freckle?**

A. A freckle is a small area of skin that contains more melanin than the surrounding skin. Exposure to the sun sometimes causes freckles to form.

Q. **Why does skin fit?**

A. Skin grows as much as is necessary to fit over the growing person. Skin does stay baggy in some places; the skin over the elbows and knuckles has to be loose so that it continues to fit comfortably when people bend their arms and fingers.

SKIN

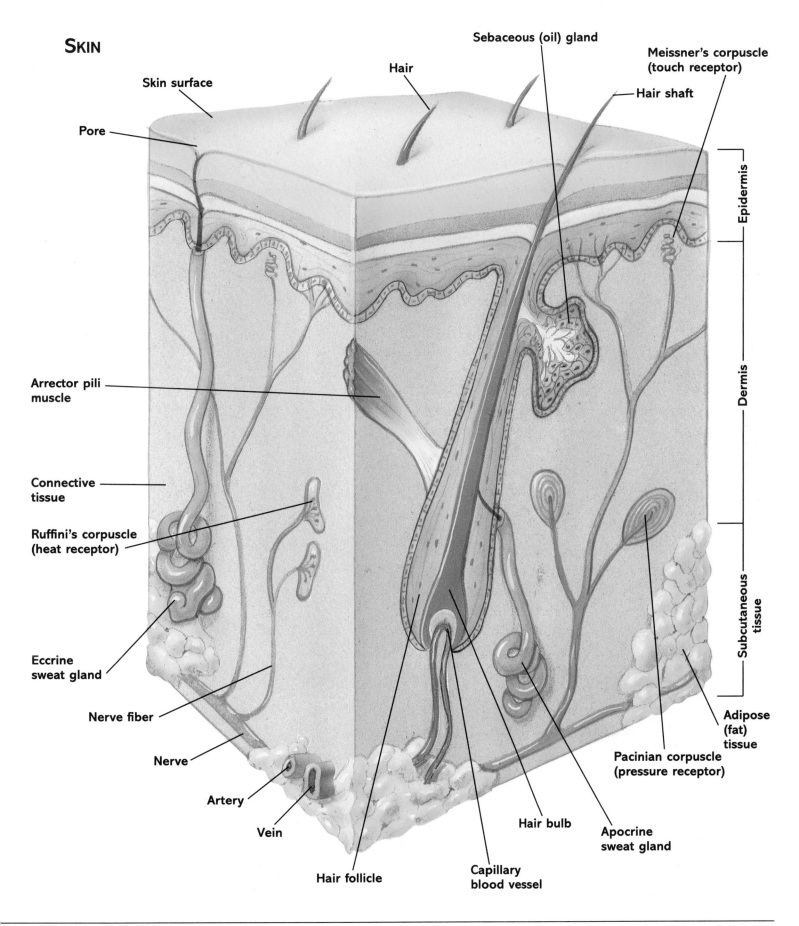

Skin surface

Pore

Sebaceous (oil) gland

Hair

Meissner's corpuscle (touch receptor)

Hair shaft

Epidermis

Arrector pili muscle

Connective tissue

Ruffini's corpuscle (heat receptor)

Dermis

Eccrine sweat gland

Subcutaneous tissue

Nerve fiber

Nerve

Artery

Adipose (fat) tissue

Pacinian corpuscle (pressure receptor)

Vein

Hair bulb

Apocrine sweat gland

Hair follicle

Capillary blood vessel

Q. How do muscles work?

A. The muscles that your body uses to move are attached to your bones by tough strips called *tendons.* Because muscles cannot push—they can only pull— they usually work in pairs. For example, when you bend your knee, the muscles at the back of your thigh pull back, or contract. When you straighten your knee, the muscles in back relax and the muscles at the front of your thigh contract.

A Muscle You Can See

You might be surprised to learn that the tongue is a muscle. For its size, the tongue is one of the body's strongest and most movable muscles. The mighty tongue has many jobs to do. It allows a person to taste, it helps grind food, it moves food around the mouth, it helps with swallowing, it helps to clean the teeth of small pieces of food that have become caught, and it helps form sounds that become speech.

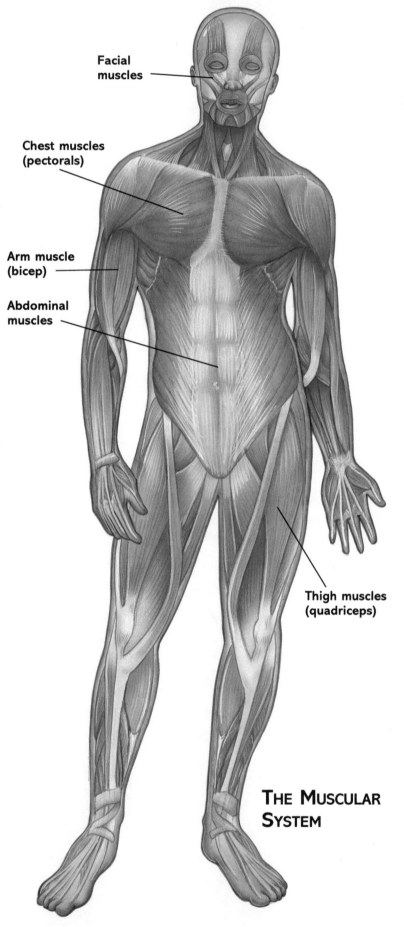

Facial muscles

Chest muscles (pectorals)

Arm muscle (bicep)

Abdominal muscles

Thigh muscles (quadriceps)

THE MUSCULAR SYSTEM

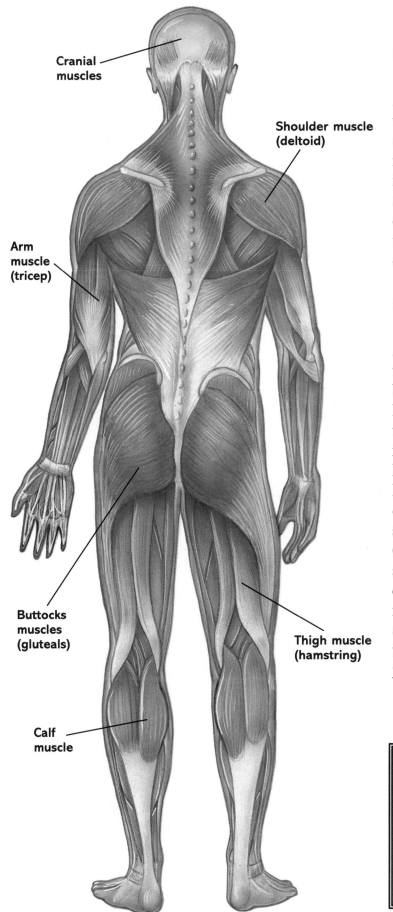

Cranial muscles

Shoulder muscle (deltoid)

Arm muscle (tricep)

Buttocks muscles (gluteals)

Thigh muscle (hamstring)

Calf muscle

Q. Are all muscles in the body the same?

A. Although all muscles are made of muscle cells, there are different kinds of muscles. The body's muscles are grouped into three categories. *Skeletal* muscles move the bones of the skeleton; we use them for walking, lifting, bending, and other physical activities. *Smooth* muscles respond automatically to the brain's commands even when you are not thinking about it; they move food through the intestines and perform other basic tasks. *Cardiac* muscles make up the heart.

Q. How do we build up our muscles?

A. We can all see that our muscles are larger now than when we were born, yet there are the same number of muscle fibers now as then. (Muscle fibers are long, thin groups of muscle cells that have bonded together and work together.) So, how did the muscle fibers grow? Muscle fibers grow by adding to their length and bulk. As a person's bones grow larger and longer, muscle fibers grow, too. The thickness, or bulk, of muscle fibers is what makes a person's muscles strong. Muscles thicken when they are made to work. Ordinary play, walking, and work help to make muscles strong enough to do most of the things people need to do. However, in this age of modern technology—with machines, cars, and elevators to do work for us—people are not as strong as they once were. In order to keep their muscles strong, many people exercise, lift weights, jog, take aerobics classes, or participate in sports.

Muscle Bound

Did you know that you have about 650 muscles in your body? The largest muscles are in the buttocks; the smallest are in the ears. In order to walk a person makes use of over 200 muscles.

Q. **How do bones grow?**

A. When a baby is born, only part of its skeleton is made of bone. The rest is cartilage—the flexible material we still have in our ears and noses. As a baby grows, the cartilage is slowly replaced by bone. Calcium and other minerals that come from food collect in the bones, making them strong. Bones are handy things in which to store the different minerals that are needed by the body's cells.

Q. **If bones store minerals, why aren't they as hard and as heavy as rocks?**

A. Rocks are solid through and through. The inside of a bone is not hard and solid like a rock. The inside part of a bone is living tissue and looks something like a sponge. The holes in it are filled with a soft substance called *marrow*. Some bones, including the skull and backbone, contain a special red bone marrow. This marrow produces red blood cells that go into the bloodstream. Your bone marrow produces about two million new red blood cells every second.

Bare Bones

For hundreds of years, the skeleton has been a symbol of danger, disease, death, and destruction. The skull-and-crossbones flew on the flags of pirate ships, indicating that any who approach should beware. During the Middle Ages, the skeletons of criminals were often left hanging in a hangman's noose as a warning to others.

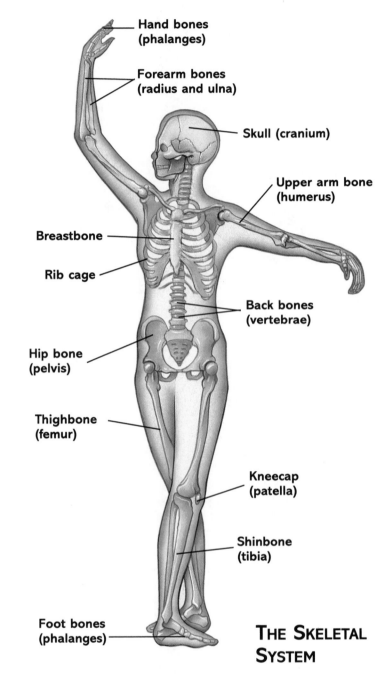

Hand bones (phalanges)

Forearm bones (radius and ulna)

Skull (cranium)

Upper arm bone (humerus)

Breastbone

Rib cage

Back bones (vertebrae)

Hip bone (pelvis)

Thighbone (femur)

Kneecap (patella)

Shinbone (tibia)

Foot bones (phalanges)

THE SKELETAL SYSTEM

Q. **What are the biggest and the smallest bones in the body?**

A. The biggest bone in the human body is in the thigh. It is called the *femur*. The smallest bones are deep inside the ears.

Q. What are joints?

A. The separate bones in the body meet at places called *joints.* They are sort of like the hinges on a door. Strong tissues called *ligaments* hold bones together. A fluid between the bones helps some of them to move easily at the joints. Different kinds of joints help a person make different kinds of motions.

Q. How do broken bones heal?

A. When a bone breaks, it begins to heal itself right away. First, clotted blood collects and creates a cushion around the break. Then, a cuff of cartilage forms around the break—just like a natural splint or cast. And then, on either side of the break, new bone cells begin to grow toward each other until they meet halfway.

JOINT STRUCTURE (KNEE)

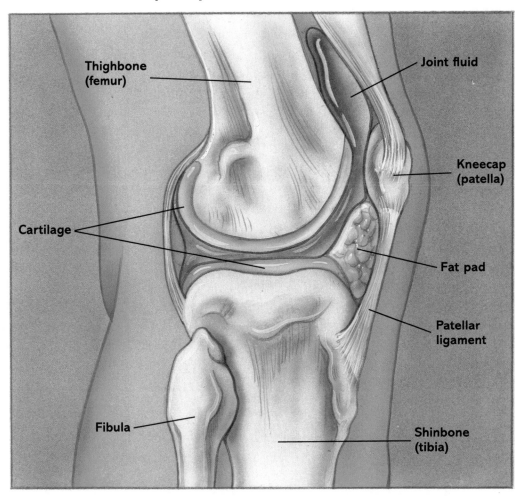

Thighbone (femur)

Joint fluid

Kneecap (patella)

Cartilage

Fat pad

Patellar ligament

Fibula

Shinbone (tibia)

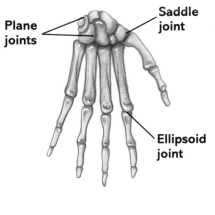

Plane joints

Saddle joint

Ellipsoid joint

HAND

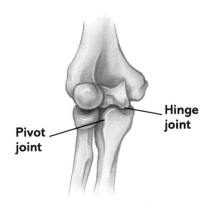

Pivot joint

Hinge joint

ELBOW

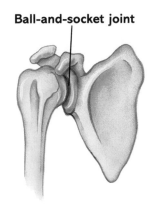

Ball-and-socket joint

SHOULDER

Q. What are nerves?

A. Nerves are something like tiny wires located throughout the body. In fact, this network of nerves is often referred to as the nervous system. All kinds of messages run along the nerves and are transmitted to and from the brain. The brain functions as the control center of the body.

Q. What is inside the brain?

A. The brain is composed of three main parts: the *cerebrum* (suh REE brum), the *cerebellum* (sair uh BELL um), and the *brain stem*. The cerebrum is much bigger than the cerebellum. Only the cerebrum thinks. The cerebellum helps muscle coordination, reflexes, and balance. The brain stem takes care of automatic functions such as your heartbeat.

BRAIN ANATOMY

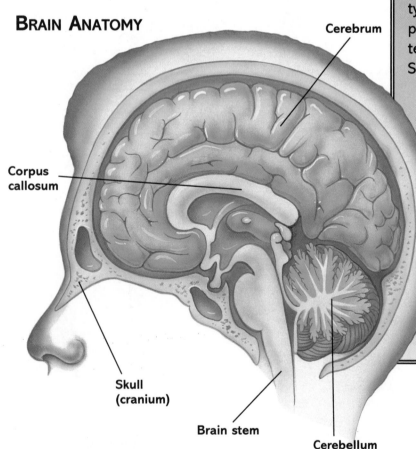

Cerebrum

Corpus callosum

Skull (cranium)

Brain stem

Cerebellum

On Your Nerves

There are two main parts of the nervous system: the *central nervous system,* which contains the brain and spinal cord, and the rest of the network of nerves, called the *peripheral* (puh RIH fur al) nervous system. The peripheral nervous system has about 46 miles of nerves that can deliver signals at speeds of 250 miles per hour. There are two main types of nerves in the peripheral nervous system: *sensory* and *motor.* Sensory nerves transport messages to the brain from the eyes, skin, ears, nose, and other sense organs. Motor nerves carry signals from the brain to the muscles, telling them to move, and to the glands, telling them when to secrete their hormones.

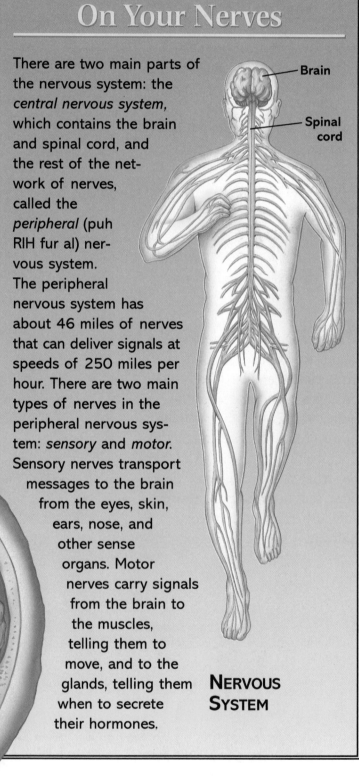

Brain

Spinal cord

NERVOUS SYSTEM

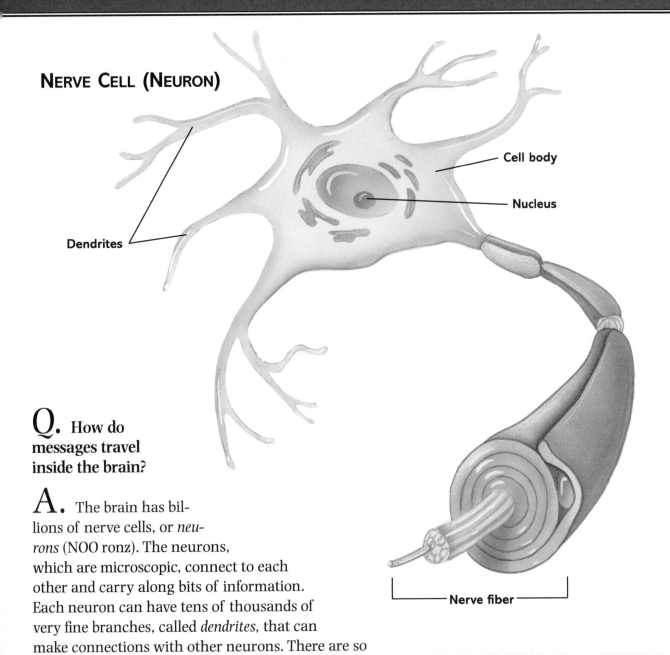

NERVE CELL (NEURON)

Cell body

Nucleus

Dendrites

Nerve fiber

Q. How do messages travel inside the brain?

A. The brain has billions of nerve cells, or *neurons* (NOO ronz). The neurons, which are microscopic, connect to each other and carry along bits of information. Each neuron can have tens of thousands of very fine branches, called *dendrites,* that can make connections with other neurons. There are so many branches that the brain can make trillions of different connections. Information can be linked in a seemingly infinite number of ways. That is why people can think very complicated thoughts. That is also why people can keep lots of information in their memories.

Q. What is a mind?

A. The brain and the mind are not the same thing. A person's mind is that person's collection of thoughts and memories. The brain stops growing when a person reaches adulthood, but the mind does not. The mind continues to grow as long as a person lives.

Half Brain

The cerebrum is divided into two halves, or hemispheres, that are connected by a thick bundle of nerve fibers called the *corpus callosum* (KOR pus ka LO sum). This connection allows the two halves of the brain to communicate with each other. For most people, the left side of the brain receives sensory messages from and sends signals to the right side of the body, while the right side of the brain receives messages from and sends signals to the left side of the body.

THE CIRCULATORY SYSTEM

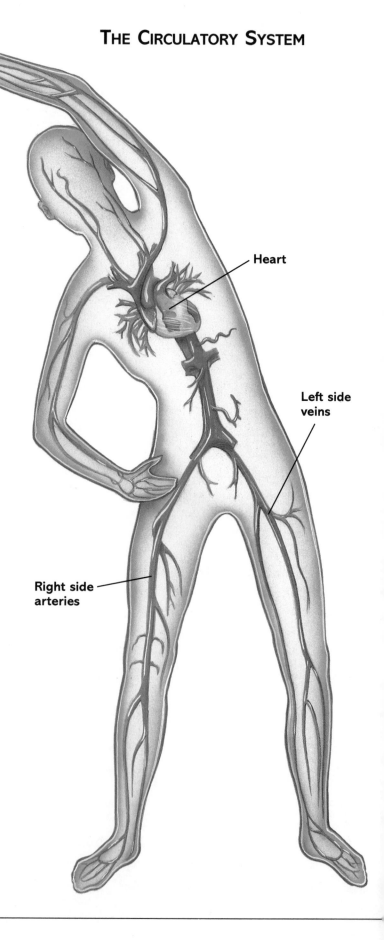

Heart

Left side veins

Right side arteries

Q. What is the circulatory system?

A. The heart, blood, and the system of veins and arteries that carry blood to all parts of the body make up the circulatory system. The circulatory system is the body's highway system, allowing fuel, oxygen, and wastes to be carried to and from every cell.

Q. Is blood the same in all people?

A. Everyone's blood performs the same important job—transporting nutrients and oxygen to the body's cells and removing wastes. However, there are four different types of blood, which are grouped into the categories A, B, O, and AB. All people have blood that is one of the four types. If a person is ever in need of extra blood, doctors will make sure that the blood that is given is compatible with the person's blood type.

Q. What is the difference between an artery and a vein?

A. Arteries are tubes that carry blood from the heart to the rest of the body. Arteries are strong and flexible and have thick walls so they can withstand the pressure of the pumping heart. The blood in arteries is carrying oxygen to the body's cells. Veins carry blood back to the heart after the oxygen has been deposited in the body's cells. The walls of veins are thinner because veins do not need to withstand the pressure of the pumping heart.

Q. Is blood always red?

A. Oxygen makes blood bright red. After oxygen has left the blood, it darkens to a somewhat purplish color. Purplish blood is blood that has already dropped off its load of oxygen to cells in the body. Generally, bright red blood is found in arteries, and purplish blood is found in veins.

Q. What does the heart do?

A. All of the cells in the body need nutrients and oxygen in order to survive and do their work. In order for blood to move these things around the body, it must be pumped, and that's the heart's job. The heart is an extremely strong muscle that is about the size of a fist. It pumps the blood by beating. In healthy adults, the heart beats about 70 times per minute.

Q. What is a heart attack?

A. Just like every other part of the body, the heart itself needs oxygen and nutrients. When part of the heart has its blood supply cut off by a blood clot or other blockage, that part stops working and a heart attack happens. A person having a heart attack will die if the heart stops pumping blood to the rest of the body for more than a few minutes.

Q. Can people with weak hearts be helped?

A. Parts of the heart can be replaced or repaired. Healthy blood vessels can be used to make a path for blood around arteries that have become blocked. Blockages can sometimes be cleared by inflating tiny balloons inside tight arteries. The valves inside the heart can also be repaired or replaced if they become worn.

Pulmonary valve

Aorta

Superior vena cava

Left pulmonary artery

Left atrium

Right pulmonary artery

Left pulmonary veins

Right pulmonary veins

Mitral valve

Right atrium

Aortic valve

Coronary artery

Coronary vein

Tricuspid valve

Left ventricle

Inferior vena cava

Right ventricle

Descending aorta

HEART

What the Heart Doesn't Do

Since ancient times, there have been many misconceptions about the heart. Ancient peoples believed that the heart was the center of love, courage, honor, loyalty, jealousy, and many other emotions.

Although we know now that the brain and not the heart controls the emotions, we still say "take heart" when we talk about courage and "broken heart" when we talk about lost love.

Q. How do the lungs work?

A. The lungs move air in and out of the body. Unlike the heart, the lungs are not muscles, but they are surrounded by muscles that inflate and deflate the lungs like balloons. One of these muscles is the *diaphragm*—a huge sheet of muscle that stretches beneath the lungs, all the way from the breastbone to the backbone. Other muscles that help to pump air are attached to the ribs. When the brain gives the signal, all of these muscles tighten up and get short. They pull the ribs up and out, and the diaphragm flattens. This makes the chest cavity bigger, and there is less pressure in the lungs so the outside air rushes in.

RESPIRATORY SYSTEM

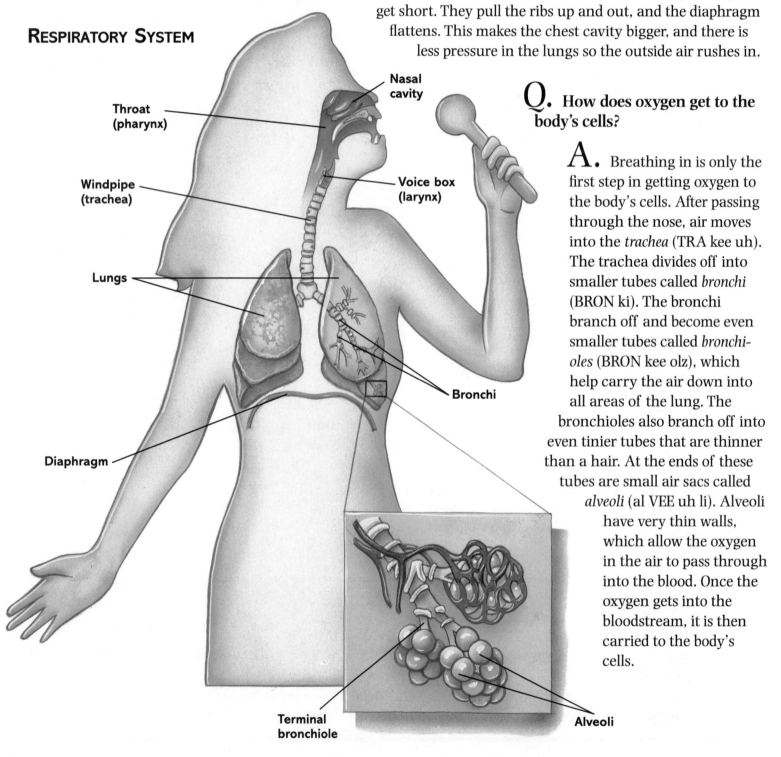

Throat
(pharynx)

Nasal
cavity

Windpipe
(trachea)

Voice box
(larynx)

Lungs

Bronchi

Diaphragm

Terminal
bronchiole

Alveoli

Q. How does oxygen get to the body's cells?

A. Breathing in is only the first step in getting oxygen to the body's cells. After passing through the nose, air moves into the *trachea* (TRA kee uh). The trachea divides off into smaller tubes called *bronchi* (BRON ki). The bronchi branch off and become even smaller tubes called *bronchioles* (BRON kee olz), which help carry the air down into all areas of the lung. The bronchioles also branch off into even tinier tubes that are thinner than a hair. At the ends of these tubes are small air sacs called *alveoli* (al VEE uh li). Alveoli have very thin walls, which allow the oxygen in the air to pass through into the blood. Once the oxygen gets into the bloodstream, it is then carried to the body's cells.

Q. **Why does the body die if it cannot breathe?**

A. All of the cells in the body need oxygen in order to stay healthy. If they don't get oxygen, they cannot survive. All of the body's organs are made of cells; if enough cells die, organs can no longer function and the body dies.

Q. **Why is oxygen so important for living things?**

A. You already know that the cells in the body need oxygen in order to stay healthy, and that without oxygen, the body's cells eventually die. Oxygen is so important because it combines with food to produce the energy the body needs. When people exercise they need extra energy. That is why people breathe harder and faster when they are exercising.

Q. **Why do people yawn?**

A. Sometimes, if a person's breathing becomes quiet and shallow, there may be a slight lack of air to the lungs. When this happens, the amount of oxygen in the blood decreases, and there is a rise in the amount of carbon dioxide in the blood, which is usually exhaled in normal breathing. The body responds to this change by taking an extra-deep breath, or yawn, which rids the body of excess carbon dioxide, allowing the lungs to obtain more oxygen.

Alveoli, Anyone?

There are hundreds of millions of alveoli in the lungs. If they were spread flat, all of the alveoli in one person's lungs would have the same surface area as a tennis court.

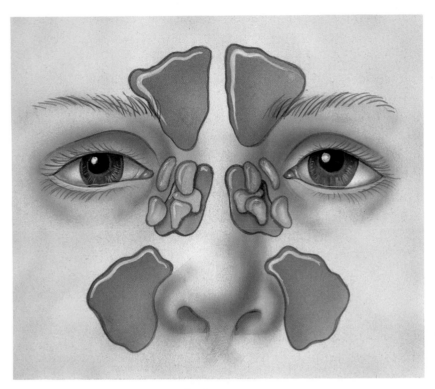

SINUSES

Q. **Why is it better to breathe in through the nose rather than the mouth?**

A. When air is breathed in through the nose, tiny hairs called *cilia* (SIH lee uh) help to clean it of dust. In back of the nostrils is a hollow cavity whose lining creates mucus. This mucus catches dust and impurities, and it moistens the air so that it does not do damage to the delicate tissues of the lungs. When air is breathed in through the mouth, it cannot be cleaned or moistened before proceeding into the lungs.

Q. **What are sinuses?**

A. A sinus is an empty chamber or space in the body. Usually when people talk about sinuses, they are talking about the ones located in the head behind the eyes and cheeks. These sinuses make the head lighter so that it's easier to hold upright, and they amplify or enrich the sound of the voice.

Q. **What happens to food after it is swallowed?**

A. When people eat, they rarely think about what happens to the food or where it goes after they finish chewing. Food takes a long journey through many organs and tubes. These organs and tubes make up the digestive system. From the mouth, food is pushed along a tube called the *esophagus* (ih SAH fu gus) to the stomach. There, it mixes with juices and gets broken down to a semiliquid form. It spends about three hours in the stomach, and then it travels through the small intestine, where more juices are added. Most of the food is digested in the small intestine, and the nutrients that the body needs are absorbed into the bloodstream, which carries them to all the cells in the body. Any parts of the food that are not digested and absorbed go into the large intestine. From the large intestine, this waste material passes through the anus and out of the body.

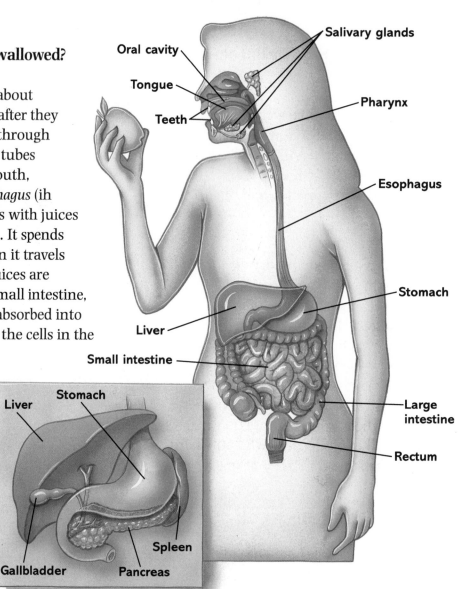

THE DIGESTIVE SYSTEM

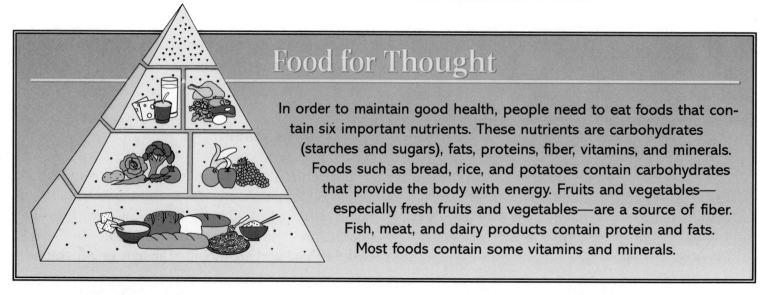

Food for Thought

In order to maintain good health, people need to eat foods that contain six important nutrients. These nutrients are carbohydrates (starches and sugars), fats, proteins, fiber, vitamins, and minerals. Foods such as bread, rice, and potatoes contain carbohydrates that provide the body with energy. Fruits and vegetables—especially fresh fruits and vegetables—are a source of fiber. Fish, meat, and dairy products contain protein and fats. Most foods contain some vitamins and minerals.

Q. What are teeth made of?

A. Teeth are the beginning of the digestive process. They chew food and mix it with saliva, which contains enzymes that begin to break food down. The inner core of a tooth is the *pulp,* which is soft tissue filled with blood vessels and nerves. Surrounding the pulp is the middle layer, called *dentin,* which is like a kind of bone. The third, outside layer of a tooth is called the *enamel.* Enamel is the hardest substance that the body makes. It is even harder than bone. Enamel forms a tight covering that protects the inside layers of a tooth.

Long in the Tooth

No one really knows what causes teeth to grow. At first, dentists believed that teeth grew from roots in the jaw. Scientists later discovered that the tips of the teeth, or crowns, grow outward even when they become detached from the roots. Today, some dentists believe that hormones give the signal for teeth to grow, but no one has yet proved this theory.

TOOTH STRUCTURE

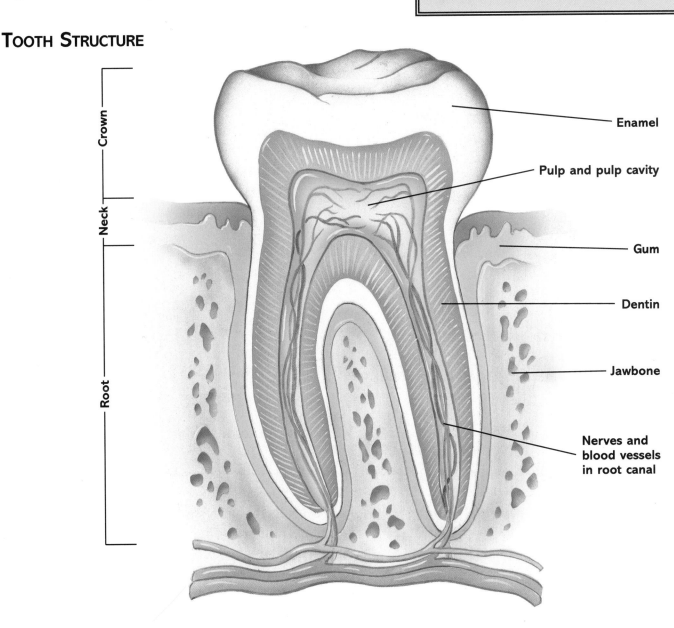

Crown

Neck

Root

Enamel

Pulp and pulp cavity

Gum

Dentin

Jawbone

Nerves and blood vessels in root canal

INTERNAL STRUCTURES OF THE EYE

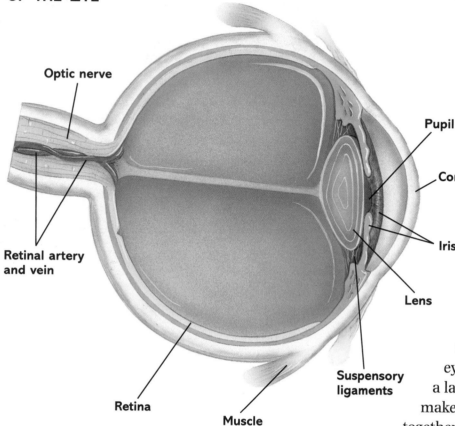

Optic nerve

Retinal artery and vein

Retina

Muscle

Pupil

Cornea

Iris

Lens

Suspensory ligaments

Q. How do people see?

A. People are very dependent on their eyes and on their sense of sight to give them information about the world around them. Light passes through the front of the eye and an image, or picture, is projected on the back of the eye. We see clearly because light is focused by a lens. The lens can change shape in order to focus rays of light from far-away objects or objects that are up close. At the back of the eye is a layer of nerve cells called the *retina*. There are two kinds of nerve cells in the retina—cones and rods. Cones see color. Rods see only black and white. When light hits the rods and cones, the nerves in the retina send messages from the eyes to the brain. These messages travel along a large nerve called the *optic nerve*. The brain makes sense of these signals and puts them together as the picture that is seen.

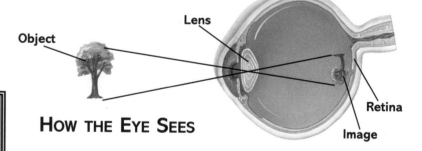

Object

Lens

Retina

Image

HOW THE EYE SEES

The Dominant Eye

Did you know that one of your eyes is used more than the other? The eye that is used more is the dominant eye. To find out which eye is dominant, hold a pencil at arm's length. With both eyes open, line the pencil up with a distant object. Take turns closing each eye and open them both again. When one eye closes, the pencil seems to jump to one side. The eye you are closing when this happens is your dominant eye.

Q. Why do some people have to wear glasses?

A. People wear glasses or contact lenses because their eyes have an abnormal shape. Near-sighted people have eyeballs that are longer than usual. They can only see things that are a short distance away. It is just the opposite for far-sighted people. They have trouble seeing things close up because their eyeballs are shorter than usual. Wearing glasses or contact lenses helps the eyes to focus correctly.

STRUCTURES OF THE EAR

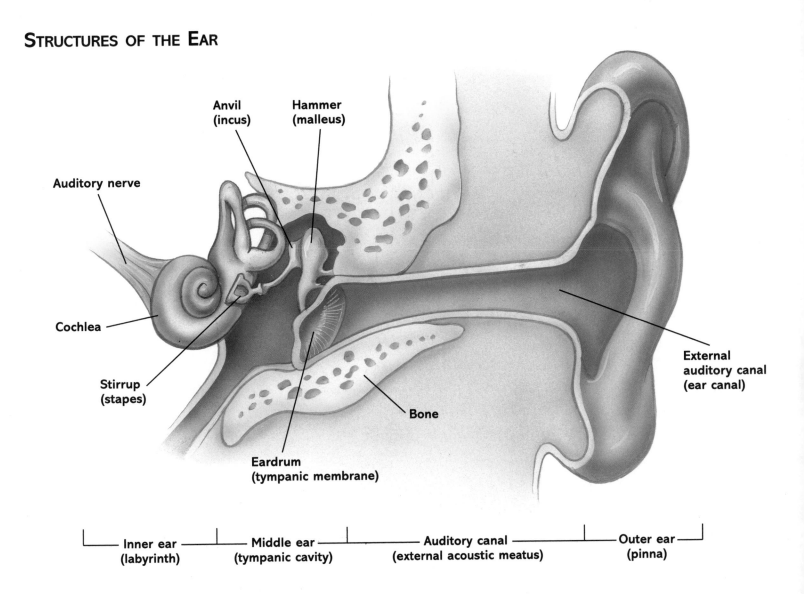

Anvil (incus)

Hammer (malleus)

Auditory nerve

Cochlea

Stirrup (stapes)

Eardrum (tympanic membrane)

Bone

External auditory canal (ear canal)

Inner ear (labyrinth) — Middle ear (tympanic cavity) — Auditory canal (external acoustic meatus) — Outer ear (pinna)

Q. How do people hear sounds?

A. Sounds are actually vibrations in the air called *sound waves*. Fast vibrations make high-pitched sounds and slow vibrations make low-pitched sounds. The outer part of the ear helps funnel the vibrations into the ear and down into the ear canal to the eardrum. Once vibrations reach the eardrum, the eardrum vibrates in much the same way as a musical drum. From the eardrum, these vibrations travel to three small bones deep within the ear: the anvil, the hammer, and the stirrup—the smallest bones in the body. These tiny bones resemble the things they are named after. From these bones, vibrations continue their journey to the *cochlea* (KO klee uh). The cochlea is a coiled tube that is filled with liquid. Cells in the cochlea turn the vibrations into electrical signals that are transmitted to the brain along a nerve called the *auditory nerve*. The brain sorts out the signals and recognizes them as sounds.

How Do We **TRANSPORT** PEOPLE & PRODUCTS?

Trucks, trains, boats, and planes are powerful vehicles that transport goods all over the world. People also use these and other vehicles for travel and recreation.

Q. **How does an airplane fly?**

A. An airplane can fly because the shape of its wings affects *air pressure*. Air pressure is the force created by the weight and movement of the wind; you feel it every time the wind blows on you, and you can see the power it has if you blow on a piece of paper or blow the wrapper off a straw.

To learn how a plane flies, you have to know two things. The first thing is that as air moves faster, it creates less pressure; this idea is called the *Bernoulli* (bur NOOL yee) *principle*. The second thing is that air moves faster over a curved surface than it does over a flat surface. An airplane's wing has a curved top side and a flat bottom side. As a plane moves forward, the air passing over the curved top side moves faster and creates less pressure than the air passing over the flat bottom side. The stronger air pressure creates lift—it pushes up. If enough lift is created, the wing and the plane will be held up in the air.

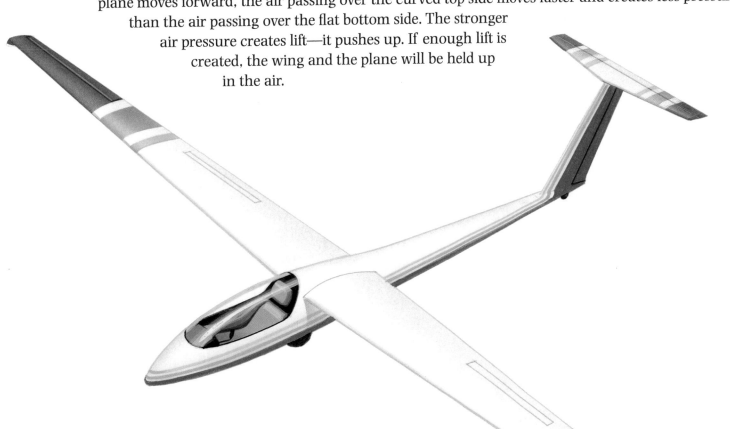

Q. **Can an airplane fly without engines?**

A. Yes. The Bernoulli principle produces lift anytime air flows over the proper shape of wing. The airflow can be caused by engines pushing the airplane through the air, or it can be caused by the airplane moving forward as it glides downhill. Sailplanes and gliders do this all the time. Their wings are specially designed so that they create lots of lift from very little airflow. Gliders also use the lift in currents of warm, rising air to stay up.

GLIDER

Q. Are there different kinds of engines on airplanes?

A. There are basically two kinds of engines. One is called a piston engine, and it works very much like the one in a car. Fuel and air are mixed together and compressed, and then the mixture is ignited. The mixture expands as it burns, and the force created by the expanding mixture pushes a piston, which turns a shaft, which turns a propeller.

The other kind of engine is a jet engine. Jet engines compress the air first using two sets of *compressors*, which look like fans. Jet fuel is sprayed into the compressed air, and the mixture is ignited. As it burns, the mixture expands and pushes out the back of the engine through a set of *turbines*, which look like the compressors only smaller. This makes the turbines spin, and a shaft connecting the turbines to rotor blades at the front of the engine makes the rotor blades spin also. The spinning rotor blades force air backward, which moves the plane forward.

TURBOFAN JET ENGINE

Nose cone
Air bypass duct
Fuel intake
Combustion chamber
Propulsion nozzle
Air exits
Gas exits
Air in
Air exits
Exhaust cone
Air in
Turbine
Turbine guide vanes
Second-stage compressor
Shaft
Stationary vanes
Rotor blades
Primary-stage compressor

BOEING 757

JET AIRPLANE

Airplane Control

Airplanes use air to steer in the same way that they use it to fly. By controlling air flow over the wings, pilots can control the force of lift on different parts of the plane and make it change direction

The back edges of an airplane's wings have small, movable panels called *ailerons* (A luh rons). If an aileron is moved up, the wing on that side has less curve and therefore less lift. If the pilot makes the aileron on one wing go up and the aileron on the other wing go down, lift increases on one wing and decreases on the other, and the plane *rolls* to one side.

The fin of a plane has a panel called a *rudder* that controls the *yaw* of the plane the same way the ailerons control the roll. If the rudder is turned to one side of the fin, that side will have more lift, and it will push the back of the plane in the other direction.

Making the plane go higher or lower is called changing its *pitch*, and it works the same way as changing the yaw and roll. The small wings on the tail of the plane have panels called *elevators*. The two elevators move up or down together to change the shape of the small wings. If they move down, they increase the lift under the tail; this makes the back of the plane go up and the front of the plane go down, so the plane goes lower.

Rudder

Elevator

ROLL AXIS

Controlled by ailerons

YAW AXIS

Controlled by rudder

PITCH AXIS

Controlled by elevators

Aileron

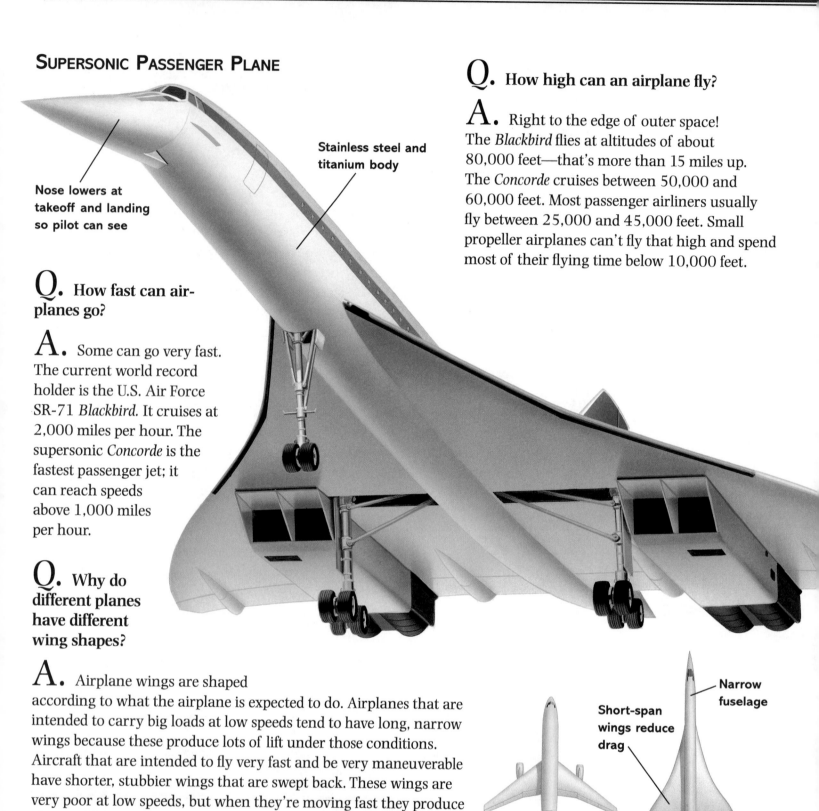

SUPERSONIC PASSENGER PLANE

Nose lowers at takeoff and landing so pilot can see

Stainless steel and titanium body

Q. How fast can airplanes go?

A. Some can go very fast. The current world record holder is the U.S. Air Force SR-71 *Blackbird*. It cruises at 2,000 miles per hour. The supersonic *Concorde* is the fastest passenger jet; it can reach speeds above 1,000 miles per hour.

Q. Why do different planes have different wing shapes?

Q. How high can an airplane fly?

A. Right to the edge of outer space! The *Blackbird* flies at altitudes of about 80,000 feet—that's more than 15 miles up. The *Concorde* cruises between 50,000 and 60,000 feet. Most passenger airliners usually fly between 25,000 and 45,000 feet. Small propeller airplanes can't fly that high and spend most of their flying time below 10,000 feet.

A. Airplane wings are shaped according to what the airplane is expected to do. Airplanes that are intended to carry big loads at low speeds tend to have long, narrow wings because these produce lots of lift under those conditions. Aircraft that are intended to fly very fast and be very maneuverable have shorter, stubbier wings that are swept back. These wings are very poor at low speeds, but when they're moving fast they produce plenty of lift without making lots of air resistance, or *drag*. Some aircraft have wings that are shaped like a triangle—like the *Concorde*. These triangular, or delta, wings combine the best of both low-speed and high-speed. At low speeds, their large surface area provides plenty of lift. At very high speeds, the sharp sweep of the wings' front edge makes for very low drag.

Narrow fuselage

Short-span wings reduce drag

Delta wing shape

SUBSONIC PLANE SHAPE

SUPERSONIC PLANE SHAPE

Q. How does a helicopter fly?

A. Helicopters fly the same way airplanes do: by the lifting force made when air flows over a specially shaped surface. On a plane, that surface is the wing; on a helicopter, it's the rotor blades that spin on top of it. Of course, it takes a great amount of power to spin the rotor blades fast enough to lift the helicopter up. The force created by the spinning blades makes the body of the helicopter want to spin in the opposite direction. To prevent this, helicopters have a small propeller, called a tail rotor, at the back end. The tail rotor pulls the tail in the opposite direction that the body wants to spin. This balances out these forces, so the body of the helicopter can stay pointed in one direction.

Q. Why is it that helicopters can hover and planes can't?

A. You know that a plane flies because of the lift created as air flows over its wings. To create enough lift, an airplane has to move forward at a great speed. If it stops moving forward, not enough air flows over its wings to create the lift it needs to stay up. A helicopter flies because of the lift created when air flows over its rotor blades, and it can create enough lift to fly simply by spinning its rotor blades fast enough; it doesn't have to move forward to create lift, so it can hover in one place.

Q. How do you steer a helicopter?

A. Helicopters do not have ailerons, rudders, or elevators like planes do. Instead, the angle of the rotor blades can be changed as they spin so that they create more lift on one side and less lift on the other side. The tail rotor can also be controlled to create force that moves the tail of the helicopter in either direction.

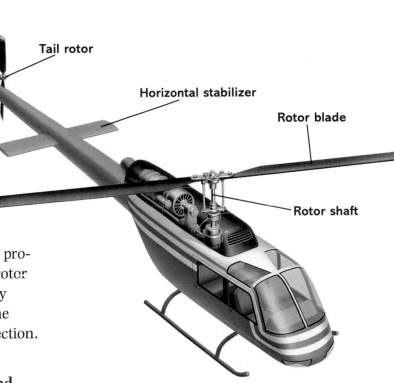

Tail rotor

Horizontal stabilizer

Rotor blade

Rotor shaft

HELICOPTER

Q. How much can helicopters carry?

A. Helicopters can haul tremendous loads. Some types are called skycranes because they can lift so much. In many areas of the country, helicopters are used to lift trees weighing many tons out of the forest, carrying the trees to lumber mills to be cut up. And in many cities, helicopters are used just like cranes to put heavy equipment like air conditioners on top of buildings too tall for a crane on the ground to reach.

Q. How fast can helicopters fly?

A. Helicopters are slower than airplanes. The fastest helicopters can go about 250 miles per hour, and most travel at speeds below 150 miles per hour.

Q. What makes a hot-air balloon fly?

A. A hot-air balloon flies because hot air is lighter than cold air—the hotter it gets, the lighter it is. A hot-air balloon actually floats in the colder air outside the balloon. The balloon is made of a lightweight cloth that won't let the hot air escape, and the basket hung from the balloon has a tank of gas and a burner. When the person in the basket starts the burner, it heats the air going into the balloon, and when the air is hot enough, the balloon takes off. If the burner is turned off, the air in the balloon cools down, and the balloon comes down. The balloon's pilot can control how high the balloon goes by turning the burner on and off.

Q. Why are hot-air balloons so big?

A. The bigger the balloon, the more lift it has. A small balloon would be dragged down by the weight of the basket, the fuel, and the burner, as well as by the weight of the crew.

HOT-AIR BALLOON

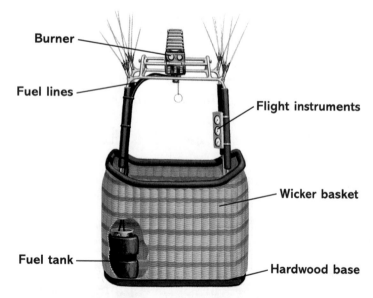

Burner

Fuel lines

Flight instruments

Wicker basket

Fuel tank

Hardwood base

HOT-AIR BALLOON BASKET

Q. Can you steer a hot-air balloon?

A. Although a balloon will travel wherever the wind pushes it, it's possible to control a balloon to some degree. The wind at different heights, or altitudes, blows in different directions, so you can pick a direction by making the balloon go up or down until you locate a wind current that's going in the direction you want to travel.

Q. How does a blimp work?

A. A blimp works in very much the same way as a hot-air balloon, except that it's filled with helium, a gas that's lighter than air even if it's cold. The helium is stored in a bag inside the blimp. Instead of a basket, the crew rides in a gondola underneath the blimp. Early blimps were filled with a different gas called hydrogen, but hydrogen can burn and explode, while helium can't.

Q. How does a blimp take off and land?

A. There's an air bag all around the helium bag, and the pilot can pump in outside air to squeeze the helium bag and make it smaller. This will make the blimp sink. If the pilot pumps out the air from the air bag, the helium bag gets bigger, and the blimp rises.

Q. How do you steer a blimp?

A. A blimp has an engine and a propeller so that it can travel in any direction. To make it move through the air more easily, a blimp is made with a streamlined shape, and it has rudders and elevators at its rear. The vertical rudders allow the pilot to steer from side to side, while the horizontal elevators allow the pilot to steer up and down.

Q. What are blimps used for?

A. A blimp can stay up in the air in the same place for a long time. This makes it very useful for taking pictures from the air. You've probably seen pictures taken from a blimp on TV, during sporting events.

BLIMP

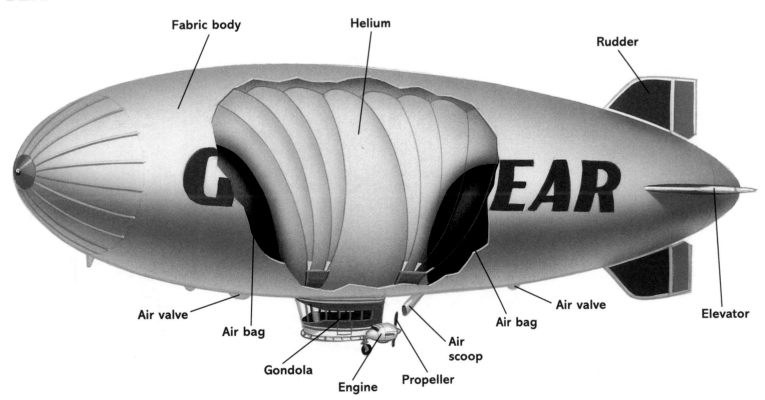

Fabric body • Helium • Rudder • Air valve • Air bag • Gondola • Engine • Propeller • Air scoop • Air bag • Air valve • Elevator

Q. Why don't boats sink?

A. Boats float because they are lighter than water, in the same way that hot-air balloons and blimps float because they are lighter than air. Boats are full of air, so even if the boat is made of a very heavy material like steel, the air keeps it afloat. If the boat gets a leak and fills up with water, though, it can sink. Submarines fill up with water and sink on purpose: They pump enough water into the boat to make it heavier than the surrounding water.

Q. What makes a boat go?

A. There are many different kinds of boats. A canoe or a kayak moves because the person in the boat moves it forward with a paddle dipped into the water. A rowboat works the same way but uses a pair of oars. Sailboats use the wind to propel them; they can't go if the wind stops. Powerboats use gas, diesel, or electric motors to turn propellers that push the boat. Some boats are powered by big fans that are mounted above the water.

Q. How does a sailboat sail in different directions when the wind doesn't change?

A. A sailboat's sails catch the wind. These sails are curved, so that when the wind fills them, they act like airplane wings. The wind blowing across the surface of a sail creates a force that moves the boat forward. A sailboat can't sail directly into the wind, though, so it has to steer a zig-zag course to make any progress in the direction the wind's coming from.

Q. Why does a sailboat have more than one sail?

A. Most sailboats have two sails—a mainsail and a jib. This lets you have more sail area to catch more wind without having to have a bigger mast. Having two small sails instead of one big one also makes it easier to raise and lower the sails.

Q. What are sailboats used for?

A. Until about 150 years ago, most boats—cargo ships, battle-ships, passenger ships—were sail-boats. Steamboats were made in 1807, and later on, gas-pow-ered and diesel-powered boats came along. These powered boats were faster than sail-boats and could be used even when the wind wasn't blowing. Today, sailboats are used mainly as pleasure boats.

Mast

Jib

Mainsail

Boom

Stern

Bow

Rudder

Centerboard

SAILBOAT

Q. What kind of powered boats are there?

A. Powerboats typically are small boats used for fishing or waterskiing. These boats range from about 10 feet to 50 feet long. Larger powered boats include passenger cruise ships, tankers, container ships, and military vessels. Smaller boats often use outboard motors, which are gasoline engines that are attached to the back of the boat. Larger boats usually have inboard engines that are located inside the boat and have a long shaft that goes through the boat's hull to drive the propeller.

POWERBOAT

Q. What's a hydrofoil?

A. To make a boat go very fast, you have to eliminate some of the drag caused by the boat traveling through the water. One way of doing this is to use a *hydrofoil* (HI druh foil), which is a type of wing mounted under the boat. When the boat starts to travel fast enough, the wing lifts most of the boat out of the water, allowing it to reach very high speeds. Such boats usually have two hydrofoils, one at the front and one at the back. A *hovercraft* (HUH vur kraft) eliminates drag a different way: It uses big, downward-pointed fans to actually lift the boat a few inches or more above the water, and air propellers make the boat go forward. A hovercraft is really more like a low-flying airplane than a boat.

HYDROFOIL

HOVERCRAFT

CONTAINER SHIP

Q. Why are container ships used?

A. Cargo usually is delivered to a ship by truck and then put on a different truck once the ship reaches its destination. A container is actually the box that a truck carries its cargo in. Instead of unloading the cargo, workers load the entire box onto the ship with a large crane. When the ship arrives where it's going, the box is picked up and loaded onto another empty truck. As a result, a container ship can be loaded and unloaded very quickly.

DIESEL-ELECTRIC LOCOMOTIVE

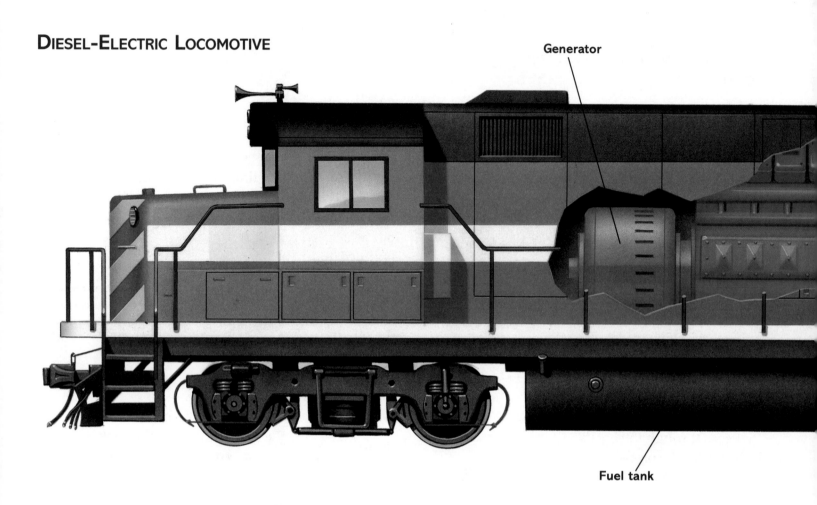

Generator

Fuel tank

Q. What are trains good for?

A. A train can carry heavy loads long distances in a short amount of time. A train runs on steel rails that are very smooth and allow the railroad cars to roll easily. One engine can pull many cars, so a train doesn't use much fuel when you consider how big a load it moves.

Q. Why aren't there more trains, then?

A. The steel rails are very expensive to install. Unless the people who own the railroad expect to send a lot of trains between two places, it doesn't pay to lay the track. When railroads were first built in this country in the 1800s, there weren't many roads and there weren't any trucks or airplanes. Railroads were the only fast way to move passengers and freight. Many towns were built along the tracks so that people and goods could be moved in and out of town. When more roads were built and cars and trucks were introduced, it wasn't necessary to build towns near the railroad, and other means of hauling freight and moving people became more popular. Trains still provide a low-cost, high-speed means of moving things a long way, though.

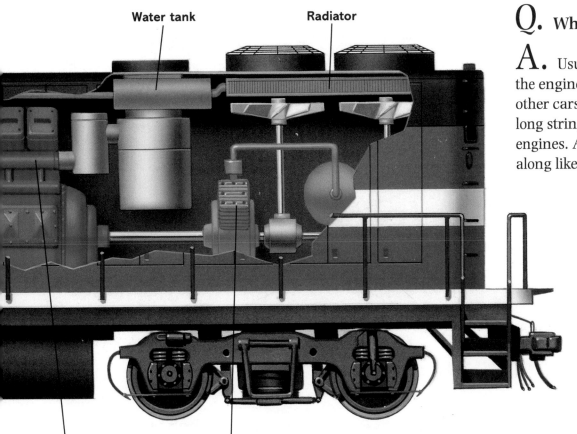

Water tank   Radiator

Diesel engine   Air compressor

Q. **What makes a train move?**

A. Usually, only one railroad car—the engine, or locomotive—pulls all the other cars, although sometimes a really long string of cars will use two or more engines. All the other cars are pulled along like trailers. In the early days of railroads, locomotives were powered by steam engines that burned wood or coal. That's the kind of engine you sometimes see in old movies, with a thick cloud of smoke coming out of its stack. Today, most long-distance trains use diesel power. The most modern ones use a diesel-electric system: A diesel engine is used to drive an electric generator that powers an electric motor that moves the train's wheels.

Subway trains and other trains that run on shorter lines often are powered with electric motors. They get their electricity from an overhead wire, called a trolley wire, or from an extra rail, called a third rail. Electric-powered trains don't have to carry their own fuel, so there's more room for passengers or cargo. They also don't pollute the air as much.

SUBWAY TRAIN

Q. Why are there so many different kinds of freight cars?

A. Different kinds of cars are used to make loading, carrying, and unloading different types of freight easier. A boxcar, for instance, has sides and a roof to protect its cargo from the weather. It has a large door on each side so that a tractor can be driven into the car from a freight platform to make cargo handling faster and more efficient.

An open hopper car has several sections that are loaded from the top and unloaded by opening a door at the bottom. It's best suited for iron ore, crushed rock, or any similar loose material that won't be harmed by the weather. Enclosed hopper cars are similar to hopper cars, but have covers at the top and side for weather protection.

An automobile carrier is a special type of box car with ramps so that cars can be driven into and out of the carrier. Automobile carriers have racks inside so that several cars can be stacked one over the other without damaging them. Tank cars are used to move pressurized gases and liquids such as corn syrup, oil, and chemicals; some tank cars are heated to keep the liquid from freezing.

A flatbed car is just what it sounds like: a flat platform on wheels. It's used for moving heavy machinery, which can be tied down to the platform. A special type of flatbed car is a piggyback car. This is used to carry an entire trailer, load and all. A truck delivers the trailer to the train, and then the trailer is loaded on a piggyback car. When the train reaches its destination, the trailer is unloaded and hooked up to another truck, which takes it to its final destination. This system makes it much easier to get cargo to and from a train.

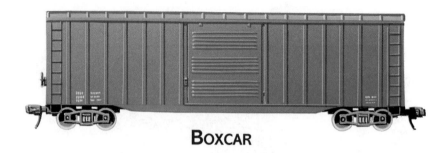

BOXCAR

OPEN HOPPER CAR

ENCLOSED HOPPER

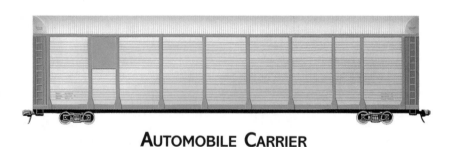

AUTOMOBILE CARRIER

PIGGYBACK CAR

Q. How can trains running in different directions share the same track?

A. At various places along a railroad line, there are *sidings.* These are sections of track where a train can stay while another train goes by on the main track. Sidings are connected to the main line by switches. These are movable sections of track that allow the train to be directed from one section of track to another. At one time, a worker called a dispatcher had to keep track of which trains had to be switched onto sidings and when. Now a computer handles all the switching.

Q. Do all the cars in one train go to the same place?

A. Sometimes, but not necessarily. It's never been practical to build a railroad track between every two places that the railroad serves. Instead, there is a system of tracks and switching terminals. A freight car can get delivered to a terminal where it will be disconnected from its train and hooked up to another train. This second train will then travel to another terminal, where the car can be dropped off, and picked up by yet another train, until it gets where it's going. Let's say you wanted to send some cars from Detroit to Houston, for instance. They would be loaded onto an automobile carrier in Detroit, and a train would take them to Chicago. From Chicago another train would haul them to a terminal in Kansas City, where they would be switched to yet another train bound for Houston.

Q. Are all the railroads owned by the same railroad company?

A. No. There are many different railroad companies. They all connect together, though, so that cargo can travel all across the country. That's why you often see so many different company names on the freight cars from one train.

Q. How fast do trains go?

A. Most trains travel at speeds between 30 and 80 miles per hour. In recent years, high-speed passenger trains have been built in several countries that travel at over 100 miles per hour. These high-speed trains are very useful for trips between major cities that are too close together to make airplane travel practical.

HIGH-SPEED TRAIN

Q. **Why are some large trucks made in two or more sections?**

A. Large heavy-duty trucks are often made in sections. The forward section is called the *tractor.* It contains the engine, transmission, and fuel, and it's where the driver sits. Behind the tractor is the *semi-trailer.* It's called a semi-trailer (or semi for short) because it doesn't have any front wheels.

TANK TRAILER

Having the truck in two pieces helps in several ways. It makes it much easier to steer, especially around corners. More important, a semi can have its cargo loaded and unloaded when it's not attached to the tractor. Drivers can deliver their load, leave the entire semi-trailer behind, and go to pick up another one somewhere else right away. Also, the same tractor can be used to haul different kinds of loads—tank trailers filled with liquids, for instance, or auto haulers carrying cars.

SEMI-TRAILER

TRACTOR

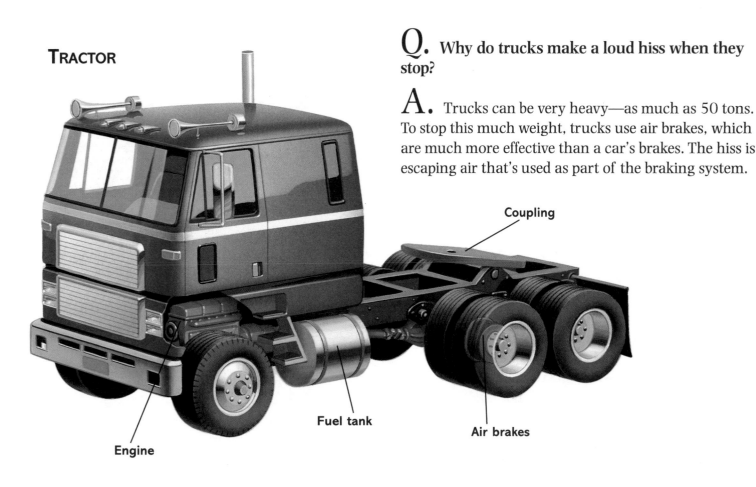

Coupling

Fuel tank

Engine

Air brakes

Q. **Why do trucks make a loud hiss when they stop?**

A. Trucks can be very heavy—as much as 50 tons. To stop this much weight, trucks use air brakes, which are much more effective than a car's brakes. The hiss is escaping air that's used as part of the braking system.

Q. **Are there smaller kinds of trucks?**

A. The smallest truck is the pickup truck. Usually, pickups are a bit larger than cars and have an open cargo area behind the driver instead of a back seat

PICKUP TRUCK

and a trunk. Originally, pickups were used primarily by farmers, who could load tools and supplies into the bed and still use the truck as a car the rest of the time. Today, they have become widely popular because of their versatility. Some pickups are made with four-wheel drive, which lets you drive them in slippery conditions like snow and mud.

A van is a closed truck with a big, boxy cargo area. It provides better weather protection than a pickup and often comes with removable seats so that it can carry either more people or more cargo. Vans made for family use have many windows, while ones used for freight have closed sides.

Both pickups and vans can be used for general transportation and light hauling. Both are popular as family transportation and for small businesses.

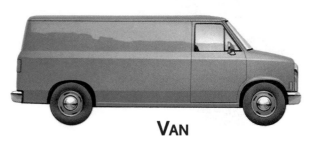

VAN

Q. Are all fire trucks painted red?

A. Not all fire trucks are painted red. However, they all are painted in a bright, noticeable color, so other drivers will see them and get out of their way.

Q. Why are there so many different kinds of fire engines?

A. Just like other trucks and trains, different fire engines are designed for different jobs. A pumping truck's job is to make sure that water from the fire hoses will have a high enough pressure to reach the top of a burning building. A pumper connects to a fire hydrant with suction hoses and then uses powerful pumps to increase the water pressure. It also has compartments for storing the fire hoses and nozzles that are used to control a fire.

An elevating platform truck has a folding stairway mounted on top of the truck, with an open platform at its top. Powerful hydraulic cylinders unfold the stairway so that it provides a working platform six stories high. Firefighters can work safely from this platform without having to try to climb dangerous stairways in a burning building.

PUMPING TRUCK

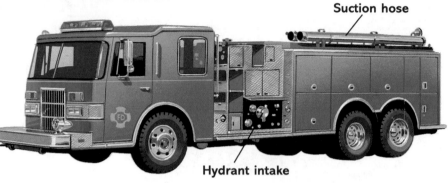

Suction hose

Hydrant intake

Q. Do any fire trucks have ladders on them?

A. An aerial ladder truck has a ladder that opens like a telescope in several sections to allow firefighters to get up even higher than an elevating platform truck can reach. The tallest ladders, for very high buildings, are carried by a hook-and-ladder truck. A hook-and-ladder is really a semi-trailer, but it's so long that some of them have a separate steering wheel at the rear. A firefighter rides in a seat at the back and helps steer the long semi around corners.

Telescoping ladder

AERIAL LADDER TRUCK

Work bucket

Q. How do they change light bulbs in streetlights?

A. When streetlight bulbs go out, workers use an aerial lift crane, or cherry-picker, to change them. A cherry-picker has a work bucket that's big enough to hold one or two persons, with high sides so that nobody will fall out. The work bucket is attached to a long jointed arm that's operated by hydraulic cylinders. The arm is controlled by the person in the bucket. Once the truck is parked near the burned-out streetlight, the repair person climbs into the bucket and raises and turns it until the lamp is within reach.

AERIAL LIFT CRANE

STREET SWEEPER

Q. When a street sweeper sweeps the street, where does the dirt go?

A. A street sweeper is a three-wheeled truck with large brooms mounted on its underside. Usually it has two flat brooms that spin horizontally and a roller behind that brushes dirt and debris forward into the two flat brooms. A pump sprays water from a tank onto the dirt, making it stick together. The brooms sweep the mixture of dirt and mud into a collecting bin inside the street sweeper.

Q. What does a snowplow do with the snow?

A. A snowplow is a heavy truck—often a dump-truck—with a curved blade at the front. The angled blade pushes snow to one side of the street as the truck drives; often, the truck also drops salt behind on the street to melt any remaining snow. If the snow is deep, another dump truck equipped with a loader will pick up the piles of snow and load them into the truck's storage bin. The snow is then carried off and dumped where it won't be in the way.

SNOWPLOW

Control cabin

Boom

Pulley

Cable

Q. How does a crane work?

A. There are actually many different types of cranes, and each is used for a particular type of work. One of the most common that you'll see at construction sites is the crawler crane. This is a crane mounted on a set of crawling treads. These cranes use their long booms to hoist heavy objects, like beams and pre-formed walls. One type of crawler crane uses two sets of cables to raise or lower the boom by shortening or lengthening the cables. The lifting is done by a single main cable that runs along the boom to the tip and hangs over a pulley system.

Tower cranes are used to build very tall buildings. Typically, these cranes are mounted right in the middle of the building under construction, and they are long enough to reach over the sides of the building. When heavy equipment and materials need to be hoisted to the floor under construction, the boom swings out and lowers the hook to the ground so workers there can attach whatever needs to be sent up.

Straddle cranes are used for moving cargo containers around and are generally found in dockyard areas. A straddle crane like the one shown here would pick a container off the back of a truck and stack it on the dock so it can be loaded onto a container ship. Similar straddle cranes are used by boatyards and marinas to lift cabin cruisers and other big boats out of the water or put them back in.

TOWER CRANE

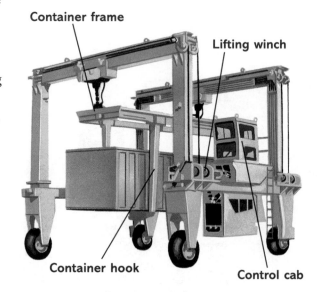

Container frame

Lifting winch

Container hook

Control cab

STRADDLE CRANE

ROLLER

Q. Why do they call it a steamroller?

A. Steamrollers are used to press down asphalt or soil, making it hard and dense so it can carry the weight of cars, trucks, or whatever drives over it. At the turn of the century, roadbuilders used a steam-propelled tractor with huge steel drums instead of wheels to press down the soil and make it firmer before paving it. This was a steam-powered drum roller, or steamroller for short.

Q. **Why do some construction vehicles have treads and others have wheels?**

A. Treads give greater traction than wheels, so the truck doesn't slip, but they make it harder to steer. Bulldozers have treads because they need tremendous traction to be able to push piles of dirt and rock around. A front-end loader, though, scoops up loads of rubble or dirt and carries it to a truck or a dumping spot; having tires makes it faster and easier to drive.

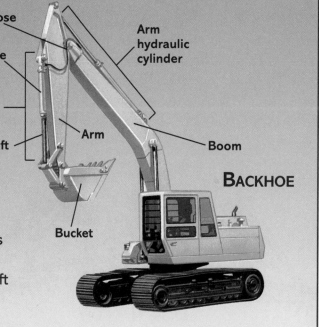

BULLDOZER

FRONT-END LOADER

Liquid Strength

Much of the power of modern construction equipment comes from *hydraulic* (hi DRAW lik) systems. Hydraulics, which comes from a Greek word meaning water, use liquids under pressure to make things move. A typical hydraulic system has a pump that forces liquid through a hose and into a cylinder. The cylinder consists of a tube and a shaft inside the tube; when the liquid is forced into the shaft, it pushes the tube out, and anything attached to the tube will move. The backhoe pictured here uses two main cylinders—one for the arm and one for the bucket. If fluid is pumped into the bucket's hydraulic cylinder, the shaft pushes the bucket and moves it in a scooping motion toward the boom. When the fluid is pumped out of the cylinder, the shaft and the bucket return to their original positions.

Hose

Arm hydraulic cylinder

Tube

Bucket hydraulic cylinder

Shaft

Arm

Boom

BACKHOE

Bucket

Q. **What are tractors used for?**

A. Tractors do the job that teams of horses used to do on farms. Their main job is to pull other pieces of equipment behind them. They can pull heavy farm machines over large areas of land, and they go much faster than horses. Farmers use tractors to prepare the soil, to plant seeds, and to care for the young crops as they grow.

Tractors have treaded rubber tires that grip the soil and provide good traction when the ground is loose or slippery. The small wheels in front steer the tractor, while the big ones behind provide power. Tractors are also very noisy, especially when you are sitting on them. For this reason, some tractors have enclosed cabs where the farmer can sit away from the noise of the engine. Here, many farmers like to listen to the radio while they work and be cooled by the breeze from a fan. Some tractors are even air-conditioned!

TRACTOR

Q. **How do machines help farmers plant crops?**

A. Farmers use many machines pulled by their tractors to take care of crops. A *disk harrow*, or disk, has many metal disks set at angles that break up clumps of dirt and make the soil fine and even. When the land is ready to plant, the farmer hooks a *seeder* onto the tractor. This machine puts seed, and sometimes fertilizer, into the soil. As the crop grows, weeds will appear along with it. To get rid of the weeds, the farmer uses a *cultivator*, which has hooks that penetrate the soil around the crops and drag out weeds by the roots. Finally, a farmer may use different kinds of sprayers to put pesticides on the crops to protect them from insects and other pests.

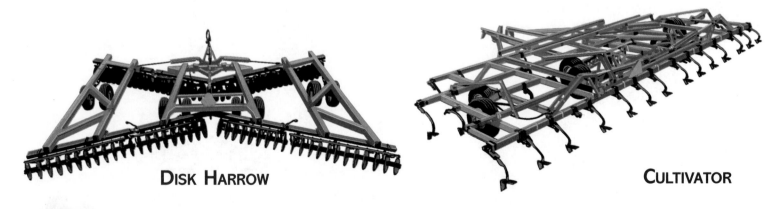

DISK HARROW

CULTIVATOR

Q. **What happens when the crops are finished growing?**

A. To harvest a crop, farmers must cut or pull the plant and then remove the part that they want from the rest of the plant. Luckily, there is one machine that combines both of these steps in one operation—a *combine* (KAHM bine). Combines are huge machines that move quickly over the land, gathering up the standing crop. A *thresher* inside the combine then separates the edible crop from the stem. It stores the crop in bins it carries onboard and shoots the stems and stalks back out into the field or into a container. Different kinds of combines are used for different kinds of crops.

Many farmers do not own combines. Instead, they hire professional combine operators to harvest their crops. These combine operators travel around the country and cut farmers' fields. That way, the combines work all the time and the farmer doesn't have to buy such an expensive machine to use just once or twice a year.

COMBINE

Q. **What machine makes those big rolls of hay?**

A. Farmers who have livestock try to grow much of their own feed, most often in the form of hay. Hay is nothing more than grass. When it's growing in the ground, it's called grass. The moment it's cut, it becomes hay. Hay must dry on the ground before it is baled, or else it will get moldy. You can't use a combine on hay. The standing grass is first cut with large mowers and allowed to stay on the ground for a few days to dry. Then the farmer pulls out his tractor and hooks a machine called a baler onto the back. Balers are available that make either large rolls of hay or square bales. The rolls can weigh up to 1,500 pounds!

HAY BALER

Where Does ENERGY COME FROM ?

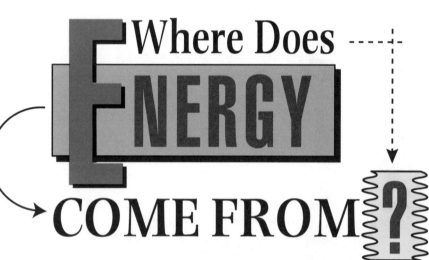

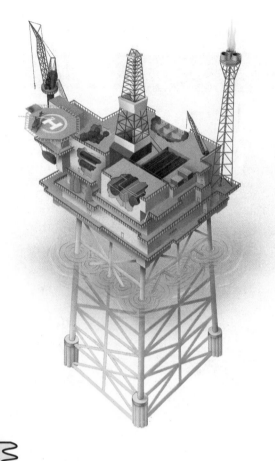

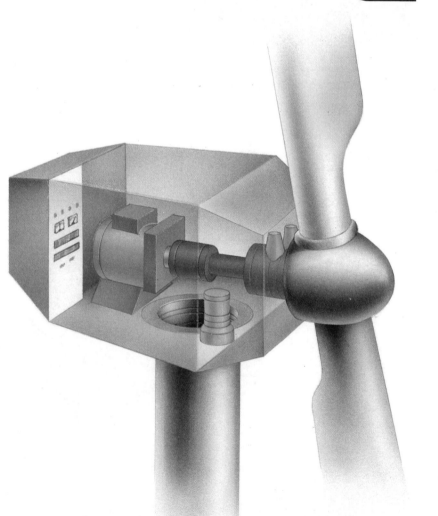

Almost everyone relies on electric lights, gas heat, petroleum-burning cars, and battery-operated devices. The energy that runs these everyday devices comes to us from many different sources.

Q. What is energy?

A. Energy is what makes things happen. Every time anything moves, speeds up, slows down, gets hot, or gets cold, energy plays a part.

People use several different forms of energy in a variety of ways. The major forms of energy we use are *thermal* energy or heat, *chemical* energy, *electrical* energy, and *nuclear* energy.

Q. How do we get energy to where it's needed?

A. The electricity generated at a power station travels to your house through power lines, or wires, either underground or up on tall poles. Once the electricity reaches your house, wires inside the walls connect it to sockets or to light fixtures.

To send more energy over its power lines, the electric company uses a *step-up transformer* to raise the voltage of the electricity before it reaches the power lines. At the end of the main power line, a *step-down transformer* reduces the voltage enough so that it can be sent to homes.

Q. Can other forms of energy be stored and delivered?

A. Yes. Natural gas for heating and cooking comes to your house through pipes under the ground. Gasoline and other liquid petroleum products that we use for energy are delivered in large tanks by trucks and trains. Batteries store chemical energy that we use for toys, flashlights, and other things that aren't convenient to plug in to a wall socket.

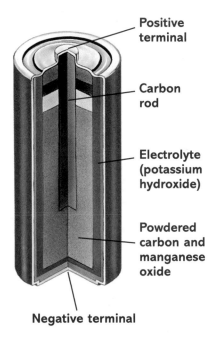

Positive terminal

Carbon rod

Electrolyte (potassium hydroxide)

Powdered carbon and manganese oxide

Negative terminal

DRY-CELL BATTERY

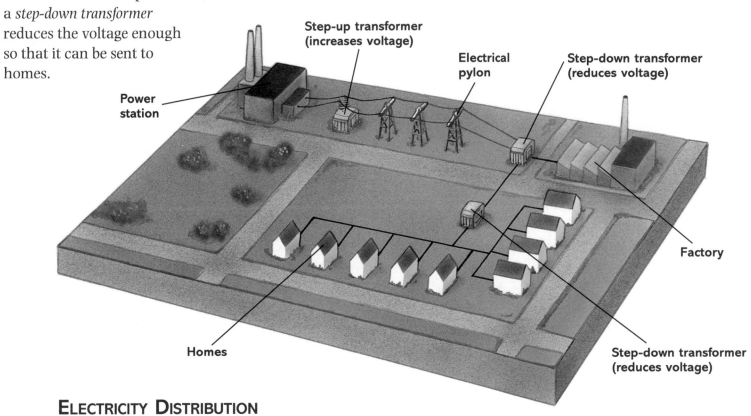

Step-up transformer (increases voltage)

Electrical pylon

Step-down transformer (reduces voltage)

Power station

Factory

Homes

Step-down transformer (reduces voltage)

ELECTRICITY DISTRIBUTION

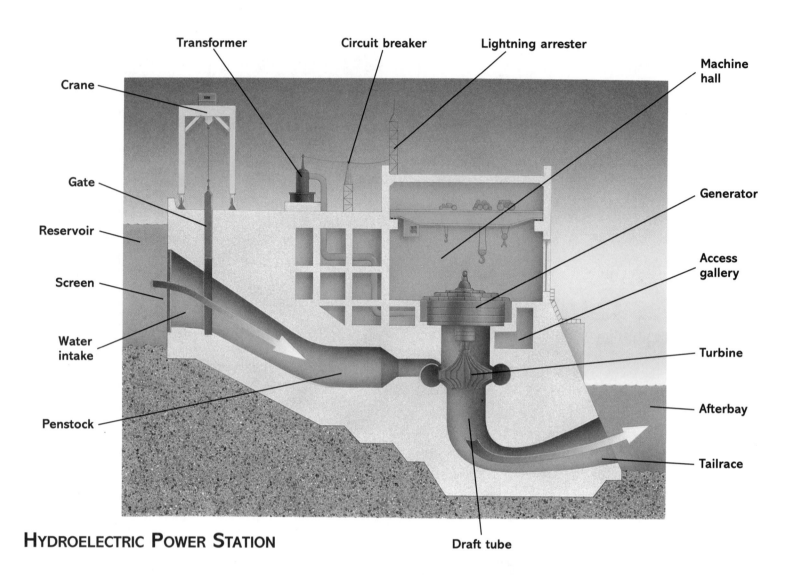

Labels: Crane, Transformer, Circuit breaker, Lightning arrester, Machine hall, Gate, Generator, Reservoir, Screen, Access gallery, Water intake, Turbine, Penstock, Afterbay, Tailrace, Draft tube

HYDROELECTRIC POWER STATION

Q. Where does electricity come from?

A. All electrical power stations make electricity in basically the same way. They spin a generator made up of magnets and wire, and the movement of the magnetic fields produces electricity.

A hydroelectric (HI dro ih LEK trik) power station uses water to spin the generator. In a typical hydroelectric station, a dam is built across a river. This allows water to collect on the upstream side of the dam. Tubes called *penstocks* lead through the dam and direct water onto giant turbines. These turbines are like huge pinwheels, and as the water flows past them, they spin. A shaft connects the turbines to the generators, and the spinning force of the turbine turns the generator, making electricity.

Q. Can a hydroelectric power station be turned off?

A. Yes. Most hydroelectric dams have gates at the front of each penstock that control the flow of water. By raising or lowering the gates, the dam operators can turn on or off as many turbines as they need. On a hot summer day when people run their air conditioners, the operators can open all the gates and generate lots of power. On a cool spring day when very little electricity is needed, they can close most of the gates and generate only a small amount of power.

Q. How much power can one of these dams generate?

A. Hydroelectric dams can generate enough electricity to power entire cities. Big ones like the Hoover Dam on the Colorado River or the Grand Coulee Dam on the Columbia River provide enough electricity to run all the houses for hundreds of miles.

Q. What happens if something gets sucked through the turbines?

A. That depends on what that something is. Hydroelectric turbines are big, but they can be damaged. Big, hard objects like tree trunks would destroy the turbines in a hydroelectric dam. To prevent this, the dam is fitted with a heavy screen on the intake (upstream) side to block logs, tree trunks, and similar debris from getting to the turbine. Smaller things do get through, but they usually just pass right through the turbine without causing any harm.

Q. Do hydroelectric dams cause any pollution?

A. Hydro-power is very clean, especially when compared to other types of power plants. Because these power stations run on water, they do not make any polluting by-products. In fact, once a hydroelectric power station is in operation, it doesn't need anything from the outside except water and the occasional replacement part.

A dam will have a big effect on the environment of a river, though. Putting the dam in can flood thousands of acres of land along the upstream side of the river, destroying the habitats of many living things. The turbines can also destroy fish populations. In the Pacific Northwest, hydroelectric dams kill countless young salmon trying to go to the ocean, which is one reason that some salmon species are in danger of extinction. Finally, the dam changes the natural water flow of the downstream side of the river, which can have a big impact on the plants and animals that live there.

HYDROELECTRIC DAM

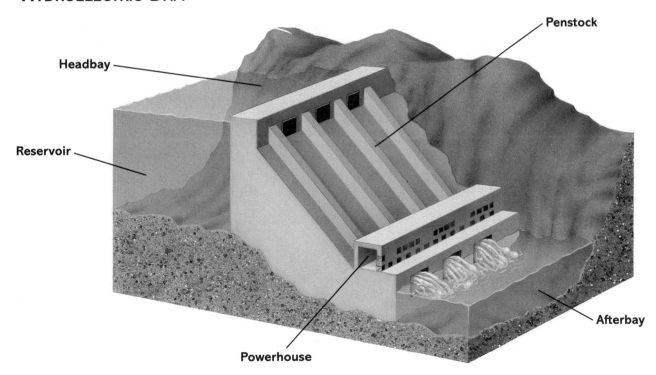

Headbay

Penstock

Reservoir

Powerhouse

Afterbay

NUCLEAR POWER

Q. **Where does nuclear energy come from?**

A. Atoms have two major parts: a *nucleus* at the center and negatively charged *electrons* that orbit the nucleus. The nucleus contains two types of particles: *protons,* which have a positive charge, and *neutrons,* which have no charge. Normally, an atom has the same number of neutrons and protons in the nucleus, and it takes a great deal of energy to hold them together.

Some atoms, like Uranium-235 (U235), have nuclei (the plural of nucleus) that don't have the same number of protons

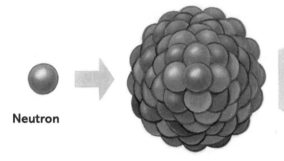

Neutron

Uranium-235 nucleus

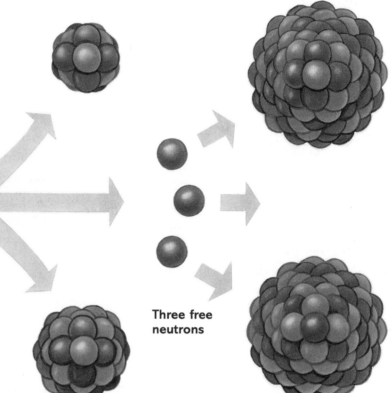

Two smaller nuclei

Three free neutrons

Uranium-235 nuclei

NUCLEAR CHAIN REACTION

and neutrons, and this makes them very unstable. They break apart easily and release energy, neutrons, and other things. If the nucleus of a U235 atom is struck by a neutron, the atom will break into two smaller atoms and release three of its neutrons. If each of those neutrons hits another U235 nucleus, those three atoms will also split, shooting off a total of nine neutrons. And if each of those neutrons strikes the nucleus of a U235 atom, they will shoot off 27 neutrons. This chain reaction is called nuclear fission. It takes a great deal of energy to hold an atomic nucleus together, and when one is split, some of that energy is released. Splitting all the nuclei in one pound of U235 would release as much energy as burning three million pounds of coal.

Q. Wouldn't that chain reaction cause an explosion?

A. It would, unless you controlled the speed of the reaction. An atomic bomb doesn't control the rate of fission once it starts. A nuclear power plant uses *control rods* that absorb neutrons to keep them from hitting other U235 nuclei. If you slide the control rods into the core of the reactor where the fuel is, the reaction slows down or stops; if you slide them out, the reaction speeds up.

Q. How does the energy get used?

A. At a nuclear power plant, the energy from nuclear fission is used to heat water into steam. The steam turns a turbine, the turbine drives a generator, and the generator produces electricity. Some plants heat the water directly, and others first heat a gas or pressurized water and then use it to make steam.

Q. Is nuclear energy dangerous?

A. If a nuclear power plant is operated properly, it's fairly safe. The leftover fuel and other by-products, however, are radioactive and are very dangerous to all living things. Used nuclear fuel will remain dangerous for thousands of years, and many people are afraid that it can't be stored safely for that long. Also, accidents have occurred at nuclear power plants that released some radiation into the environment.

Some people feel that nuclear power is too dangerous to use. Others think that it's a safe, environmentally friendly source of energy.

NUCLEAR POWER PLANT (PRESSURIZED-WATER POWER PLANT)

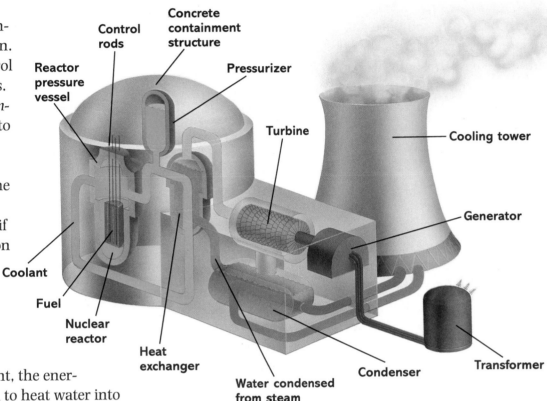

Control rods
Concrete containment structure
Reactor pressure vessel
Pressurizer
Turbine
Cooling tower
Generator
Coolant
Fuel
Nuclear reactor
Heat exchanger
Water condensed from steam
Condenser
Transformer

GAS-COOLED REACTOR

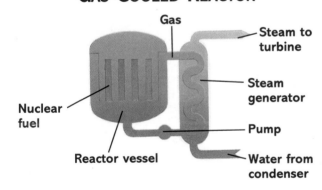

Gas
Steam to turbine
Steam generator
Nuclear fuel
Pump
Reactor vessel
Water from condenser

BOILING-WATER REACTOR

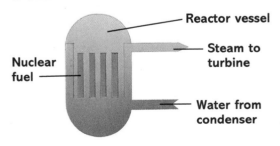

Reactor vessel
Steam to turbine
Nuclear fuel
Water from condenser

Q. **How can the sun's rays be used to heat water?**

A. If you've ever gotten into a hot car that's been sitting in the sun, you have an idea how we harness solar energy. The car gets hot because the sun's rays pass through the glass windows, strike the seats and dashboard, and change to thermal energy, or heat. Thermal energy won't pass through glass as easily as the sun's light energy will, so the heat is trapped inside the car.

A solar water heater uses a *collector*, which is a box with a glass or plastic cover and some pipes inside. The sun makes the pipes hot, so that if you run cold water through them, it becomes heated. A pump circulates water through the pipes as long as the sun is shining. The hot water in the pipes is used to heat a tank of household water. The pipes then bring the water back to the collector to be heated again.

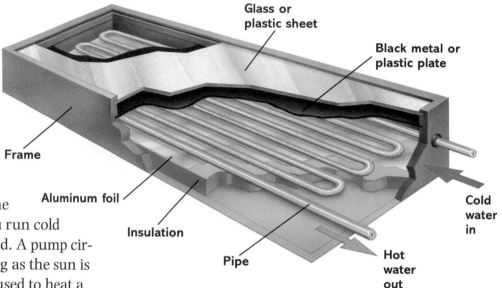

Glass or plastic sheet

Black metal or plastic plate

Frame

Aluminum foil

Insulation

Pipe

Cold water in

Hot water out

FLAT-PLATE SOLAR COLLECTOR

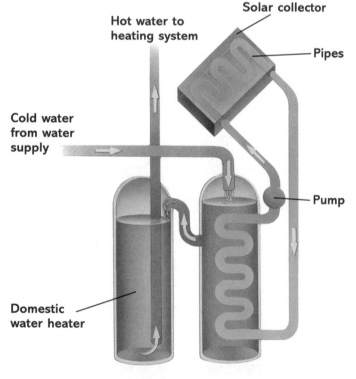

Solar collector

Hot water to heating system

Pipes

Cold water from water supply

Pump

Domestic water heater

SOLAR WATER HEATER

Primary Energy Source

Solar energy, or energy obtained from the sun's rays, is indirectly the source of almost all the energy we use. When we build a campfire, the energy stored in the wood that's burned came from the sun while the tree was growing. A windmill uses the energy contained in the wind, which results from the sun's heating of the Earth. Water, or hydroelectric, power is made possible by streams and rivers, which get their water from rain and snow that the sun's heat helps to create.

Q. Can solar energy be used for anything else besides hot water?

A. Yes. Solar-powered electric generators have a large number of solar reflectors, or mirrors, aimed at a single large solar collector. When the sun is shining, these mirrors reflect enough solar energy at the collector to maker water boil, creating steam. The steam, in turn, makes the fan-shaped blades of a turbine spin. The turbine drives an electric generator, which makes electricity. A condenser cools the steam so it turns back to water, which is then sent to the collector to be heated again.

There's another way to make electricity from solar energy. A special flat plate of material called a *photovoltaic* (fo to vol TA ik) cell converts the sun's rays directly to electricity. Photovoltaic cells can't generate high voltages, but they're very handy for charging boat and car batteries, and they are used regularly to power satellites and various spacecrafts.

Q. Why don't more places use solar energy?

A. Solar energy is non-polluting and doesn't use up oil or gas or coal or wood, but it is costly to harness. Although the sun's rays are free, the equipment needed to collect and use them can be expensive and takes up a lot of room. Right now, solar energy is used mainly when other forms of energy are not available or are more expensive.

SOLAR POWER PLANT

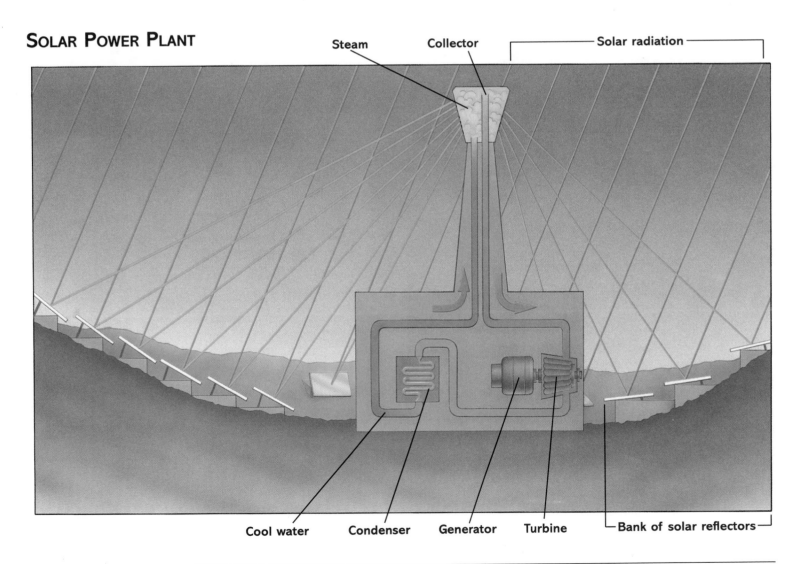

Steam   Collector   Solar radiation

Cool water   Condenser   Generator   Turbine   Bank of solar reflectors

Q. How do windmills make electricity?

A. Windmills use the power of wind to run a generator that produces electricity. The force of the wind blowing against the blades of the windmill makes the windmill spin. The blades' hub connects to a gearbox, and the gearbox connects to the actual generator. Of course, the windmill must be kept pointed into the wind, so the top is able to rotate. Some windmills have sensors to detect the direction of the wind and small motors that turn the windmill. Others have a large vane behind the windmill that acts kind of like a sail. The wind blows the vane and turns the windmill in the right direction.

WIND TURBINE

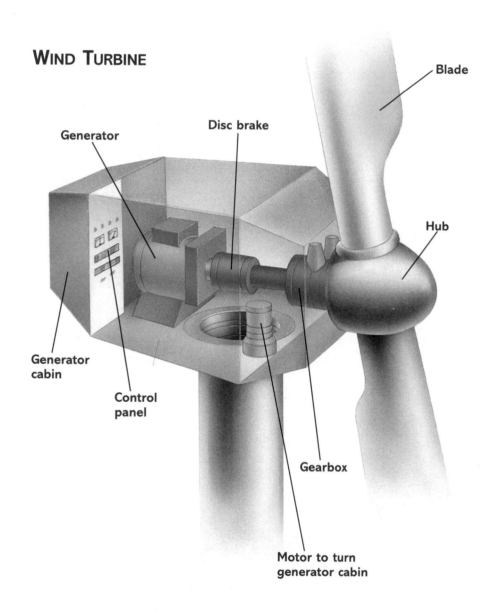

Generator

Disc brake

Blade

Hub

Generator cabin

Control panel

Gearbox

Motor to turn generator cabin

Blade

Hub

Nacelle

Tower

Q. Why are windmills mounted on top of such tall poles?

A. Windmills are up high to get away from interference with the wind from trees, buildings, and other large objects on the ground. The wind also blows more steadily at higher altitudes than it does near the ground.

HORIZONTAL-AXIS WIND TURBINE

Q. Are windmills used a lot?

A. Windmills are not practical in most areas because the wind doesn't blow consistently enough. In parts of California and Hawaii, however, the wind blows most of the time, and people have built windmill farms with dozens or even hundreds of windmills generating electricity.

Q. Do all windmills look alike?

A. Not all windmills look like a fan or an airplane propeller. Scientists and engineers are always looking for better designs for windmills, and several have been tried over the years. Two of the more unusual designs that have worked are the cross-arm rotor and the Darrieus rotor. Both of these spin around the windmill tower. Because of this, the wind will make them spin no matter what direction it blows, so they don't need any kind of pointing device to make the windmill face the wind.

Q. Are windmills a new idea?

A. Although using windmills to generate electricity is a new idea, they have been around for thousands of years. In the past, people used them to grind grain into flour. Some farmers today use the multi-bladed farm windmill to pump water to irrigate crops and provide drinking water for animals.

Q. Do windmills cause any pollution?

A. Windmills don't produce any pollutants, but they're not entirely environmentally friendly. Many birds such as hawks and eagles like to perch on tall objects, and they find the windmill towers very attractive. Unfortunately, the birds can't see the whirling blades, and many fly into the blades and are killed. Scientists are working to overcome this problem.

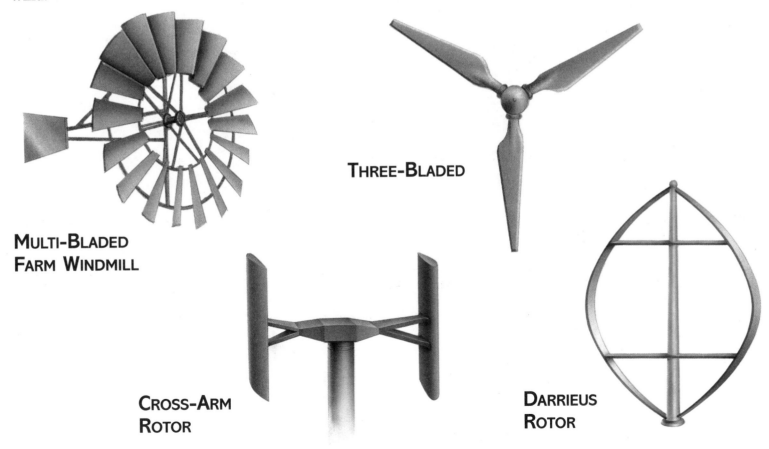

MULTI-BLADED
FARM WINDMILL

THREE-BLADED

CROSS-ARM
ROTOR

DARRIEUS
ROTOR

OIL DERRICK

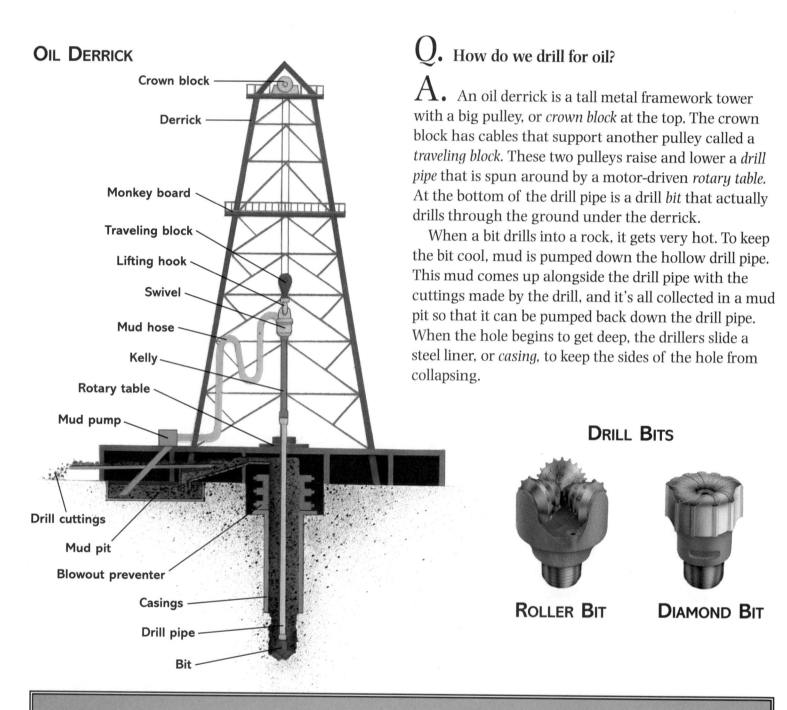

Crown block
Derrick
Monkey board
Traveling block
Lifting hook
Swivel
Mud hose
Kelly
Rotary table
Mud pump
Drill cuttings
Mud pit
Blowout preventer
Casings
Drill pipe
Bit

DRILL BITS

ROLLER BIT   **DIAMOND BIT**

Q. How do we drill for oil?

A. An oil derrick is a tall metal framework tower with a big pulley, or *crown block* at the top. The crown block has cables that support another pulley called a *traveling block.* These two pulleys raise and lower a *drill pipe* that is spun around by a motor-driven *rotary table.* At the bottom of the drill pipe is a drill *bit* that actually drills through the ground under the derrick.

When a bit drills into a rock, it gets very hot. To keep the bit cool, mud is pumped down the hollow drill pipe. This mud comes up alongside the drill pipe with the cuttings made by the drill, and it's all collected in a mud pit so that it can be pumped back down the drill pipe. When the hole begins to get deep, the drillers slide a steel liner, or *casing,* to keep the sides of the hole from collapsing.

Fossil Fuel

Oil and natural gas provide about 60 percent of all the energy used in the United States. Oil—or petroleum—was formed millions of years ago when plants and animals died and sank to the bottom of the ocean. Mud and sand covered them over, and water pressure packed them down. Heat and more pressure from the Earth's crust converted the fossilized remains to deposits of oil and natural gas. This oil-forming process is a very slow one, and although it's still going on, people are using oil much faster than it's being formed. Sooner or later, we'll have to depend on other energy sources.

Q. Are there oil wells out at sea?

A. Yes. The ocean has great deposits of oil beneath it. As more and more dry-land oil wells run dry, oil companies drill offshore for petroleum.

Q. Can we use the oil just as it's pumped from wells?

A. No. Crude oil, as it's called, is a mixture of different oils that must be separated before it's useful. An oil refinery will heat the oil until it evaporates, and then pass the gas that's formed through a series of coolers, each a little colder than the last one. This process separates the crude oil into heating oil, kerosene, gasoline, and other useful products.

Q. Where does natural gas come from?

A. Natural gas is found most often in underground deposits of oil, and it's drilled for in the same way. If a gas deposit is small, the driller just sets fire to it to get rid of it. If it's large, the hole is capped and connected to a large pipe that goes to a gas refinery. The gas refinery cleans the gas to remove impurities and then adds a bad-smelling gas to it, so it will be easy to detect if someone leaves a stove burner on by mistake.

Q. How do we drill really deep holes?

A. A derrick is tall enough to hang one length of drill pipe up in the air over the hole. When the driller reaches the end of the drill pipe, it's disconnected from the cables, and another length of drill pipe is fastened on. This process continues until they strike oil. Many wells use hundreds of drill pipes and reach thousands of feet into the ground.

TYPES OF DRILLING RIGS

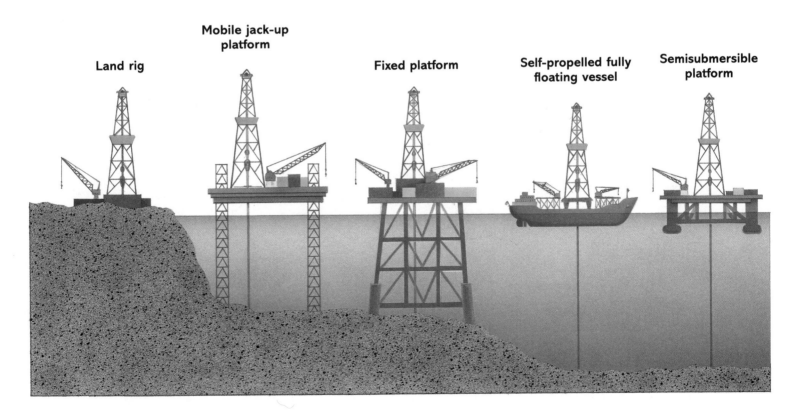

Land rig   Mobile jack-up platform   Fixed platform   Self-propelled fully floating vessel   Semisubmersible platform

COAL

Q. Is coal widely used as a source of energy?

A. Yes, it is. Almost a quarter of the energy used in the United States comes from coal. Coal is the most abundant of the fossil fuels.

Q. If there's so much of it, why isn't it used even more?

A. Coal has more pollutants in it than gas or oil. The most troublesome one is sulfur. When coal is burned, it releases sulfur compounds that combine with the moisture in the air to form acid. This causes acid rain, which can harm the environment and even damage buildings and outdoor statues. Until 50 years ago, coal was widely used for heating homes. Today most homes use natural gas because gas furnaces are cleaner and easier to operate.

Q. How do we use coal?

A. Many electric power plants burn coal to heat water and make steam. The steam then drives a turbine that makes electricity. A modern power plant doesn't burn lumps of coal the way old home furnaces did. Engineers have found that they can make coal burn more cleanly if they first pulverize it into a fine powder. After it burns, the smoke is passed through an electronic cleaner, or *precipitator*, to remove the fine ash. Then it passes through a *scrubber* where most sulfur compounds are removed.

COAL-FIRED POWER STATION

Cooling tower · Electric generator · Steam turbine · Air intake · Boiler · Coal hopper · Flue gas reheater · Conveyor · Stack · Condenser · Burners · Pulverizing mill · Electrostatic precipitator · Sulfur dioxide scrubber

Q. Where do we get coal?

A. The first people to use coal probably found it lying in chunks on the ground. Later, they found large underground deposits and began mining it. Today, there are several major types of coal mining. Surface mining, or strip mining, is the least expensive way to get coal out of the ground, but it can only be used if the coal is fairly near the surface. A big excavating machine will dig into the edge of a coal deposit, or vein, that's exposed at the side of a hill. This kind of mining has been used widely, but many people object to it because it can seriously damage the hillside.

Drift mining is more expensive. It involves digging a tunnel into the exposed coal at the side of a hill, without removing the rest of the hill. Slope mining is a method of digging an angled shaft down from the surface into the coal deposit. Since the actual mining takes place down under the surface, it's necessary to provide a separate air shaft for ventilation.

The most expensive and most dangerous type of mine is the shaft mine. Here, miners dig a vertical shaft and then make horizontal tunnels branching off from it. A shaft mine lets miners dig out deep veins of coal, but all the coal must be hauled up the main shaft. Working underground, the miners build wooden supports to keep the tunnels from collapsing. Air shafts are required to provide breathable air.

Plant Power

Most of the coal we use started out as plant life about 300 million years ago. Many swampy areas were buried under sand and mud; earthquakes and other changes to the landscape buried them further and subjected the dead plants to heat and pressure, turning them into coal. Like oil and natural gas, coal is a fossil fuel.

MAJOR VARIETIES OF COAL MINES

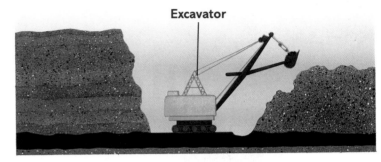

Excavator

SURFACE MINE

DRIFT MINE

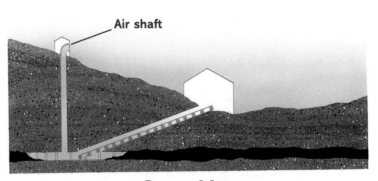

Air shaft

SLOPE MINE

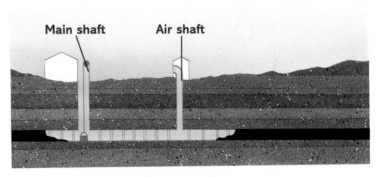

Main shaft   Air shaft

SHAFT MINE

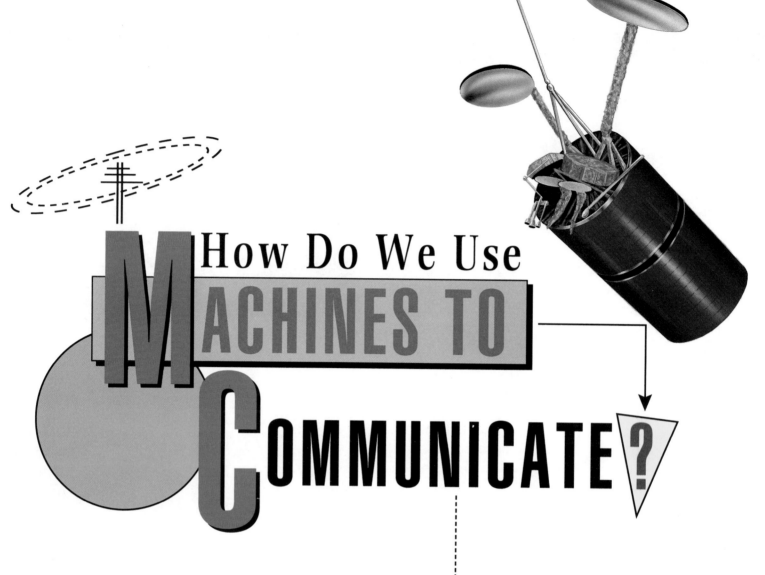

How Do We Use Machines To Communicate?

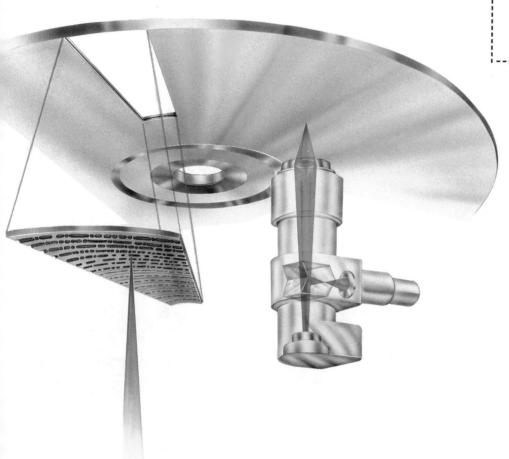

People use many different machines to communicate with each other. Modern technology helps us share ideas, feelings, and information with people who are far away.

Q. How does a radio work?

A. A radio receives signals in the form of radio waves, which are sent out from a powerful transmitter. These radio waves are made up of electromagnetic fields that oscillate (AH suh late), or change intensity, many times each second. In broadcasting a signal, radio stations combine two electromagnetic waves— a *sound signal,* which is the part you want to hear, and a *carrier wave,* which travels easily through the air.

The antenna of your radio receiver picks up all the radio waves that are being broadcast in your area, and a tuner inside the receiver lets you pick the one signal, or station, you want. A *detector* in the receiver separates the sound signal from the carrier wave. An *amplifier* in your radio then makes the sound signal stronger. The amplified signal then goes to a loudspeaker that changes the electrical signal to sound, so that you can listen to the sounds being broadcast.

Q. How can the radio tell one radio station from another?

A. Each radio station uses a different carrier wave that oscillates at a unique rate, or frequency. Using the tuner in your radio receiver, you set the tuning coil to receive a signal of one particular frequency.

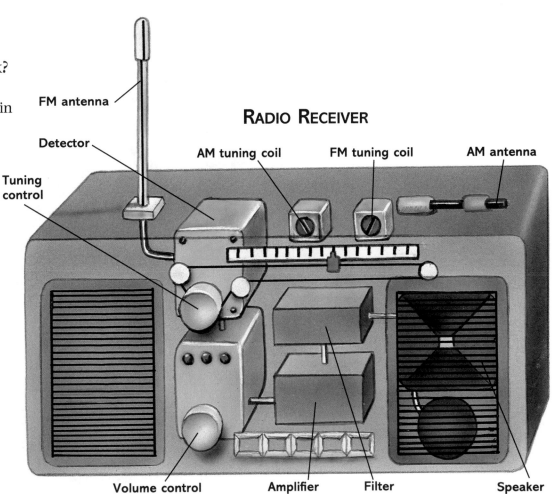

RADIO RECEIVER

FM antenna — Detector — Tuning control — AM tuning coil — FM tuning coil — AM antenna — Volume control — Amplifier — Filter — Speaker

Q. What's the difference between AM and FM?

A. AM and FM are two different ways of mixing the sound signal with the carrier wave. We said earlier that every radio wave is an electromagnetic field that oscillates, or changes intensity; *amplitude* is a measure of how much a wave oscillates, and *frequency* is a measure of how often a wave oscillates. AM, which stands for *Amplitude Modulation,* mixes the carrier wave and the sound signal by changing the amplitude of the carrier wave to match the amplitude of the sound signal. FM, or *Frequency Modulation,* mixes them by changing the frequency of the carrier wave to match the frequency of the sound signal. Thunderstorms and other electrical occurrences can interfere with AM signals. FM signals have less of a problem with interference.

Q. **Where does a TV picture come from?**

A. Television stations take the picture and sound from a show and convert them into two electronic signals. The stations then transmit the signals as radio waves through the air, and your TV picks them up through its antenna. Each television station uses a signal with a unique frequency, so you can tune your television to a particular channel that will pick up only that signal.

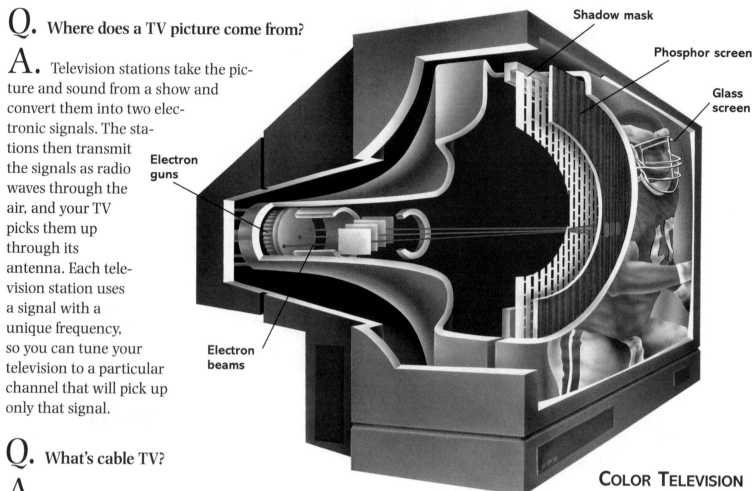

Shadow mask

Phosphor screen

Glass screen

Electron guns

Electron beams

COLOR TELEVISION

Q. **What's cable TV?**

A. Cable TV is another way to transmit TV signals. The signals are sent over wires instead of through the air as radio waves. This has several advantages over transmitting through the air—there's less interference with the picture part of the signal, making for clearer reception; there are no restrictions on how far the signal can travel, so you can watch TV stations from California if you live in Texas, for example; and you can get many more channels because the signal on the wire can go up into frequencies that would be used for other things transmitting through the air—like cellular telephones and aircraft radios—without interfering.

Q. **How does the TV actually make the picture?**

A. The screen on a TV is actually a sheet of glass with a special *phosphor* coating on the back. The coating glows when it is hit by an electron. Electron guns at the back of the TV shoot electrons at the coating and make it glow wherever an electron strikes it. The signal from the TV station tells the electron gun when to shoot and where to shoot at the screen, making some parts glow and other parts stay dark. In a black-and-white TV, these light and dark parts make up the picture you see on the screen. Color TVs work pretty much the same way, but they have three electron guns and use red, blue, and green dots that combine to make different colors on the screen.

Q. Where's the picture on a video tape?

A. The picture on a video tape is actually a series of signals encoded magnetically on the tape. Each picture is made up of a series of magnetic lines, or swipes, made diagonally across the tape. Your VCR is able to read these swipes to get a description of the picture.

The sound part of a video tape is a separate signal that is recorded as a continuous line along one edge of the tape. Your VCR reads the encoded sound information and turns it into an electronic signal that can be sent to the television speakers through an amplifier.

Q. How does the picture get from the VCR to the TV?

A. When you stick a tape in your VCR, the door on the front of the cassette is opened up and the tape is threaded through rollers and wrapped around the spinning video head drum. This is what makes the noises you hear when you put a tape in.

The video head drum in the VCR spins rapidly against the tape, and heads on the drum read all of the magnetic swipes on the tape, one at a time. The heads convert the information in the magnetic swipes to an electronic signal. The signal travels through wires to the TV and then directs the electron guns in the TV to create the picture.

VIDEOTAPE PLAYER

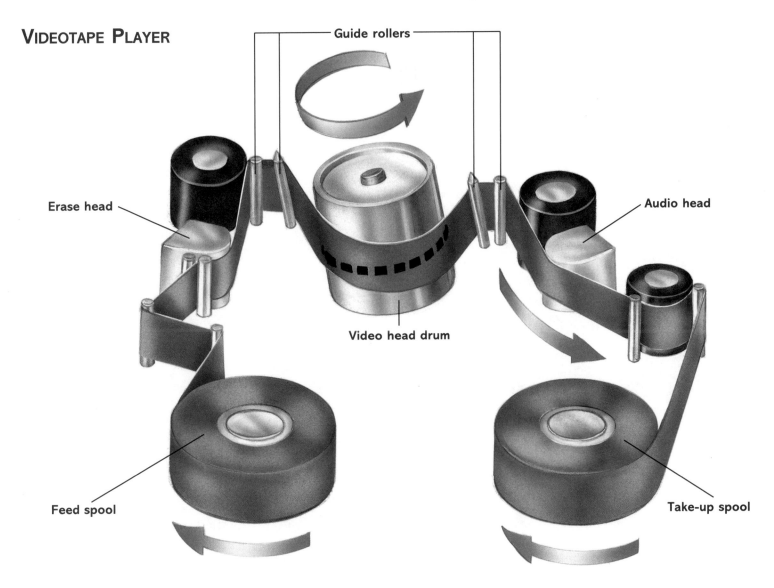

Guide rollers

Erase head

Audio head

Video head drum

Feed spool

Take-up spool

Q. How can a satellite help in broadcasting?

A. Most broadcasting transmitters can only reach receivers within 30 miles or so of the transmitter. There are many places where it isn't practical to build enough transmitters to reach everybody who wants to receive signals.

One way of solving this problem is to install relay stations between the transmitter and the places that the transmitter can't reach. These relay stations have a receiver and a transmitter to pick up and retransmit the signals sent by the original transmitter. Another way to increase the range of a transmitter is to bounce the signal off the *ionosphere* (an electrically charged layer of the Earth's atmosphere). The most effective way to transmit a signal over a distance, though, is to send it to a communications satellite that will receive the signal and retransmit it back to Earth.

COMMUNICATIONS TRANSMISSION

Communications satellite
(23,000 miles above Earth)

Radio
waves

Ionosphere
(50-600 miles
above Earth)

Transmitting stations

Relay station

Receiving stations

Q. Isn't the satellite moving?

A. Yes, but it's moving in a geostationary orbit around the Earth. Think of riding a bike in a circle around a merry-go-round. If you pedaled at the right speed, you could keep up exactly with one of the merry-go-round horses as it traveled around. A communications satellite does much the same thing; by traveling at the right speed, it stays in place over one spot as the planet rotates.

Q. Are there many satellites?

A. There are many artificial satellites in orbit around Earth. Some of them are communications satellites that relay telephone, television, and radio signals. Others are used to gather and send weather information. Navigation satellites help boats and airplanes figure out where they are. Reconnaissance, or spy, satellites are able to photograph and record activity on the Earth's surface.

Q. Why don't all those satellites bump into each other?

A. Different satellites have orbits that put them over different parts of Earth, so that their paths don't cross. And, of course, it's a big sky, so there isn't much chance of two satellites coming near each other.

Q. Aren't the signals from satellites very weak?

A. Yes they are. That's why the satellite dishes you see are so large. They act as collectors for the signal, and they are curved so that they focus and strengthen the signal before it reaches your TV set. Transmitters use even bigger dishes so that they can send a very strong signal to the satellite.

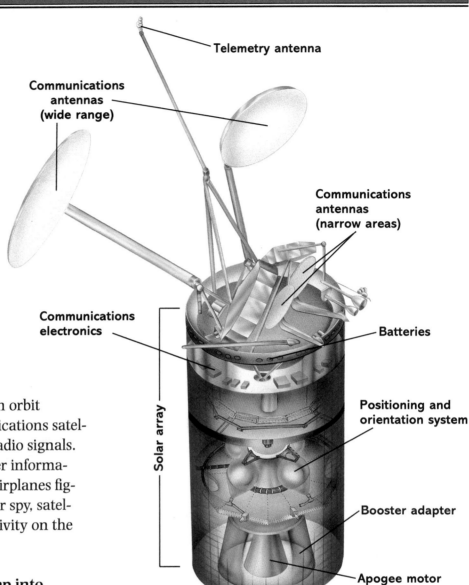

Telemetry antenna

Communications antennas (wide range)

Communications antennas (narrow areas)

Communications electronics

Batteries

Solar array

Positioning and orientation system

Booster adapter

Apogee motor

INTELSAT TELECOMMUNICATIONS SATELLITE

The First Satellites

Echo I was a simple satellite launched in 1960. It was really just a big balloon treated with a thin metallic coating so that it could reflect radio waves. *Echo I* wasn't a very useful satellite.

Two years later, *Telstar I* was launched. *Telstar I* used *transponders* to send signals. A transponder consists of a receiver, an amplifier to make the signal stronger, and a transmitter to send the stronger signal back to Earth.

Q. What is a compact disc?

A. A compact disc, or CD, is a plastic disc that stores music in digitized form and uses a laser beam to play it back. The new CD technology has pretty much replaced older forms of recording, such as vinyl records. People have come to prefer CDs because they sound better, are free of noise, and last longer. They're called compact discs because they're much smaller than the older records were.

Q. How does a CD store music?

A. A CD stores its digitized signals as very tiny pits, or dimples, in a spiral pattern on a plastic disc. This disc is coated with a thin coat of aluminum to reflect light and then given a protective plastic coating over the aluminum.

Q. How does the CD player get the music from the disc?

A. To play a compact disc, a CD player directs a very tiny laser beam at the disc, and the disc reflects the light back to an electric eye, or *photodiode.* The places on the disc with pits reflect the light differently than the smooth places without pits, and the photodiode senses the differences. Different combinations of smooth and pitted places make a message, in much the same way that different combinations of dots and dashes make a message in Morse code. The photodiode converts the message in the reflected laser beam to an electrical signal. This signal is then sent to an amplifier and a loudspeaker, where it comes out as music.

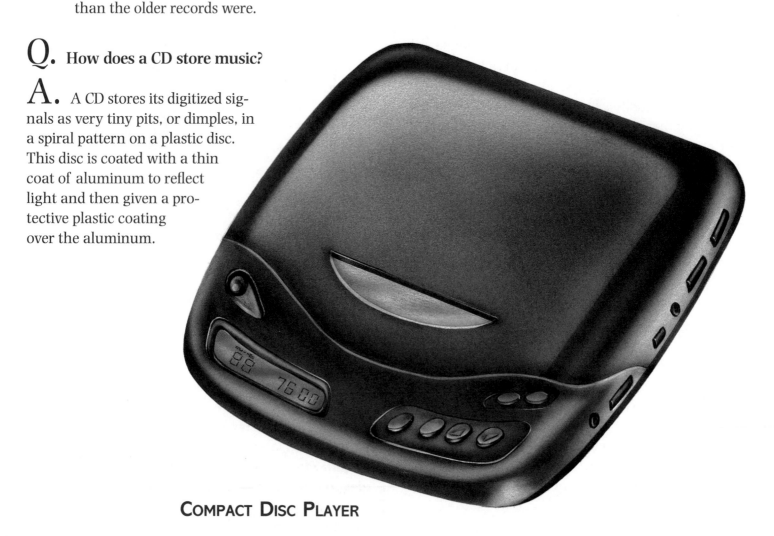

COMPACT DISC PLAYER

COMPACT DISC PLAYER INTERIOR

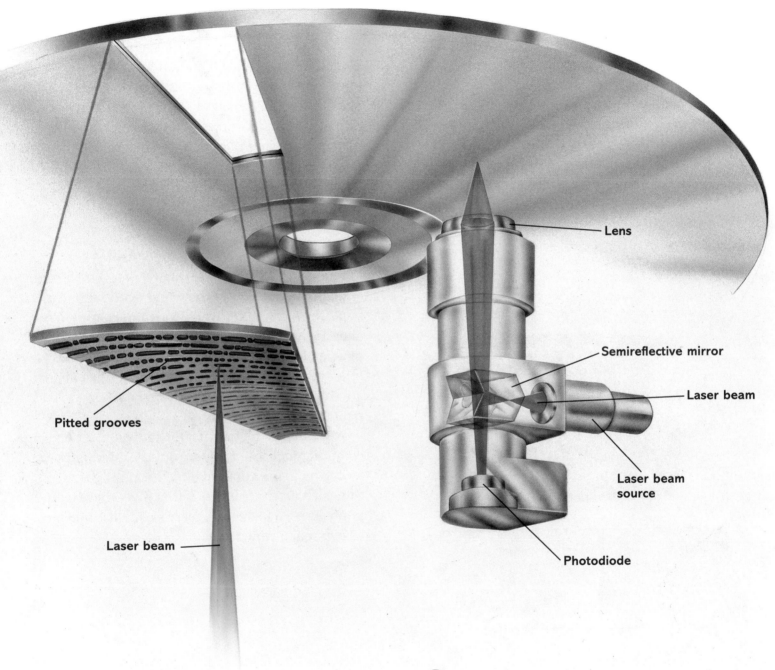

Lens

Semireflective mirror

Laser beam

Laser beam source

Photodiode

Pitted grooves

Laser beam

Q. Do CDs wear out?

A. Since nothing except a laser beam is used to play the CD, there's no wear during playback. If a CD is handled very carefully (to avoid scratching it) and is stored out of direct sunlight (which can damage the plastic), it may never wear out.

Q. Can you store anything besides music on a compact disc?

A. Yes. A CD can store anything that can be digitized. Special CDs—called CD-ROMS—are used to store computer programs, movies, and even books.

Q. What is the Internet?

A. The Internet is one of the newest methods of allowing people to communicate with each other. The Internet lets computers "talk" to each other by sending words, pictures, movies, and music over telephone lines.

The thing that makes the Internet possible is the fact that all of these different kinds of messages can be *digitized.* When a signal of any sort is digitized, it is converted to a series of electrical signals called *bits.* A computer can take this string of bits and send it over telephone lines to another computer. The other computer then can change the bits back to words, music, or pictures.

Q. What's a computer network?

A. A computer network is made of a number of computers that are connected together by telephone lines. Many large computers—*mainframes*—are connected to several different networks. These mainframes can move signals from one network to another, turning a collection of smaller networks into one huge network. Computer devices called *routers* make sure that messages reach the right place.

Q. What's the Internet good for?

A. The Internet can do a lot of neat things. E-mail (short for Electronic Mail) letters can be sent easily to people all over the world, without having to paste on stamps or wait a long time for mail delivery. Newsgroups let people who are interested in a particular subject discuss it with thousands of other people. There are newsgroups for just about anything you can think of—from kite flying to classical music.

You can use the Internet for shopping, for playing computer games, for finding out the latest news, or for trying to sell your old bicycle. One of the nicest things about the Internet is that if you have a question you need to answer, there's usually someone within reach who can help.

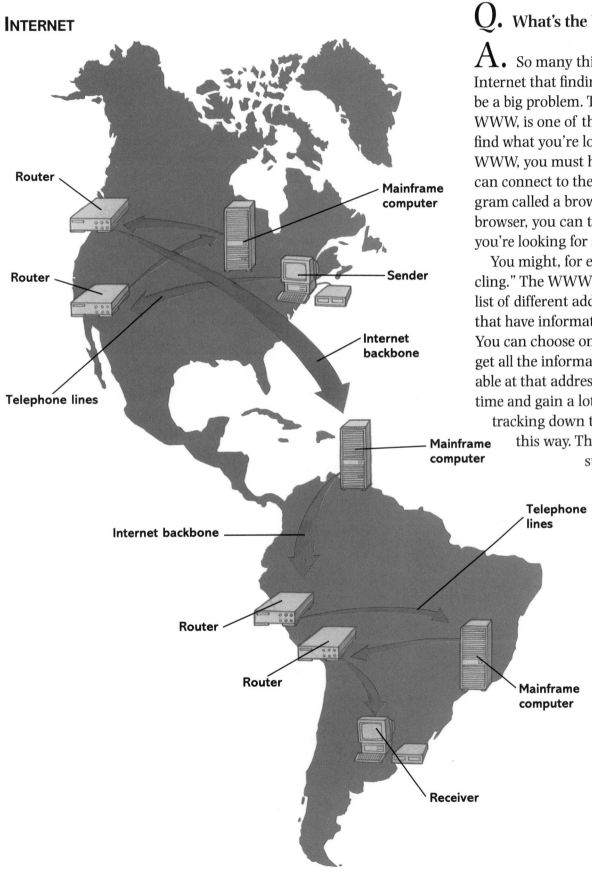

Router

Router

Telephone lines

Mainframe computer

Sender

Internet backbone

Mainframe computer

Internet backbone

Router

Router

Telephone lines

Mainframe computer

Receiver

Q. What's the World Wide Web?

A. So many things are available on the Internet that finding what you want can be a big problem. The World Wide Web, or WWW, is one of the most popular ways to find what you're looking for. To use the WWW, you must have a computer that can connect to the Internet and a program called a browser. After you start the browser, you can tell the computer what you're looking for simply by typing it in.

You might, for example, ask for "recycling." The WWW will come back with a list of different addresses on the WWW that have information about recycling. You can choose one of these, and you'll get all the information on recycling available at that address. You can save a lot of time and gain a lot of information by tracking down these Internet addresses this way. This is what people call surfing the net.

Q. How does a telephone work?

A. A telephone's mouthpiece—the part you speak into—is a microphone. It changes sounds into electrical signals. These signals travel along wires until they reach the earpiece of another telephone. Inside that earpiece is a speaker that changes them back to sounds for the person on the other end to hear.

If we had to have a separate pair of wires for every telephone that we wanted to talk to, the country would be covered with wires! Instead, *trunk lines* containing optical fiber cables connect different cities together. Each trunk line ends at a switching station, which is linked to all the phones in its area.

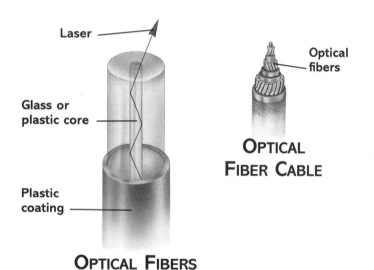

Laser

Glass or plastic core

Plastic coating

OPTICAL FIBERS

Optical fibers

OPTICAL FIBER CABLE

Q. Why are telephone numbers so long?

A. There are many millions of telephones in use today, and each one of them needs its own number. Usually, each phone is given its own unique seven-digit number. There are ten million different combinations for seven-digit numbers, so as many as ten million phones can each have a unique number.

Q. What are area codes?

A. Telephones have become so popular that even ten million numbers is not enough. To help provide more numbers, we use area codes—extra three-digit combinations in front of the regular seven-digit phone number. Each area code represents an area of the country. A number with an area code of 312, for example, is in Chicago, while an 802 number is somewhere in Vermont. That way, a person in Vermont and a person in Chicago can both have the same seven-digit number without getting each other's phone calls. In places where there are a lot of people, one city may have several area codes; in places with fewer people, an area code may cover an entire state.

How May I Direct Your Call?

A long time ago, operators directed people's phone calls to the right telephone. Callers would tell the operator the number they wanted, and the operator would connect each caller's phone to the phone of the person they wanted. As telephones became more popular, it was hard for operators to keep up with all the calls. An automatic switching system was developed, and telephones were made with dials, so that callers could dial a number directly. Each number on the dial sent a different electrical signal along the wires, and the signal would operate the switches. Later, engineers invented faster switches that work with musical tones made by buttons on the telephone. These touch-tone phones are the kind we use today.

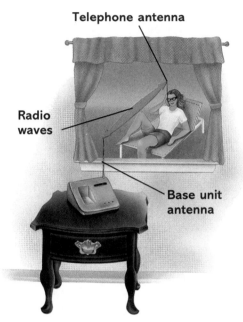

CORDLESS TELEPHONE

Telephone antenna

Radio waves

Base unit antenna

Q. How does a cordless phone work?

A. A cordless phone has a small, low-power radio transmitter and receiver built into it. The phone's base unit, which plugs in to your telephone line, also has a transmitter and receiver. Radio signals that can carry a telephone conversation are sent back and forth between the cordless phone and the base unit, linking you to your telephone line. Because the radio's power is so low, a cordless phone won't usually broadcast far enough so that your neighbors can hear what's being said on your phone; to make eavesdropping even less likely, different cordless phones are tuned to different frequencies, and some have voice-scrambling systems for added security.

Q. How does a cellular phone work?

A. A cellular phone lets you make and receive calls from anywhere, even from a moving car or boat. In a cellular telephone system, the area covered by the system is divided into circular sections, or *cells*. Each cell has a transmitter/receiver combination (transceiver) that's connected to the telephone company's central switching office and has only enough power to reach that one cell.

Like a cordless phone, a cellular phone has a built-in radio transmitter and receiver, but instead of linking you to your telephone line, it links you to the transceiver of the cell you're in, which in turn links you to the central switching office and the telephone company. A computer in the switching office keeps track of which cell you're in, so that if you leave one cell, your call automatically switches to the next cell you enter. That way, you can communicate over a very large area without needing a very powerful radio, which would interfere with other people's phone calls.

CELLULAR TELEPHONE NETWORK

Central switching office

Local telephone company

Transmitter

Cell site transceiver

Cell

Radio waves

Cellular telephone

Q. How does a fax machine send a letter?

A. When you send a fax, the machine slowly draws the original letter through a set of rollers. As the page goes through the machine, a light-sensitive scanner passes back and forth over it. The rollers tell the machine exactly where on the page the scanner is, and the scanner tells the machine whether it sees white, black, or some shade of gray at any particular spot on the page. That information is changed into an electrical signal that can be sent over phone lines.

Q. How does a fax machine receive the letter?

A. When a fax machine is receiving a transmission, it gets an electrical signal that tells it where all the white, black, and gray spots on the original document are. Using that information, the receiving fax machine can make a copy of the original document.

Resolution: Lots of Dots!

The way fax machines scan a sheet of paper has a lot to do with why the copies they send usually look so fuzzy. In most fax machines, the scanner moves in a straight line across the page from left to right. It starts at the top of the page and works its way down, scanning across the page about 100 times for every inch of paper in a typical fax machine. As it's scanning, it's breaking the image of the page down into dots. There are usually about 100 of these dots per inch along each scanning line in most machines. The number of dots and number of scanning lines per inch determine the machine's *resolution,* or how clear the image it sends to another fax machine will be. The more dots and lines per inch, the higher the resolution and the clearer the image. With fewer dots and lines, the image becomes fuzzier. Very high resolution fax machines, like those used to send photographs, can send an image almost as clear as the original photo. These machines use many hundreds of dots and lines per inch, but they're very expensive.

SENDING

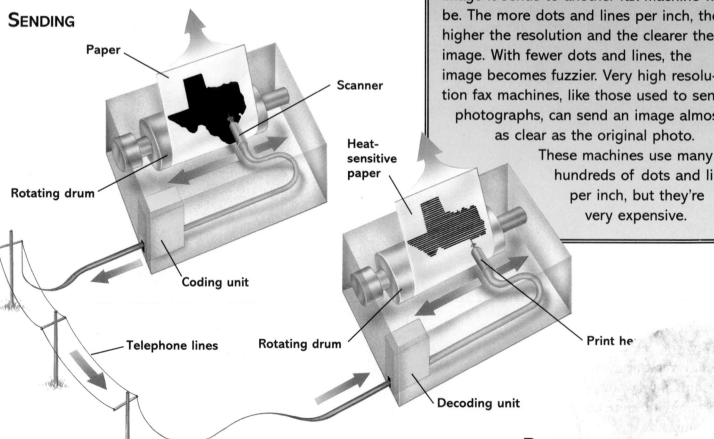

Paper

Scanner

Rotating drum

Coding unit

Heat-sensitive paper

Telephone lines

Rotating drum

Print he

Decoding unit

RECEIVING